As Green as Grass

As Green as Grass

*Growing Up Before, During and
After the Second World War*

Emma Smith

BLOOMSBURY

LONDON · NEW DELHI · NEW YORK · SYDNEY

First published in Great Britain 2013

Copyright © 2013 by Emma Smith

The moral right of the author has been asserted

This is a work of non-fiction based on the life, experiences and recollections
of Emma Smith. In some cases names have been changed.

Bloomsbury Publishing Plc
50 Bedford Square
London
WC1B 3DP

www.bloomsbury.com

Bloomsbury Publishing, London, New Delhi, New York and Sydney

A CIP catalogue record for this book is available from the British Library

ISBN 978 1 4088 3561 6

10 9 8 7 6 5 4 3 2 1

Typeset by Hewer Text UK Ltd, Edinburgh
Printed and bound in Great Britain by CPI Group (UK) Ltd, Croydon CR0 4YY

For my beloved family, as usual, with gratitude for kindnesses too many to mention.

PART ONE

BEFORE

We have said goodbye to the rocks and cliffs and sands and the rough seas of the north Cornish coast, and exchanged them for a Devonshire village ten miles inland on the very edge of Dartmoor. The reason why we have moved so far away from Newquay, the small seaside resort where I was born twelve years ago, is because my father has been transferred by the Midland Bank to one of its bigger branches in Plymouth. Daddy says it means he has been promoted, but I think that secretly he misses the importance he had in Newquay, where he was the only cashier to be working behind the bank's high shiny counter. Perhaps, though – probably, in fact – he still is unique, even in Plymouth, no matter how many cashiers there are, because of having a DSO after his name. Our father, as we well know, is a war hero.

For me and my older sister Pam the main difference about our new life – apart from losing the sea – is that we shall be going to a real school. In Newquay, instead of school, we shared lessons every morning with a group of three or four other girls. Our teacher was called Miss Howard, and our classroom was in her minuscule flat, situated at the top of a steep narrow staircase behind a grocery shop, a short distance from the harbour with its fishy smells, and close by the glamorous distractions of the Victoria Cinema. We wore our ordinary clothes at these morning lessons in Miss Howard's flat, and were free each afternoon to do whatever we wanted. During the summer we did nothing much. What my sister Pam and I wanted then was simply to spend hours and hours down on the Great Western Beach. But now, besides wearing a uniform, we will be having lunch at school, and staying on there all day, and not getting home until teatime.

Plymouth has a cathedral, and is consequently more than just a large town; it counts as a city. And as if that weren't enough grandeur for Plymouth, it is also, we have learnt, a chief port of the Royal Navy. The brochure provided by Moorfields (the school we shall very soon, according to Mummy, be attending) informs us that its particular purpose is to educate the daughters of officers and gentlemen. Our father, of course, isn't a naval officer; he is merely a clerk in a bank. But we Hallsmith children have had it impressed upon us most forcibly all our lives by Daddy that in spite of his lowly employment he is – and we must never forget it – *a gentleman*. So this makes it quite all right for Pam and me to go to Moorfields, which, although expensive, our mother has chosen in preference to the Girls' High School, where the pupils might not necessarily be the daughters of either officers or gentlemen.

Yesterday Mummy took us by bus the ten miles into Plymouth so that we could be fitted out in Dingle's Department Stores with the required uniform: a navy-blue gymslip, navy-blue blazer, white shirt and a silky striped scarlet-and-navy tie; black shoes and stockings; a round navy-blue velour hat, and – mysteriously – things called galoshes, which I have never seen before. Also a satchel. We are now equipped for school. I am thrilled. I have always wanted to have a uniform. In Newquay I used to observe the girls who went to Thelema School or the County School and envy them the distinction that, it seemed to me, their uniform bestowed on them. And the fictitious girls in such Angela Brazil novels as I succeeded in borrowing from Boots' Lending Library – they too wore gymslips in the illustrations I pored over, and now I shall be able to feel I am the same as those heroines.

The name of our village is Crapstone, and the semi-detached house we have just moved into is called Melrose. Semi-detached means a building that is joined on to another house exactly like it: a sort of mirror image, or an identical twin. My older brother and sister, Jim and Pam, are twins, but not identical – quite on the contrary. Except for both being fair-haired and blue-eyed (I wish I had blue eyes) they aren't in the slightest bit alike.

Our new next-door neighbours, Mr and Mrs Brown, have three children. They live so close to us we are able to hear their muffled voices and footsteps through the partition that separates our hall from their hall. Laurence Brown is about the same age, I think, as Pam and Jim, and Phoebe and Philip Brown are not as old as me, but older than my younger brother Harvey, who was four in June. Their house is the last in the road, with a much more extensive garden than we have. Beyond its boundary wall stretches a wilderness of gorse and heather: the actual beginning – or, if you were going in the opposite direction, the end – of Dartmoor itself.

We don't really have a garden at all. How can you have a garden if there aren't any flowers? The only flower bed is a weedy triangular patch of ground squeezed into a corner on the farther side of a short gravel drive that leads up to a garage at the back. Since our house, Melrose, stands on a higher level than the road running past it, the overgrown unkempt lawn in front is also on two levels, connected by a steepish daisy-strewn slope intended, Harvey thinks, especially for him to have the fun of rolling down; which he does, at every opportunity.

Instead of the customary border display of pinks and pansies, hollyhocks and snapdragons, what we've got, on the upper lawn, is a single exotic shrub: a pampas grass. Huge and flamboyant, its clump of long thin trailing green leaves – resembling a monster's wild uncombed hair – is topped by spikes of beautiful silvery-golden plumes. Pampas grasses, being tropical plants, usually grow in hot countries, Africa or India, not on the edge of Dartmoor. I've always loved flowers, and I'm truly sorry we haven't any, but who would not be proud to possess, as we now do, a plant so remarkable and distinguishing.

When we children first arrived and were shown what was to be our new home, I had felt a twinge of disappointment, I must admit, because of the rather dreary grey colour of its blotchy plaster façade, and its peeling paintwork. But my disappointment was gone in less than a minute. In addition to the spectacular pampas grass, Melrose's other redeeming features were immediately obvious: a balcony, jutting out from the floor above, and supported on a row of wooden pillars, has the effect of creating a shady veranda underneath; and French windows (that is to say, double full-length glass doors) open on to the veranda from one of the ground floor rooms. We have never before lived in a house with a balcony, and a veranda, and French windows, and a pampas grass on the front lawn.

Nor is this all. When we went inside and upstairs yet another marvel awaited us. The previous tenants of Melrose have left behind them in the attic, either on purpose or else from sheer forgetfulness – wonder of wonders, a ping-pong table! Nothing in the world could have so surprised us or given such promise of enjoyment in the days ahead as a ping-pong table. These novel and entirely unexpected assets more than compensate for my hasty first impression of our new home's dingy outside appearance.

A ping-pong table!

People have been calling on us and leaving little two-inch cards with their names and addresses printed on them. This never used to happen in Newquay, but it's what they do here, apparently, whenever there's a new arrival in the village. It isn't in the least like playing ludo or snakes and ladders, but it strikes me, nonetheless, as being a sort of grown-ups' game, with a set of clear, although unwritten, rules. This is how the game is played:

Somebody we don't know, a Crapstone resident, who usually turns out to be a wife – she seldom brings her husband with her – rings our bell and is invited in for tea and biscuits. She doesn't stay more than fifteen or twenty minutes: a very short visit (subsequent visits can be longer). We find, when she has departed, that the silver salver in the hall has had one or two, or perhaps even three, little white cards deposited on it, like the eggs a hen has laid and left in its nesting box. Ever since Daddy was presented by Newquay Tennis Club's Committee with a sparkling expensive silver tray in appreciation of the work he put into being the Club's Honorary Secretary, we have wondered what possible use there could be for such an object. What was it *for*? Well, here we have the answer: it was, and is, intended for the reception of visiting cards.

After about a week the call has to be returned. Our mother, wearing gloves and a hat, and probably taking Pam (but not me) with her, calls on the caller, and leaves her cards. Once this is done, all the participants are deemed to be officially acquainted: we now know each other. And so now, if we should chance to meet in the road, say, outside the post office, we can stop and chat; a conversation it wouldn't have been correct for us to have had before the completion of the card-calling game.

During the summer, while we were still living in Newquay, our mother was warned by old Mrs Mulroney that because of the village we were moving to being so close to the Royal Naval port of Plymouth, only ten miles off, this is the way things would be done; and that's why Mummy prepared herself by having cards printed, and why she has no difficulty, it would appear, in following the rules for Crapstone visiting.

Moreover, she listened to the advice her strait-laced imperious old Irish friend gave her on other matters as well. Nor did Mummy protest when Mrs Mulroney reprimanded her quite severely – I was present, and heard the rebuke – for not fulfilling the duty she owed her husband (*the dear brave man, God bless him*) by failing to bring us four up in a manner befitting the sons and daughters of an English gentleman. She had been deeply shocked, Mrs Mulroney declared, on learning that the family's general factotum, Lucy Coles – (my dear Lucy) – was allowed to refer to the Hallsmith children without the deferential prefix of a Miss or a Master. Standards had to be maintained; had, indeed, to be enforced. If the lower orders were not reminded constantly that they *were* the lower orders, the resulting loss of respect, in Mrs Mulroney's opinion, could spell disaster. Look at Russia – bloody revolution!

Our father, it's true, has always fervently believed his rightful place in society is that of a gentleman, whether English or Scottish, but it isn't a consideration which has ever much bothered Mummy – not until our removal to Crapstone. She must have remembered and pondered on her old friend's words, and come to the conclusion that perhaps there was reason in them; that Mrs Mulroney did, perhaps, know best, after all. For when our move, a few weeks ago, had been finally accomplished, and Mummy set about hiring a sixteen-year-old girl from the nearby village of Buckland Monachorum to be our daily cleaner, Mary Northey was instructed to call my brothers Master Jim and Master Harvey, and my sister Miss Pam; and I am to be spoken to, and of, as Miss Elspeth. Furthermore, on the trip to Plymouth, having bought the necessary school uniform for Pam and me, Mummy went on to buy a selection of lacy caps and little frilly aprons for Mary Northey to change into once she had done the morning's cleaning and scrubbing and furniture polishing, and finished washing up the dirty dishes. Mrs Mulroney's parlourmaid had been trained to wear just such a frilly cap and apron, freshly laundered, when serving afternoon tea.

It feels funny to me, being called *Miss Elspeth*. Mary doesn't seem to think it funny, but I do. I shall have to get used to it, I suppose. Generally I look forward to change, and expect it to be exciting. But with some changes, I'm bound to say, I don't feel altogether comfortable.

Pam and I have started going to Moorfields, our new school in Plymouth. It's the second half of the winter term. We weren't able to start at the beginning of the first half because that was when we were moving from Newquay to Crapstone. I think it's a considerable disadvantage for a new girl to have to begin at her new school halfway through the term. It makes it much harder, somehow, to fit in. Although actually, if I'm truthful, I'm not sure that I'd have fitted in anyway. I had thought that school would be exactly like the Angela Brazil books I'd been reading, but I was wrong; it's not. It isn't like them at all.

Every day we have to gobble our breakfast down in order to catch the eight o'clock bus that stops to pick up passengers at the Crapstone war memorial. Pam always does catch the bus, but I've sometimes fallen asleep again after she's woken me at seven o'clock, and as soon as I've rushed, helter-skelter, out of Melrose and got to the end of the Browns' garden wall, I can see that I've missed it. There it goes, trundling off without me over the moor's flat empty landscape, disappearing into the distance. In another half-hour Daddy will be driving to his work in the Midland Bank, but a lift with him would come too late. I must make the best of a bad job, covering the two miles to Yelverton on foot as fast as I can run, so as to reach the crossroads in time to clamber, panting, aboard the next bus, a double-decker travelling from Tavistock to Plymouth.

Never mind that in the scramble to get dressed I may have completely forgotten about the essential stripy tie; or that a shoelace may have to do as an emergency replacement for my hair-ribbon, blown away on the windy moor. *Never mind!* – it could be worse! By catching the Tavistock bus I ought, if I'm lucky, to be able to creep, dishevelled and breathless, into Form 2's classroom, where morning Assembly is held, and join a line of my classmates a few desperate seconds before Miss Bailey and Miss Pocock enter, closely followed by their staff of teachers, filing in, one by one, glumly, to position themselves under the notice board. Despite some semi-muffled sniggers, I will, by the skin of my teeth, have avoided utter disaster.

But if I'm not so lucky I shall find on arrival – as I have twice miserably done – the door already shut, and hear Miss Carlisle banging out a tune on the piano, and voices singing the opening hymn. Any lateness here is disgraceful, and such extreme lateness inexcusable. It will mean – has meant – that I am unworthy to be a pupil in this punctual, bell-ringing, uniform-wearing, pukka establishment. It means that I'm a failure. I had never imagined that I should be a failure, going to school, but I am.

The future looked altogether different on the Saturday before half-term when Mummy took me and Pam to meet – or, rather, to be inspected by – Miss Bailey and her friend, Miss Pocock. Miss Bailey is the owner and the chief head-mistress, and Miss Pocock is her second-in-command.

'Oh, what a charming house!' our mother had exclaimed as we approached the wide flight of shallow steps leading up to a pillared porch. 'Don't you agree, girls?' And yes, of course we did.

Everything we saw was charming: the velvety smooth lawns under spreading beech trees, the big windows, framed in climbing roses and ivy – everything. And here my sister Pam and I – lucky us! – were to go to school! A delightful prospect, we thought it then. The disappointments came later.

We were ushered inside, into an elegant drawing-room, and introduced to Miss Bailey. And straight away I thought how very odd it seemed that Miss Bailey, this fat little unsmil-ing person, didn't at all match the house or the garden. I decided, immediately, that I didn't care for her, and I could tell at once that she didn't care for me. But it's my belief now, after several weeks of observing Miss Bailey, that she doesn't, in fact, care for children; not for any children, no matter who they are. Which really is extremely odd. Because, if so, why did Miss Bailey choose to have a school for girls?

I hate school. I hate everything about it. Well, almost every-thing. It isn't that the girls in my class are horrid; or not exactly. Mostly they take no notice of me. They ignore me, as though I'm some sort of an outsider who ought not to be there. It's only Monica Harris who goes out of her way to be as nasty to me as possible. I don't know why she does, unless it's to amuse Doreen Cohen and make her laugh. Doreen Cohen is really, I think, by nature quite amiable – or she would be if it weren't for the bad influence of Monica Harris. They are bosom friends, inseparable, although they look, and in every particular are, complete opposites: Doreen Cohen being dark and big and lazy and clumsy, whereas Monica Harris is fair-haired, quick and smallish, with a very turned-up nose and a permanently spiteful expression.

She has nicknamed me Spitty, not because I spit, which I don't, but because my name is Elspeth Hallsmith. And she calls me Teacher's Pet whenever I'm top of the English or History or French lists that are pinned on the notice board at the end of each week. And once, when we were sitting side by side during Geometry, she stuck the point of her compass into my leg, on purpose.

When I said *Ow!* very loudly because of the surprise, and because it hurt, everybody looked at me, and Mrs Eliot, our Geometry teacher, paused in the middle of chalking an isosceles triangle on the blackboard and asked me crossly – she's always cross, anyway – what was the matter.

'Nothing,' I said. 'It was nothing – I'm sorry, Mrs Eliot.' I felt ashamed for interrupting the lesson and attracting such disapproving attention to myself. I couldn't explain that I had yelled out because Monica Harris had stuck the needle of her compass into my leg.

When we lived in Newquay and had lessons each morning from Miss Howard, my sister Pam and I used to enjoy learning. We wanted to learn. It never occurred to us that being taught was boring, or a waste of time. In every lesson we tried to please Miss Howard, our teacher, by doing as well as we could. And when we did manage to do well, she *was* pleased. Which meant, of course, that we were too. But now if I get good marks at school, and beat the other girls, they think I'm showing off.

It would be better, I've realised, to give up trying altogether; better to get low marks and be considered a dunce, than to get high marks and be unpopular. And since I must endure somehow, as best as I can, life in this hateful school, I've decided to stop working hard; to stop, in fact, making any effort to succeed at anything – with the exception, that's to say, of my two favourite subjects. Apart from them, instead of attempting to be top of the weekly lists, I plan in future to be bottom.

With English Literature, though, and English Grammar I shan't – I can't – give up trying to learn. I don't mind if that beastly Monica Harris or anyone else calls me Teacher's Pet. Miss Ruddock (nicknamed Ruddygore) is our English teacher, and I *love* her lessons. I only wish they were longer and that we had them more often. At present in our Literature class we are studying *Silas Marner*, the story of an old miser and a little orphan girl he adopts, and when my turn comes to read a paragraph aloud I feel positively dizzy with the sheer pleasure of it.

So at least there is something that I do truly enjoy and look forward to in school; *something*, after all.

Lady Astor has been taken on a tour of Moorfields by Miss Bailey, finishing in our classroom, where she talks to us for ten minutes or so about being Plymouth's elected Member of Parliament, and how it's only recently that women, thanks to the Suffragette Movement, have been allowed to vote at all, let alone sit as Members in either the House of Commons or the House of Lords. When we girls are older, she says, we must be sure to use our vote: it's up to us to see that more women are elected to Parliament, instead of it being simply men, as now, who make the laws and govern the people of this country.

She is quite old, Lady Astor, but still beautiful, and beautifully dressed, and she smells divine. She has an American accent, because she's an American, although married to Lord

13

Astor, who is English. She doesn't put on airs or try to be superior, but smiles and laughs, and waves her hand at us when she leaves.

Miss Bailey is puffed up and almost bursting with pride at the honour she plainly feels the visit confers on her. But as she must so greatly desire her eminent visitor to receive a favourable impression of Moorfields, it would surely have been advisable to keep her well clear of these scruffy back premises on the tour of inspection. Lady Astor will have arrived at the front of a house my mother described as charming, although, unlike Mummy and me and Pam, she was no doubt driven up the tree-lined avenue, and between the velvety lawns, and under the spreading beeches, by a chauffeur in a Rolls-Royce. The charms I glimpsed on that memorable afternoon of our interview with Miss Bailey I have not seen since.

For it is by way of the tradesmen's entrance, opening off a side street, a rough narrow cul-de-sac, that I and the rest of the pupils come daily to school. The cloakroom where we hang our coats and change our shoes and go to the lavatory is a square brick shed squeezed into and occupying almost the whole space of what would once have been a backyard.

Inside the school's back door, directly ahead, is a short flight of linoleum-covered steps leading into the dining hall, bare except for its long tables and benches of scrubbed wood. Immediately to the right a dark passage vanishes in the direction of invisible kitchens and sculleries and servants' quarters, while to the left lies the cramped classroom of Form 1, where the youngest pupils, eleven-year-olds, are taught; and beyond this is my Form 2 classroom. Its high windows, pointed at the top, are the same shape as the windows in churches, which makes me think it must originally have been a private chapel.

Certain rich families in times past had the habit, I've heard, of tacking on a convenient chapel to their own residence, thereby saving themselves the trouble of having to traipse off to wherever the nearest proper church might be; and before Moorfields became a school for girls it was indeed the home, I've been told, of just such a wealthy family. This would account for everybody nowadays trooping through Form 1 and crowding into my classroom every morning for Assembly. If my Form 2 classroom was previously a chapel it would naturally be chosen as the appropriate place, whether crowded or not, in which to sing hymns and say prayers.

On further reflection I've come to the conclusion that Miss Bailey, who must have been extremely unwilling to conduct her guest away from the elegant atmosphere of the main building down to the makeshift muddle of our school's nether regions, did so because, and only because, Lady Astor asked especially to speak to Elizabeth Drax, daughter of Admiral Sir Plunkett-Ernle-Erle-Drax; and Elizabeth, as it happens, is in my class, Form 2.

Since moving from Newquay to Crapstone my sister Pam and I don't any longer have much to do with one another, either in or out of school. Pam was fifteen in October, so she went into the top class at Moorfields, joining company in the Fifth Form with the head-girl, Louise Turner, and the prefects, amongst them Mary Dawkes, whose father has just retired from being Bishop of Plymouth, and a second Pam – Pam Prince. Their classroom is at some distance from mine, on the far side of the main school building, overlooking the gardens. Most of the Fifth Form seniors are as tall, or nearly as tall, as my sister. I see them strolling round the playground during morning break, in groups of two or three, sometimes arm in arm. Pam doesn't ever stop to speak to me. She doesn't so much as glance at me in passing. You would never guess we were sisters.

15

The playground, situated across the little cul-de-sac road at the back of the school, is an area occupied first and foremost by a netball pitch, its cracked and blackish macadam surface badly in need of repair. Beyond it, higher up, are two tennis courts, one grass and one hard. Both courts are out of use at present, because it's the wrong season for tennis. What we play at school this term, and next term too, apparently, is netball, and, once a week, hockey.

Although neither she nor I have played netball before, Pam at once achieves renown as a champion shooter of goals. Her height is a distinct advantage, enabling her almost, when reaching up, to drop the ball coolly and calmly into the net. I can tell, simply by watching, that my sister is a fully accepted member of the Fifth Form; is, in fact, popular.

On Tuesday afternoons a coach, hired for the purpose, transports us juniors – that is to say, Forms 1 and 2 – together with Miss Stewart, our games mistress, to a sportsground outside Plymouth, where we play hockey. This also is a new game for me: a wonderfully exhilarating game, better than rounders or cricket on the beach at Newquay. Because I run very fast I've been allocated the position of left-wing. So now I've discovered something else the school provides that I can enjoy and look forward to; something I may, perhaps, without the risk of scorn, excel at. Not that speediness on the wing will win me much, or any, approval from my team, since, unfortunately, I'm the only girl in Form 2 who really does enjoy playing hockey. The others groan when it's Tuesday afternoon again, and make up all sorts of excuses so as to be let off an activity they consider both exhausting and a bore.

Tuesday's midday dinner is always just a bowl of soup, the least hunger-satisfying meal of the week. I don't know who decided that soup by itself is the best preparation for a strenuous hockey-playing afternoon. By the time I catch my bus home to Crapstone at the end of Tuesday afternoons, I'm absolutely ravenous.

I have another problem regarding food at school. Four baskets, loaded with currant-buns, are placed by the kitchen staff on the dining-hall tables at eleven o'clock when the bell clangs for morning break. Every girl snatches a bun for herself; every girl except me. Currant-buns are an extra on the school bill, and my mother, having decreed that it is a quite unnecessary extra, has struck it decisively off the term's pay-in-advance account. When asked, as I frequently am, why I'm not behaving the same as everybody else by helping myself to a mid-morning bun, I say I don't like them. This is a fib. I do like currant-buns, very much indeed.

Another extra on the bill disallowed by my mother is elocution, a subject which gentle stooping apologetic Miss Grace Pocock teaches. She also teaches drawing; but whereas Drawing is not an extra, Elocution is. I am the only girl in my class who doesn't take Elocution. As a consequence, during this Monday morning period I am obliged to stay sitting mutely at my desk, pretending to do alternative work, while all around me my classmates are reciting, singly or in unison, the magical lines of Walter de la Mare's poem 'The Listeners'. Of course I too learn them by heart. How can I not? But I must remain dumb, head bent, the words I yearn to utter echoing inside it, unheard, unspoken: words I am sure – *sure* – I could render more passionately than Barbara, or Cynthia, or Tamsin, with their plodding sing-song repetition: *'Is there anybody there?' said the Traveller/ Knocking on the moonlit door* . . . It is a sort of agony for me, not to be free to spring to my feet and declaim them aloud.

Why, I wonder, if every sixpence is of such crucial impor- tance, why did our mother choose to send her daughters to expensive Moorfields instead of to the cheaper High School? And now we *are* here, does Mummy think, or hope, that she can make atonement for an unjustifiable extravagance – and her conscience be soothed into the bargain – by economising over currant-buns and elocution lessons? Why, otherwise, having inherited from her Uncle Stewart several years ago sufficient money (we don't know how much it was) to lift the Hallsmiths out of penny-pinching poverty and grant us a lifestyle, certainly not of affluence, but at least enough to count ourselves modestly well-off – *why* should she now refuse to sanction these insignificant items added to our school fees? Has she any idea how humiliating it is for me to be the only girl in Form 2 not to have elocution lessons or a currant-bun each morning? No! – my good kind mother has no idea. And I can't explain my feelings to her. Impossible!

I've been chucked out of Form 2 singing class. Mr Wexford, our singing master, is a tall severe rather frightening old man who doesn't have children himself, being unmarried. He lives with his sister somewhere on the outskirts, as it happens, of Crapstone. Once a week – every Thursday – he travels in to Moorfields by bus and spends half an hour with each of the five forms in turn.

Last Thursday morning, in the middle of an exercise of trills that we, his Form 2 pupils, were practising together, he quite suddenly told us all to stop singing. Mr Wexford didn't say why we were to stop. But then, to my surprise, he came close up to where I stood and commanded me to sing, on my own, the single notes of what is called a scale. And when I did – or when, at least, I tried to do as he said – with him towering over me, and the rest of the girls clustered, silent and staring, round about, he accused me, as though I was committing a shameful crime, of singing flat. He said I was singing off key. As I don't know what a key is, I may very well have been singing off it. He made me repeat the same notes again and again, growing crosser and crosser by the minute, until, when I couldn't make another sound come out of my mouth, I started to cry; not much, but a few tears trickled down, and I didn't have a hankie. Mr Wexford wasn't a bit sorry for causing me to cry. He said, disgustedly, that I was tone deaf, and as it would be a waste of his precious time to try to teach me to sing in tune, in future I was not to attend his singing class. He told me to leave the group, and to go and sit at a desk by myself while he continued the singing lesson without me.

What Mr Wexford obviously doesn't understand is that I *want* to sing. I *love* to sing – I always have loved to sing – just as I love dancing; and I think that if I'm doing it wrong, as he says I am, then I'm the one girl in his Form 2 class who is most in need of teaching, and he's a teacher of singing, so it's his *duty* to teach me.

It was, I have to admit, a truly mortifying experience, which I wish I could completely forget; only I can't. Mr Wexford is a horrible man, unkind, and I would like everybody everywhere to know that he isn't any good as a teacher. I haven't, however, so far informed even my parents of Mr Wexford banning me from his singing class. The fact of the matter is, my feelings were too badly hurt for me to have been able to mention the episode to anyone yet, including my sister Pam.

We are in the middle of the Christmas holidays and life has taken a turn for the better; has altered, in fact, amazingly. My brother Jim was away at his Exeter boarding school when we moved to Crapstone, and because of the general upheaval of settling in, our parents thought it advisable for him to stay on there throughout the half-term holiday. So it's not until now that Jim has had a chance to see his new home.

The idea of change – any sort of change – which I view as exciting, has always disturbed my older brother, and from the moment he heard that we were to leave Newquay, Jim grew increasingly upset and anxious, and his stammer got worse. But now that he's here and has been able to investigate for himself every inch of our new address, his doubts have evaporated, and as to his stammer, it's hardly noticeable. In his declared opinion (influenced, I daresay, by the ping-pong table), our present home, Melrose, is a distinct improvement on the one we had before, and he actually prefers the village of Crapstone, and the landscape of Dartmoor, to Newquay, with its beaches and cliffs. He doesn't miss the sea at all, as Pam and I do. For us, losing the sea was like losing a part of ourselves. But Jim, of course, never did care much for bathing: the Atlantic Ocean was too rough and too cold for him – it made his teeth chatter and his skin go blue and goose-pimply.

A surprising number of boys and girls who are also, the same as Jim, away at boarding schools during term-time, were suddenly, at the start of the Christmas holidays, visible in Crapstone; since when the Twins and I (our brother, Harvey, is still too young) have been invited again and again to have tea and play indoor games – Monopoly and racing demon, and charades – with Charles and Sam Pyne, Roger Hammick, Michael and Sylvia Syson. In Yelverton we have got to know Terence Dewar, the son of Admiral Dewar, and in Douseland the Monroes, and Phyllida Wharton. Every day we seem to be introduced to somebody else of our age group – a lively group into which we have been unreservedly welcomed. I perceive, with a lift of the heart, that no matter how awful my school days are, the holidays will be entirely different: they will be *fun*!

This delightful enlargement of the social scene is restricted, however, to us children; it doesn't apply to, or include, our parents. In Newquay they were seldom at home on winter evenings. We were left then with Lucy Coles in charge of us, while they went off to committee meetings, or bridge four-somes, or perhaps to a rehearsal for the next amateur dramatic production. Following what she used to describe deprecatingly as her *little windfall* – the inheritance of her Uncle Stewart's money – our mother had become something of a local celebrity, much in demand for opening fêtes and delivering after-dinner speeches: performances at which she not only shone, but immensely enjoyed undertaking. Nor was our father, although a lesser star, wholly eclipsed by his wife's successes. As a decorated hero of the Great War, he had his duly acknowledged and respected position in the firmament of a thriving seaside resort.

I don't believe they realised, my parents, that in saying goodbye to Newquay they would be saying goodbye to all of these flattering small-town triumphs. Crapstone bears no resemblance to Newquay. How does Crapstone's adult popu-lation spend its evenings? We don't know. The male half of the residents are mostly, it seems, connected in some capacity with the Royal Navy: with the naval dockyards, or possibly with Keyham College where young men are trained to qual-ify as naval engineers. Whatever occupation it is they are engaged on, when the menfolk drive out from Devonport at the end of a working day, having entered their houses and shut their front doors behind them, they are no more to be seen. Crapstone grown-ups don't, as far as we children can tell, visit one another after dark; they don't, at any rate, invite Mr and Mrs Hallsmith to visit them.

The ladies who were punctilious in coming to call and leaving their cards on our sparkling silver salver must have thought they had fulfilled their duty by carrying out every-thing the rules of correct behaviour required. We had supposed it was the initial step in a subsequent flowering of friendship, but we were mistaken: it was nothing of the kind. Our mother, on her way to the village shop, will daily exchange with, it may be, old Mrs Batson or Mrs Orr-Ewin, trivial remarks about the coldness or otherwise of the weather. They bow and smile; speak, and pass on. And that's the whole neighbourly extent of it.

I understand the uneasiness of the situation my parents find themselves in. It's a situation not dissimilar to my own at school. They are treated by the inhabitants of Crapstone as the outsiders they plainly are; and as newcomers, who are neither needed nor desired by a circle already complete, they are politely ignored. These friends of ours, which the holidays have so magically conjured out of nowhere, are like unexpected Christmas presents; but presents given exclusively to us three children: *ours*, not theirs. Although Mummy has plenty of recently made village acquaintances, there are none who count for her as the sort of real friends that we now have, and she is lonely; I am sure she is. I can feel her loneliness, her disappointment.

And as for my father, what has happened to his all-devouring, passionate ambition to be a world-famous artist? In the weeks, the months we've been living here he hasn't set up his beloved easel once; hasn't unpacked his sandalwood box of oil paints, his brushes, his canvases; hasn't touched a piece of charcoal.

If we three, the Twins and I, have avoided returning the hospitality shown to us, hoping we won't be thought rude and ungrateful not to invite back to tea in our house any of those whose invitations we have so gladly accepted, it is because we are too embarassed to usher our cheerful high-spirited new friends into an atmosphere at home darkened by Daddy's prevailing mood of brooding dissatisfaction, his angry sideways glances, his bitter silence.

I think friendship is very important. I think you have to have at least one friend you can share your thoughts with. Having just yourself isn't enough. Last term I did try to make friends with Kathleen Crowther, mainly because she seemed to be the only other person in my class who, like me, was quite on her own. Kathleen Crowther has two long brown plaits, and spectacles, and a terrible squint, and her voice is so husky and low it's difficult to hear what she's saying. She is musical, and plays the violin. But whenever I said anything in the way of conversation, instead of answering she would blush bright red and look as if she was afraid I might be planning to attack her; as a result of which I gave up attempting to make a friend of Kathleen Crowther.

After the Christmas holidays I went back to school in the gloomy expectation of it being as hateful as it had been the previous term. But I was wrong again. School isn't hateful any more, and the reason it's not is Alice Winslow: my new best friend.

Alice, and her sister Cynthia, who is a year-and-a-half younger and therefore in the form below us, were absent from Moorfields last term, visiting relations in America. They themselves are American: their father, Mr Winslow, is the American Consul in Plymouth. He has only one hand, the left; he lost his right hand in the Great War.

Both Alice and Cynthia have cornflower blue eyes, and each of them has two short fat blonde pigtails, but whereas Cynthia is rather plain in the face and extremely naughty and disobedient, not giving a hoot for any rules or regulations, her older sister, Alice, is distinctly pretty and as good as gold, rather solemn – a serious girl. She pays attention during lessons, and works hard, and nobody calls her Teacher's Pet. And because she is esteemed by the other girls in Form 2 as someone out of the ordinary and special, I have ceased to be cold-shouldered, an outsider. I've been accepted. Monica Harris wouldn't dare to stick her compass point into my leg now that I'm the best friend of Alice Winslow.

The Winslow family live in a big red-brick house on the hill above Yelverton, so Alice and Cynthia and I catch the same bus to and from school every day. But I think Alice would have become my best friend in any case. I don't worry, when I'm with her, about anything. She's always calm and smiling, even-tempered, never the slightest bit sulky or cross. It's astonishing the difference one girl can make to a person's life.

Years ago, when Mildred Walker first got engaged to Mr Bruce-Payne, she promised me that on the day of her wedding, sometime in the future, I should be a bridesmaid; and she hasn't forgotten her promise. This is why I'm travelling up by train to London now with Mummy for the ceremony. As it's taking place at the very beginning of the Easter holidays, I shan't be missing any school.

The dress I'm to wear is beautiful, made of a stiff goldeny-yellow taffeta silk with a full skirt and puff sleeves. I was measured at home for it, and the measurements were sent off to Mildred Walker, and then the dress arrived by post, ready to be worn. It fitted almost perfectly, only needing a few minor alterations, which Mummy was able to do easily.

We are staying with rich old Mrs Bazin in her big house in Finchley, London. Mrs Bazin is Mildred Walker's grand-mother, and the mother of Elsie Walker, who comes to visit us regularly every summer. Before our mother turned into Mrs Hallsmith she was called Janet Laurie, and during the Great War she had been going to marry Mrs Bazin's son, Geoffrey, and would have done if he hadn't, unfortunately, got killed the same week he was due to return on leave from France to marry her. Old Mrs Bazin is obviously devoted to Mummy, who is the daughter-in-law she so nearly, but didn't quite, have. Every year without fail she sends my mother on her birthday in July a pair of what, clearly, are exceedingly expensive gloves.

The two other bridesmaids at Mildred Walker's wedding are both grown up. Except for theirs being of a larger size, our dresses are identical, and we have all three been given a twinkly brooch of cut steel as a present from the bride and groom, which I do think is very kind of them.

After the actual marriage ceremony in church there is a party for all the many wedding guests in Mrs Bazin's extensive garden, with drinks, and masses of food, and the wedding cake, and speeches. Luckily the weather is fine and warm. I talk to a tall elderly man with remarkably bushy black eyebrows. His name is Sir Maurice Gwyer, and he has just been appointed, I'm told, the Lord Chief Justice of India. We talk about books, mostly, and I tell him I mean to be a writer. I like talking to him. We get on together extremely well.

Peggy Burton has gingery-red hair, as does her father, Commander Burton (Retd), and she looks rather like him in other ways as well. Her face is pale and pinched, but unlike his it has a permanently worried unhappy expression. She is my age, a sufficient reason, it seems, for me to have been appointed her special friend who often visits her on Saturday afternoons.

The arrangement – a parents' arrangement – was made, I suspect, with the idea of me cheering Peggy up, and getting her to be jollier. But except for the coincidence of our ages being the same, we have nothing in common. Peggy doesn't talk – she hardly says a word; and she doesn't read books, unless they are to do with horses. Companionship with her younger sister, Dido, who is a great deal livelier as well as much prettier, would be preferable, but Dido has no need of a special friend to cheer her up, being cheerful already. It's Peggy I'm invited to have tea with, and sometimes to stop on for supper with, and even once to stay the night with. She is the only member of her family whose mind is exclusively focussed on ponies. Her father, an ex-sailor, doesn't ride at all; her mother gardens; and Dido has guinea pigs and rabbits for pets.

The Burtons live in a sprawling red-brick house a mile or so outside Crapstone. It has a tennis court, and a stable wing, and what for Peggy is most essential: the paddock where she and I ride her two ponies, Darkie and Annabella, hour after interminable hour, trotting them round and round, and putting them over the low jumps of brushwood or planks that cause me, as often as not, to tumble ignominiously off. Luckily Darkie, the shaggy little pony I ride, besides being quite old, has very short legs, so that the ground, when I do fall, is fairly near.

My mother regards these invitations as a splendid opportunity for Elspeth to learn how to ride, forgetting, or deciding to ignore, a previous equally splendid opportunity I once had during the week we stayed on her brother Andrew's farm in Suffolk. There I was offered by a tribe of Laurie cousins any one of their ponies to learn to ride on; an offer I declined, my attention being fully engaged just then in the far more exciting enterprise of teaching myself to ride on one of their bicycles.

Horses were a part of Mummy's own childhood, and remain, I suppose, inseparably part of a cherished memory for her of these early lost years before James Laurie, her beloved father, agent for the Fawley estate, was drowned while sailing in Southampton Water. She – Janet – was twelve at the time; how awful that disaster, which changed everything, must have been for her, his favourite daughter. I think perhaps the dreamily faint recollection she has of a happiness long gone is why Mummy now persists in believing the Peggy Burton connection pleases me as much as it pleases her.

When a parcel arrives in the post from Mildred Martin, (Daddy's horse-loving, horse-owning second cousin) containing a pair of discarded but still serviceable grown-up jodhpurs, my mother is overjoyed and gets busy immediately with scissors and sewing machine, reducing them in a few hours of drastic alteration to a size that fits me. (*Jodhpurs*, I'm told by Mummy, is the Indian name for the oddly shaped trousers, baggy above and tight below, that all real riders wear.)

Thus it is, kitted out in authentic riding gear, and flicking carelessly at bracken fronds with the natty little riding crop also supplied by generous Cousin Mildred (and with which I will never flick at slow old Darkie's flanks to make him go faster: the slower he goes, the better!) – thus equipped I set off on several Saturday afternoons to walk the two or so miles of deserted country road alongside Dartmoor's ragged edge, in order that Peggy Burton may give me instructions in how to saddle a pony (*make sure the girths are tightly buckled*); the complicated way a handful of reins must be threaded between the fingers; and the mastering of an excrutiatingly difficult up-and-down rhythm to accommodate the seat of my jodhpurs to Darkie's awkward bumpety-bumpety trotting motion. Peggy watches my efforts impassively; she doesn't ever say *Well done*.

To what extent are these dutiful visits, parent-enforced, a pleasure for me? Some aspects of them, yes, I do genuinely enjoy. For instance, the smell of harness and hay when the ordeal of riding is over and we are unsaddling our mounts in the dimly lit stables. I enjoy the romance of growing familiar with somebody else's luxurious home; with the rooms of the house, and its gardens and outbuildings. I am grateful for, and respond to, nice Mrs Burton's warm unfussy welcome; and I revel in the cosiness of the nursery, its drawn curtains and the blazing fire, and scones and cakes for tea.

What I don't care for, not a bit, is bumping about in excessive discomfort on Darkie's broad back, and being scared I shall fall off at the next jump; and when the worst happens, falling off.

The fact I can't ultimately avoid acknowledging to myself is that I haven't any instinctive affinity with horses; and they, of course, know it. I am aware of our being very different creatures, and the difference, the unbridgeable gap which divides us, alarms me profoundly. That is the actual, shameful truth.

For a while I succeed in keeping up an outward pretence of developing an interest in ponies and riding and gymkhanas and so on, but it's a pretence I can't maintain. In my heart of hearts I know that, unlike Cousin Mildred and Peggy Burton, I am simply not a horse-lover; nor shall I ever be.

I don't know what it was gave Commander Burton, Peggy's father, the sudden idea of organising a game of hockey to be played in the Easter holidays by as many boys and girls who might find themselves home from school and at a loose end, but however the idea may have occurred to him, his proposal has been seized upon with the utmost enthusiasm.

The word got passed around, and I suppose friends must have told friends, so that on the second Saturday morning of the holidays quite a crowd of us, arriving on foot or on bicycles, or brought from further off by parents in cars, and each armed with a hockey stick, are gathered together on a patch of rough open grassy moorland not far from where the Burtons live. This conveniently open space lies to one side of the flat stretch of road I walk along by myself on those afternoons when I've been invited to have tea and to ride with Peggy Burton on her ponies, Darkie and Annabella.

Today there is no sign of Peggy Burton, or of Dido, her sister. They don't, it seems, want to participate in the hockey match their father has arranged. But both the Pyne boys,

Charles and Sam, are here, and so is Laurence Brown, who lives next door to us Hallsmiths. Also present are Michael and Sylvia Syson, and a girl called Daphne, and Josephine Pipon, and Roger Hammick, and Robert Winnicott; and Terence Dewar from Yelverton, and Rose and Xander Monroe from Douseland, and Phyllida Wharton; and others, too, whose names I don't know, and some children I've never seen before; and Pam and Jim and me.

Everyone is in high spirits, laughing and talking. Commander Burton, while not caring to ride horses or to take an interest in gardening – his wife's passion – has apparently, as well as a liking for the company of young people, an overflowing abundance of energy and enterprises. Already he's been hard at it, busily preparing in advance our improvised hockey field by marking out the boundaries, and using fencing stakes for goalposts.

We cluster round him now, ready and eager to do whatever he tells us to do. Being a Commander (even though a Retired one), he is accustomed, we respectfully realise, to commanding. Consequently, when he appoints Terence as captain of the side that will wear distinguishing scarlet cotton sashes, and Xander as captain of the rival side, wearing yellow sashes, there is no question of any argument: the Commander's word is law. And the two boys, taking it in turns, begin at once to choose their teams. Since I am probably the youngest person here, and certainly the smallest, it's hardly surprising I should be chosen last of all.

Nevertheless, I pluck up enough courage to beg Terence Dewar, captain of my team, to let me *please* be our left-winger. He looks a bit doubtful, and as if he's on the point of refusing. I expect he thinks it's cheeky of me to ask. So I hasten to assure him that I am an extremely fast runner; which is true. (To be able to run fast is essential in hockey for players on either wing.)

He still looks very dubious, but shrugs and turns away, saying: 'Oh all right, then. Do the best you can.'

We spread out, and Commander Burton blows his whistle; and we're off! It's the greatest possible fun; a *great* deal more fun than school hockey, because of the mixture of ages, and there being boys as well as girls. At half time Commander Burton, who was tearing about like a madman, up and down the length of the field, blowing his whistle and yelling, produces a crate from his car filled with Corona bottles of ginger pop and bags of currant-buns. I believe he's enjoying himself as much as we are.

Terence's team – *my* team – wins the match by three goals to two, and at the end of it he stops beside me and thumps me on the shoulder, and says, grinning: 'Well done, Ellie – very well done indeed!'

I am so pleased – so *gratified* – that Terence Dewar remembered what my name is; and so glad he said *Well done*! I didn't actually shoot any of our goals but he's bound to have seen how extremely fast I really did run, dribbling the ball near to the goalposts again and again, which helped the centre-forwards to score.

Our impromptu hockey match – Commander Burton's good idea – has been a terrific success. *Such* a success that we've agreed to repeat it, and to meet here for a return match the following Monday morning.

The popularity of Commander Burton's hockey matches, instead of waning, has increased, to the extent where they have been accepted as a regular fixture. This is because our Easter holiday mornings were inclined to be rather empty. Holiday afternoons present no problem. We and our local friends can drop in at each other's houses for tea, and games of Monopoly or demon patience or rummy; or a group of us may, alternatively, catch a bus into Plymouth and go to a matinée film. It's the mornings that until now were rather dullish.

Luckily Commander Burton seems not to mind how often we want him to take charge of the proceedings. Then, towards the end of our third exhilarating match something disastrous happens to me.

Although the grass of the clearing where we play has been cropped short by the herds of wild ponies that roam freely over Dartmoor, the surface, unlike properly maintained hockey fields, remains uneven and tussocky. A ball, vigorously propelled, instead of speeding along the ground as intended, may well take off and become airborne. And it is just such a ball, soaring through the air, that hits me, shockingly, smack in the mouth. Conducted off the field by a kindly spectator, somebody's mother, I sit in a bleeding sobbing heap on the sidelines while the last few minutes of the contest are played out to a triumphant finish for Xander Monroe's team. (Terence Dewar, of course, has lost his left-winger.)

I am given a lift home in somebody's car and handed over to my own mother. Upstairs in the bathroom she sponges my battered face and admonishes me to *be a man*; and also to be *brave as a lion*. These are the two bracing phrases our mother, who once nursed wounded soldiers in the Great War, always employs when she thinks that one of her children is making a fuss about nothing.

But how can I be a man, or be as brave as a lion, when I am in such excrutiating pain? My top lip is split, and the surrounding flesh discoloured and swollen. I can't eat anything: impossible! I drink sips of water from a glass with difficulty. To speak is equally difficult. All I say – all I can mumble is: 'It hurts, Mummy – it hurts. It *hurts*.'

Laurence Brown calls in to enquire how I am. A tremendous whack with his hockey stick was what did the damage.

He is desperately sorry, he says; and he sounds, and indeed obviously is, desperately sorry.

'Oh, good gracious, Laurence,' says my mother, 'it's not your fault. Accidents of this sort can happen to anyone in a game of hockey. It looks worse than it is. Elspeth', she says, briskly, 'will be as right as rain tomorrow.'

But in the morning I'm not as right as rain. My pillow is covered in blood, and I am still moaning beseechingly that it hurts.

My mother, after eyeing me narrowly, changes her mind and takes me on a bus into Plymouth where the dentist, who has the curious name of Mr Diamond, announces that, according to the X-ray, my top jaw is fractured, which means it's broken; and that three of my front teeth have been detached from their moorings and are now hanging loose. Given time, he tells Mummy, the fracture will mend itself unaided, and because I am so young – still growing – there is a very good chance, he says, that if the loose teeth are pushed back up into the bone and held in place by a narrow band, or splint, of silver, they may, with luck, reattach themselves.

We return to Crapstone on another bus, and as soon as we reach home my mother puts me to bed and draws the curtains across, and from then on treats me with as much tender care as though I really am a badly wounded Great War soldier.

The one beneficial result, I discover, of a broken top jaw is that, without the shameful label of *coward*, I'm excused from – saved from – ever again having to spend hours and hours riding around Peggy Burton's paddock on her pony, Darkie. The risk (which in fact is a certainty) of my falling off prohibits it.

It's now the summer term, and so instead of the school uniform of white shirts and navy-blue gym-slips we wear dresses of blue-and-white checked gingham, and our navy-blue velour hats have been replaced by lightweight panamas. We still play netball, but hockey is finished until next autumn. Each afternoon it's the turn of one of the five forms to be given a tennis coaching session by Miss Stewart – Stewey – the games mistress. I don't much like her – in fact, I don't like her at all. She has a short thick ugly neck, which reminds me of a bull's neck, and she holds herself very straight and rigid, with a habit of gazing over the tops of our heads as though she finds us too contemptible to be bothered to look at directly. I used to love playing tennis when we lived in Newquay, but I don't enjoy being taught how to play it every Thursday afternoon by Miss Stewart.

I don't enjoy Geography any more, either, because it's taught by Miss Joplin, who is fat, and quite old, with a bulgy red face and a disagreeable smell, always in a hurry and always appearing to be angry and offended – we don't know why. Miss Ashford teaches Arithmetic. She has very sticking-out teeth and seems, the same as Miss Joplin, to wish that she wasn't a teacher. Botany is taught by Mrs Owens, who doesn't live at Moorfields, as do the rest of the teaching staff, but arrives, usually late and in a fluster, from somewhere else outside the school. She's nice, but my favourite teacher is dear little Miss Ruddock, the English mistress.

At the end of this term, which is the end of the school year, there will be Parents' Day, the occasion when announcements are made and prizes distributed, in the gymnasium. Every form is required to produce some sort of a brief entertainment: it could be singing, or dancing, or perhaps a gymnastic display. Miss Ruddock has suggested that Form 2 should perform what she calls 'a sketch', and that we girls ought to write it ourselves. Her suggestion is greeted with cries of dismay.

Miss Ruddock looks at me. 'What about you, Elspeth?' she says, encouragingly. 'Why don't you have a go?'

And because, of course, I want to be able to do it, I say: 'All right, Miss Ruddock – I'll try.'

But once I'm at home, despair overwhelms me. What have I let myself in for? I confide in my father. To my relief, he immediately takes an interest, and in next to no time solves the basic problem of there being only girls to act in the sketch.

Why not have an employer – the editor, possibly, of a women's fashion magazine – sitting at her desk and interviewing a string of applicants, one by one, for a job on her journal?

Oh, what a good idea! Yes – oh, yes! And in due course, having taken shape on paper, been approved by Miss Ruddock, and rehearsed obediently by my fellow pupils (thankful as they are to be saved from the nuisance of the threatened boring task), *The Interview* is presented as part of the Parents' Day programme in Moorfields' gymnasium on the last Friday of the summer term.

It's over very quickly, in ten minutes: a success. The audience claps, and afterwards I'm congratulated. How clever of me, Elspeth, to write such an amusing piece for the stage! *What a talented child I am!* But I know what nobody else knows: that it was my father, not me, who wrote *The Interview*. I had hardly anything to do with it. Daddy, whose idea it had originally been, took over the entire project, elbowing me out of the way. The construction, the dialogue, the jokes (which I don't think are funny) are his. I copied it out laboriously at his dictation, but only the blobs of ink and marks of tears on the pages are truly mine.

I ought perhaps to be grateful to Daddy, as I was at the start, for getting me out of a hole. Didn't he rescue me? But my gratitude has gone sour. I feel ashamed and cheated – a cheat myself: mortified and miserable. The whole thing is a fraud. I know – I *know* – that I should either have done it,

34

whether well or whether badly, by myself alone, or not have done it at all.

Colonel and Mrs Batson are both very old. They live in the last house of a terrace that looks directly across a couple of hundred yards or so of rough common land to where the road from Yelverton reaches and skirts round the bus stop and the stone war memorial. Their house being at the end of the line, they have just enough space on its further side to include, before the boundary fence of the Sysons' property, a tennis court – mossy and damp, and overhung by surrounding trees, but still, a tennis court. And Sam and Charles Pyne, who live a few doors up from the Batsons, have been given permission by them to use the court whenever they want in the school holidays, and to invite whatever friends they want as well.

Since we three Hallsmiths, the Twins and I, play tennis, and are friends now of the Pyne boys, they invite us. Sylvia Syson and her younger brother, Michael, also tennis players, are also invited. Roger Hammick sometimes joins us there, and anyone else of the Crapstone fraternity who may have nothing better to do on a sunny idle morning or afternoon.

We don't, in fact, play tennis continuously, or even very strenuously, but throughout these weeks of July and August the Batsons' grassy neglected court serves as a handy place to gather and discuss other plans for meeting: plans to walk or bicycle down to Denham Bridge, perhaps, taking buns and biscuits with us and bathing in the River Tavy. The Colonel and old Mrs Batson tell us that they like to hear the laughter and shouts of young people floating in through their open windows.

For us children the summer holidays are as carefree and joyous as were the Christmas and Easter holidays, provided we can manage to spend the greater part of them not at home. We return to Melrose when, and only when, we must: for meals, and at night to sleep. Indoors we sit silently, imitating the silence of our parents. Harvey, aged five, chatters away uninhibited, but we, his older brother and sisters, leave our chattering and laughter outside in a jolly world existing beyond the dull grey garden wall of Melrose.

With the arrival of September, which is the month when our father has *his* annual fortnight's holiday, Daddy announces brusquely that he intends to travel to Switzerland for it, on his own, without his family. He does at last get out his painting gear: the brushes, the sandalwood box of oil paints, canvases, charcoal. He is going to paint landscapes, not portraits, and he means to set off alone.

We glance from him to our mother, trying to assess her reaction. Surely she must feel as glad as we do – thankful to have gained a clear fourteen days absolutely unshadowed by the wretchedness, the manifest ill-humour of her husband, our father, which has been hovering like a black thundercloud over our family life?

Surprisingly, Mummy doesn't seem to be pleased at all. Instead, she is not merely upset by this decision of his: she is mortally offended. She weeps, appearing to be cut to the heart by Daddy's total rejection of her, and us, for his fortnightly vacation from the despised Midland Bank. We overhear sounds of rage and despair as she pleads with him. Her tears, though, have not the slightest effect on our father, except maybe to cause his angry brow to grow even darker. Grimly, he packs his bag, straps together his painting equipment, and is gone.

It will be for two weeks only, the briefest of respites. But however brief, we children rejoice at this break in the clouds, ashamedly hushing our merriment for fear of wounding yet more profoundly our already stricken mother.

* * *

I've lost Alice Winslow as my best friend. Mr Winslow, the American Consul, was transferred to Canada, quite suddenly. They were abroad in the summer when Mr Winslow got the news of his posting, and Alice never came back to Plymouth, so I had no chance to say a proper goodbye to her; which is a pity. She wrote to me, and she'll write again, I expect, but letters aren't as satisfactory as having someone you can actually talk to – a companion.

I was very sorry – of course I was – to lose my friend Alice, and like that, without any warning. The reason I'm not missing her, though, as much as I thought I should, is because at the beginning of the autumn term (the beginning of the school year as well) I've moved up, together with everyone else in Form 2, to Form 3.

We have literally moved *up*. To reach Form 3 we must pass through the whole length of the dining hall, and then mount a short flight of steps that bring us to a higher level at the front of Moorfields house, where the classrooms of Forms 3, 4, and the top form, the fifth, are situated. These three spacious rooms, with big windows facing out over the lawns and the flower beds, are such a tremendous improvement on the cramped and muddly quarters of the junior classrooms we've left behind us, that it makes everything to do with school seem brighter and better.

Besides our new classroom we have two new teachers, Miss Williams and Miss Watkins, both young and both very pretty, and each of them flashing a ring on her engagement finger: an indication, presumably, that they may not be staying for long at Moorfields. Miss Watkins is Welsh, and she teaches Mathematics instead of the Arithmetic taught to us by poor dreary Miss Ashford, who – we are thankful to note – has vanished from the scene.

Miss Williams teaches us History, a subject I greatly enjoy, especially as we've made a start on the Tudors (I wasn't ever awfully interested in the Middle Ages). But I should enjoy the Tudors even more if I wasn't being distracted by worrying about Miss Williams' health. Pretty as she undoubtedly is, she appears to me to look so dreadfully ill, so deathly pale, I wonder what can be the matter with her? When she's chalking the names of battles or of kings and queens on the blackboard I see that her thin white fingers, including the finger with her diamond engagement ring, are shaking uncontrollably. Is she going to die?

We still have to endure hours and hours of the same boring Geography lessons given by surly smelly old Miss Joplin, who didn't, regrettably, decide to leave with Miss Ashcroft. Since, however, graduating to Form 3 we find that French and Scripture – subjects not taught in the lower forms – have been added to our current compulsory syllabus. From now on we are going to have to study these two extra subjects, plus everything else, in preparation for the School Certificate, an exam that some of us will be expected to take when we arrive in the top form.

It is the responsibility of Mam'selle, a nervous young woman wearing horn-rimmed spectacles, to instruct her students in the intricacies of the French language. Not many years older than we are, Mam'selle suffers from the misfortune of speaking very little English, a handicap that seals her fate, supplying us with endless material for cruel fun and her with endless misery.

We are being taught Scripture by Miss Bailey, our headmistress. Until now we haven't had the privilege of receiving tuition from the head. I observe, with a sort of fascination, this illustrious personage as she stands, dumpy and fat, in front of her Scripture class, reading aloud and commenting on parts of the Gospel of St Luke. She keeps one arm permanently crooked up at right angles like a shield across her chest, and she makes from time to time those odd little distasteful movements with her mouth that I've previously noticed, as though she's chewing on something that has a nasty flavour, something she can't get rid of either by swallowing or by spitting it out. And if Tamsin – or possibly Angela, a girl equally bold and unafraid of authority – should put Miss Bailey at a disadvantage by asking her, with pretended innocence, an embarassing question, the elbow of her tucked up arm twitches irritably, in and out, much as the corners of her mouth twitch crossly when she's uncertain how to answer.

'Please, Miss Bailey—' Tamsin's hand is stretched high above her head.

'Yes, Tamsin?'

'What does it mean – to circumcise?'

There is a pause. We watch Miss Bailey's elbow and her mouth working away busily: twitch, twitch. 'It means – well, it's a – circumcision is a small operation, Tamsin, that men – some men – sometimes have—' Angry-eyed and elbow jerking, she dares Tamsin, her tiresome pupil, to pursue the question further.

Tamsin, aware of being on to a winner, does dare: 'What sort of an operation, Miss Bailey?'

'That's not – it's not – it isn't of any importance, Tamsin, *what sort*. It doesn't concern us. Please don't interrupt again.'

'I only wanted to *know*, Miss Bailey—'

Despite her injured air of ignorance, Tamsin, I'm sure, knows very well; and so, from their half-concealed grins, do the other girls. But I myself don't know, and I would like to be told what is meant by *to circumcise*, this peculiar phrase printed in the Holy Bible that Miss Bailey feels, apparently, unable to explain.

This October the Twins, Pam and Jim, have their sixteenth birthday. But whereas Jim will continue to travel by train every term to and from his Exeter boarding school, Pam has left Moorfields. She isn't a schoolgirl any longer. She is now a student at Plymouth Art School, a branch of the Technical College. Instead of a gymslip, and a tie, and black stockings, and a navy-blue velour hat, Pam can nowadays wear whatever she chooses. Instead of pocket money, she has a small, a very small, dress allowance from Mummy. Her pigtail, divided into two plaits, she has taken to winding around her head like a coronet, and fastening with hairpins. *Hairpins*! It's those hairpins of hers that make my sister seem to be all of a sudden completely grown up, and more of a stranger to me than ever. We exchange hardly any conversation. We are worlds apart.

She doesn't talk to me – or, for that matter, to our parents – of what she does at art school, but I've seen Daddy pick up the sketchbooks and the sheets of squared paper that Pam brings home and leaves lying carelessly about, and glance through them, frowning. He doesn't ask her any questions, and she doesn't offer any information. Daddy himself never went to an art school. He was only nineteen when the Great War began, besides which his own father had somehow managed to lose all their family's money, so I expect he would have had to start earning a living at once as a bank clerk, even before joining up in the army to fight.

Daddy looks at Pam's pages of lettering, at her textile designs, her drawings of the muscles and bones in a man's arm and shoulder, at her pencilled copies of Roman pillars and archways, without speaking a single word. She, tensely attentive on the far side of the room, is pretending to read a book.

Since early childhood my sister Pam has drawn and painted pictures. Our father never showed the slightest interest in her efforts, or praised her for them; never, indeed, praised her for anything. Yet he must, however grudgingly, consider – must he not? – that she possesses artistic talent (inherited, to be sure, from him), or else why would he have agreed with Mummy to send their elder daughter to Plymouth Art School?

I can't tell what Daddy is thinking; but I watch him anxiously while he gazes, in total silence, at these examples of her classwork, revealing, as they do, the wide variety of subjects which, apparently, Pam is being taught at her college during the winter term of 1936. He frowns; he narrows his eyes; he flicks the pages over scornfully, as if to intimate that he, a natural-born and undeniably tip-top artist, had no need of any of this highfalutin art school stuff.

Supposing Daddy comes to the conclusion it's all a load of rubbish – academic nonsense – and a waste, therefore, of good money? He will, I fear, decide, quite simply, to put an end to it. And if he does, then that will be that. *No argument!*

For Pam, who is so happy, so obviously proud of her new status as an independent art student, the blow would be a shattering one. Is this perhaps, I wonder, Daddy's intention? To punish my sister Pam for her years of stubbornly defying him? They were always at loggerheads, always enemies, he and she. The reason why they were, and are, I haven't ever really understood.

I wait; we both, Pam as well as me, wait for a verdict we are both in dread of hearing. Our father tosses the sketchbooks down at last with a gesture of disgusted impatience, and turns away, and leaves the room, having still not expressed his opinion, or uttered a word to either of us.

Daddy has been what our mother describes as 'taken up' by Mrs Pipon, whose daughter, Josephine, we made friends with at a summer tennis party. Mrs Pipon is the very attractive, fashionably dressed, intimidatingly brisk and energetic wife of Commander Pipon. Having discovered that our father was a leading light in Newquay's Amateur Dramatic Society, Mrs Pipon immediately scooped him up to take part in an entertainment she is organising for a charity of some kind, connected with naval widows.

It will be staged, we gather, in Plymouth at the beginning of the New Year. That much we have gleaned from Daddy, but hardly anything else. He keeps us in the dark as to where the rehearsals are held, or who are his fellow actors, or even the precise nature of the enterprise, except that it is to be a sort of colourful extravaganza, in which he will portray a comic Irish character called Paddy the Piper.

Daddy? – our father? – to play a comic Irish character? We are frankly incredulous. He has already let slip, though, by mistake, more than he intended, and regrets it. His gratification at being invited – he on his own, without Mummy – into the charmed circle of sophisticated naval-officer's-wife Mrs Pipon, is an excitement, like a prize, he has no wish to share with anyone, least of all his family.

Two or three times a week Daddy arrives home from the Midland Bank, eats a hurried meal, changes into casual clothes, and after tying a silk cravat at the neck, drives off again, tight-lipped, but in a state of barely suppressed exuberance.

What goes wrong? We shall never know. When, in the Christmas holidays, we bump into Josephine Pipon at another party, she is not helpful.

'Oh, *that*,' she says, replying vaguely to our inquiries. And on being further pressed: 'Well, actually,' she says, 'I think the whole stupid thing was cancelled.'

Was it cancelled? Was it stupid? Possibly, yes. We can be certain of nothing except that a sudden inexplicable fiasco has resulted in our father plunging back overnight into the gloomy pit of his former depression.

Then, at Easter, there occurs what amounts to a minor

miracle. He is commissioned by Mr and Mrs Beckley to paint a portrait of their daughter, Jean. Mr Beckley, the manager of Dingle's Department Stores, is as much of a Crapstone outsider as are we. But whereas our house, Melrose, being set within the confines of the village, merits no undue attention, the Beckleys' residence appears actually to proclaim a total alienation from any naval or similar local affiliations by its bleakly isolated position, standing alone, expensively newly built, large and raw on the way downhill to Buckland Monachorum.

The sittings, it has been agreed, are to take place at the weekends. And seeming to match the spring's ever lightening, brightening evenings, our father's mood also grows daily lighter, brighter. Out comes his banished easel, his palette, the tubes of paint, the brushes, and, essentially, a blank white canvas. Sounds of whistling and snatches of song filter through the bathroom door during Daddy's Sunday morning shaving sessions, the signs, unheard by us for many a dismal month, of confidence restored.

He has reason, our father, to whistle and sing. For here, surely, is his long-awaited chance to show a previously unappreciative world who he, Guthrie Hallsmith, DSO, really is: not a mere piffling clerk, slaving away at a soul-destroying job in a wretched bank, but an artist, a free creative spirit, whose true vocation he has always passionately, deeply, doggedly believed is to be a painter. This time, though, when it all goes wrong, we do know why.

How sad, how ironic that a portrait painter's most valuable gift, with which our father was blessed at birth, the infallible ability he has to achieve an exact likeness of his model, should be what proves fatal to the latest dream of sweet success.

Mr and Mrs Beckley hadn't wanted, or counted on being presented with an exact likeness of their beloved child. Of course not! What they had anticipated having was a charmingly pretty picture of her to hang above the drawing-room mantelpiece; and Jean Beckley, a nice quiet obedient little girl with impeccably good manners, isn't – alas! – pretty. Feature for feature she resembles her father, not her mother. So when shown the finished portrait, which until then they had been prevented from viewing, the Beckley parents are aghast. This is by no means how they see their darling daughter, or how they had expected Mr Hallsmith to see her. There is, consequently, a distressing, a painful, and finally a collosal row.

Mr Hallsmith will be paid, the Beckleys insist, his promised fee, and they – almost certainly with the intention of consigning it to a bonfire – will retain possession of the picture. Our father, however, insists even more forcefully, that since his clients have stated their dissatisfaction, they can keep their paltry money, and he will keep the painting. He is the artist, he reminds them, and if he chooses not to sell it, then the work belongs to him. He plans, he says, later on, to submit the portrait he has done of Jean Beckley to the Royal Academy, confident the judges will this year select it for inclusion in their Summer Exhibition.

Mr and Mrs Beckley, more and more agitated, categorically forbid our father to exhibit his dreadful painting of Jean anywhere at all: she is their daughter, their flesh-and-blood, and they will not give him their permission. Daddy declares, furiously, that he has a lawful right to the ownership of what is *his* painting, *his* work. But in the end, exhausted, out-manoeuvred, he throws in the towel; and losing the argument, loses with it the portrait.

We, his children, listen at home, goggle-eyed, while he pours into our mother's increasingly dismayed ears a scathing blow-by-blow graphic account of this ding-dong battle. The money, which he does, eventually, with the worst possible grace, accept, is no consolation for Daddy's insulted professional pride; no balm for his despairing rage. Once again a malign Fate has interfered in his life, and has defeated him.

'Idiots! Morons! *Philistines*!'

I loved everything about my dancing classes in Newquay with Miss Luke. I loved the big empty room in her bungalow that had only a piano and a gramophone in it, and yard upon yard of golden floorboards, and sunshine pouring through the windows. And I loved Miss Luke too, because she was kind and funny and pretty and young. But most of all I loved my dancing slippers, made of pale blue very soft leather, with blue satin ribbons.

Although Miss Luke taught her class of girls how we were to place our arms and our feet in the correct ballet positions, and although we also practised a certain number of ballet exercises at the barre, it was the other sorts of dancing we performed with her that I enjoyed far more than learning to obey the strict rules of Russian ballet. I had always anyway whirled and twirled about by myself on the beach when the tide was low, and it was wonderful to be encouraged by Miss Luke, who greatly admired a famous dancer called Isadora Duncan, to use our own imaginations and invent whatever movements we felt would best express our emotions.

I can still remember the delicious sensation of wet grass under my bare feet during a garden fête that was held in the summer before we left Newquay, when I was drifting around, waving a grey chiffon scarf, pretending to be the personification of Mist.

My recently begun dancing classes in Plymouth are entirely different. I shall never, as a pupil at Madame de Villiers' Dance Academy, dance barefoot on grass.

Madame de Villiers is very severe – not a smiler – and she teaches only ballet, nothing else. Her Dance Academy is in a narrow crowded street, two floors above a butcher's shop. I catch a bus from Mannamead down into the centre of Plymouth at the end of every Friday afternoon when all I really want, being tired out after school, is to catch a bus going in the opposite direction that will take me home.

Much as I find the dancing lessons I've started this term with Madame de Villiers disagreeable, it is my ballet shoes that chiefly horrify me. They have stiff chunky squared-off block toes to enable us, her pupils, to stand, and to dance, *en pointe* – that is to say, on the extreme tips of our toes. This is meant, according to the laws of Russian ballet, to be particularly graceful, but I think it's unnatural. It cramps my feet, and makes my ankles ache, and I'm inclined to lose my balance and topple over.

In the Hallsmith family we children have become accustomed to being told by our parents what has been arranged for us, and not asked if that is what we would like to happen. In this case, though, my mother did ask me if I would like to have dancing lessons again, and I said, thinking they would be as delightful as they were in Newquay with Miss Luke, that I should. So it's absolutely my fault.

I ought to tell Mummy that I made an awful mistake. Why don't I, then? *Why* can't I manage to tell her that this isn't a form of dancing I enjoy? It ought to be easy enough to say, but, somehow, it's not.

And why is it that she, my mother, who refuses to pay extra for Elocution or currant-buns at my school, has now decided to pay goodness knows how much more for the weekly Russian ballet lessons which I secretly long not to have to endure?

These are perplexing questions, and I puzzle over them in private: conundrums of odd, irrational behaviour that I try but fail to solve.

It's a summer evening, the end of an amazing afternoon. I'm the only person sitting on the top deck of the Tavistock bus,

46

travelling away from Mannamead, Plymouth, towards Yelverton, where I shall get off and catch a connecting bus to Crapstone.

I'm glad to be alone. Without any other passengers to distract my attention I can give myself over to glorying in a state of blissful happiness. I sit bolt upright, holding my tennis racquet and the round black base of my beautiful silver tennis ball tightly, and saying to myself, again and again: *This is the happiest moment of your life – you must remember it always, because you will never, ever be happier than you are now.*

When I heard my name called aloud in front of the crowd of people assembled outside the Carhallen Tennis Club's pavilion, I was dumbfounded. All the cups for winners and runners-up in the Junior Tournament had been distributed. Nothing remained on the green baize cloth except for a single sparkling silver tennis ball, the trophy awarded annually (I was informed by a spectator) to the most promising tennis player under fourteen. And today – I could hardly believe my ears – today it was being awarded to me. To *me*!

This morning Pat Turner, my friend, and I were competing against each other in the finals of our under-fourteen class. It was the last morning of the Junior Tournament, and the hottest. I didn't realise anyone in particular was watching us; but somebody must have been. Pat, who goes to the Girls' High School, not Moorfields, is a much better tennis player – far steadier – than I am. The Turners have their own tennis court, and playing against Pat is like playing against a brick wall, whereas I'm hopelessly erratic; which means it's luck, mostly, either good or bad, whether my shots (and I always hit them as hard as possible) fly *over* the net, or *into* the net.

So Pat, in the end, of course, beat me, as she was bound to do. But we managed to keep the match going between us for ages – ding-dong, dong-ding – and I suppose that's why the judges decided to entitle me *most promising*. There were also, I have to admit, very few under-fourteen entrants. I was only just able to squeeze into the category myself: next month I shall have my fourteenth birthday; and Pat has her birthday even sooner – ten days before mine.

Pam and Jim were each knocked out of their under-eighteen contests early in the tournament, and they neither of them turned up for the prizegiving ceremony; but I stayed on for it in spite of having lost the match this morning, simply so as to enjoy the fun and excitement of the occasion – and thank goodness I did!

Sitting by myself on the top of the Tavistock bus, rattling homewards, I've been thinking about the curious coincidence of a hockey ball causing me excrutiating agony during last year's Easter holidays, and then, in the summer holidays this year, being presented, out of the blue, with a glittering silver prize tennis ball. It's almost as if my guardian angel was wanting to compensate me for that initial misfortune: two balls, the first a disaster, and the second such a thrill! Awful things do happen sometimes, quite unexpectedly; but I mustn't forget that also, just as unexpectedly, something truly marvellous can happen.

I was wondering on the bus who I should find at home to entertain with a graphic account of my triumph, and am disconcerted, after bursting noisily into the house, by its total silence – the rather creepy silence, it seems to me, of a surprising emptiness. Where is everybody?

The Twins, I now recollect, were invited to Pamela Prince's tennis party, and Harvey may very likely be out to tea with Eddie Orr-Ewing. As for Mary Northey, our Mary, she will have departed on her bicycle as soon as she finished preparing a cold supper ready for us to eat at seven o'clock. But my father ought to have been home from his work in the Bank at least an hour ago. I could tell at once, by the car not being in the garage, that he isn't here. Perhaps, I think, he did return, and then for some reason drove away again. If so, has my mother gone with him? Where is my mother?

I place the precious tennis-ball trophy carefully on the hall table and listen. Not a sound! But yes – there is a sound: a door upstairs closes; footsteps.

'Mummy!' I shout. 'Hullo, Mummy – I'm back. *Mummy*!'

She doesn't answer me, but appears on the landing at the head of the stairs, and comes down, step by step, descending very slowly to where I'm standing waiting for her, puzzled, at the bottom.

'Mummy,' I say, '– what's the matter? Are you all right?'

She doesn't look all right, although I can't be sure exactly what it is that looks wrong. There is a certain frightening blankness about her face, her expression, that makes her seem different: a stranger.

She stares at me, but it's as if she doesn't see me – as if I'm invisible to her. And then, still not having uttered a word, she goes by me, through the hall, the porch, the front door, leaving it open behind her, out of the gate, leaving that open as well, and starts walking slowly, slowly, as if in a trance, down the middle of the road.

I run after her. 'Mummy, where are you going?' She doesn't answer. 'Can I come with you?' She takes no notice of me. I put my hand in hers and clasp it, and we walk on together, without speaking, side by side, until we get to the T-junction where we can turn either way; and here we stop.

Our house, Melrose, is built on a semi-circular loop off the road that leads over the moor from Yelverton to Crapstone and on downhill to where it diverges, one branch dropping sudden and steep to Buckland Monachorum, Mary's village, and the other continuing a short distance further to reach the lovely River Tavy, a favourite spot with us children in hot weather for picnics and for bathing in the deep dark pool under Denham Bridge.

When we've been standing motionless for one whole minute, two minutes, three, I give my mother's hand a timid shake, to rouse her.

'Mummy – let's go home now. Shall we?'

'Yes,' she says, nodding, and as though having become, at last, aware of my presence. 'Yes – home, yes. Yes.'

We turn to the left, and proceed at the same slow pace through the village meeting no one; past Miss Crooke's General Stores and Post Office; turn left again; past the Sysons' house, and the terrace where Colonel and Mrs Batson and the Pynes and Mr and Mrs Coede and Commander Roberts live; left again, and so, completing the circle, home to Melrose.

Once we are safely inside, my mother speaks to me clearly and firmly in her normal voice. She tells me that she means to lie down for a bit.

'Have you got a headache?' I ask her. Mummy often does have headaches; recently more often than usual.

'Yes,' she says, 'I have – I have a headache.' She touches my shoulder; touches, briefly, my cheek. 'Thank you, Elspeth.' Then she goes upstairs and I hear her bedroom door close.

I haven't told her, or anyone yet, about the silver tennis ball awarded to me today for being the most promising tennis player under fourteen.

The first fortnight in September is when our father always has his annual holiday from the Midland Bank. Last year he astonished everyone by packing a bag, apparently on impulse, and setting off alone for Switzerland.

Mummy had regarded her husband's behaviour as a deliberate insult and was deeply offended, which may be the reason why this year we've been booked, all six of us, into a bed-and-breakfast establishment (a glorified pub, although calling itself an hotel) in the very small village of Porth on the

50

north coast of Cornwall, a few miles outside Newquay, where I was born.

When we lived in Newquay it wasn't so much the tiny Porth hamlet with which I was familiar as the many little easily accessible sandy coves lying at the base of low cliffs on the far side of the long wide estuary. This is where we would drive out to on countless fine weekends for Sunday picnics; and where stood, also, the Rose Café, owned and run by our two elderly Newquay friends, the Miss Clark-Ourrys, who used to insist on treating us free of charge to their delectable strawberry-and-cream teas.

The Rose Café was, and still is, a large whitewashed weather-boarded weatherbeaten shed, originally a boathouse for fishing vessels and the fishermen's tackle. In front of it is a row of bollards resembling big black mushrooms growing at intervals out of the cracked uneven concrete surface of what was a wharf, now reduced to a level not much above the shingle piled up against it by every high winter tide.

Owing to the increasing age and deteriorating health of Miss Isobel and Miss Veah Clark-Ourry, no cream teas have been either sold or given away throughout the present summer season. The café is closed; its doors are shut and locked. But in the September of 1935 they lent it to us, and the rusty corrugated iron roof of their treasured café provided the Hallsmith family with shelter during the huge upheaval of John Julian's removal vans transporting our furniture and possessions from Newquay, Cornwall, to Crapstone, Devon.

For our parents to be obliged – as they were, because of a last-minute failure of plans – to accept an offer of accommodation so unorthodox and rudimentary, was a severe blow to their pride and a measure of their desperation in an emergency. For my sister Pam and me, on the contrary, those few days and nights of camping like gypsies in the ramshackle old Rose Café, lulled by the closeness of waves and wind, were the height of romance: unforgettable!

And here we are again, two years later; not in the Rose Café, but again in idyllic dreamed-of Porth, and within yards of the sea – the sea that I have missed almost unbearably. The fortnight ahead is like an answer to prayer, a gift from the gods, and I won't, I've resolved, allow anything or anyone to spoil it for me.

If, though, the resolve I've made is to be effective it means I have somehow to distance myself from the worsening situation between my father and my mother. It means that I mustn't pay attention to their rows, or be upset by my mother's tears, which will be difficult. Nothing she does or says to Daddy nowadays pleases him. More and more frequently his habitual gloominess is punctuated by explosions of ungovernable fury, directed chiefly at Mummy. I have thought, sometimes, that he hates her. This, I know, is a dreadful wicked thought, and it can't be true – not really. How could he possibly hate my kind and gracious, tall, beautiful mother, who is admired and loved by everyone she meets?

In any case I've decided, for the length, at least, of this year's holiday, to lead an independent existence from the rest of the family, so as to be able to enjoy myself wandering about alone, exploring, bathing, revisiting my favourite remembered nooks and crannies along the shoreline, uninterrupted. And for three whole perfect mornings and afternoons this is exactly what I do. Nobody bothers me with questions, asking where I'm going or where I've been. But it's just because I'm ignored – as I wish to be – by the others, that I remain correspondingly ignorant of the gathering storm clouds. And as a result, when a thunderbolt falls out of the sky in the middle of Wednesday night, it takes me shockingly by surprise.

Pam and I, with our little brother Harvey, have been

sharing a room together in an annexe at the rear of the Bridge House Hotel. By Wednesday midnight, as well as being out of earshot, we are all three fast asleep, and the screams of our mother fail to wake us up. But Jim, in the bedroom next to our parents, is woken up.

I can't, of course, give a description of the catastrophe from personal experience, having had no knowledge of it until I come down to breakfast on Thursday morning to find that Daddy is not at the table. His chair is unoccupied. Our father – Daddy – in fact, is gone!

The various fragmentary accounts I gather from different sources, and assemble like bits of a jigsaw, do eventually give a fairly complete picture of the disastrous events that began yesterday afternoon, while I was happily observing a colony of seals bobbing about in the green Atlantic swells off the tip of Porth island.

My father, in an access of rage, had all at once attacked Mummy and knocked her down flat on the sand of a small secluded bay, and left her there, lying unconscious. The tide was coming in and would soon have swamped the little beach. Revived when the cold sea-water washed over her feet, she looked up and saw Daddy, with six-year-old Harvey beside him, standing on the cliff above, watching her.

That night – last night – he attempted to strangle Mummy. Jim, roused by his mother screaming for help, burst into their bedroom, to be greeted by the sight of Mummy crouched on the floor in a corner, both hands protecting her throat, and his father in the act of clambering across the bed to reach her and renew the assault. Grabbing hold of his infuriated father by the legs, Jim dragged him clear of the bed and shook him and shook him, saying through gritted teeth: 'If you lay so much as a finger on my mother again, I'll kill you – I will!'

This was the heady moment of revelation, a moment of mixed emotions when my brother Jim realised how he, so

53

mocked in Newquay's County School for his puny size (*Old Tom Toddy, All head and no body* ...), had grown at seventeen to be bigger, taller, stronger than the man who used to flog him, as a terrified child, with the leather razor-strop.

What then happened was that Daddy tore himself free, and rushed out of the room, and out of the Bridge House building, wearing only his pyjamas, and drove off in our maroon-coloured Austin tourer, into the night.

He drove, as we learnt this morning, to Newquay, and on through Newquay to Pentire Head, and turned up in a state of wild incoherent disarray at the house of Mr and Mrs Jenkins, parents of our friend Oliver. Mr Jenkins immediately rang Dr Mitchell, who got out of bed, and got dressed, and motored over to Pentire, and administered some sort of medicine to calm and sedate our demented father.

Uncle Malcolm, our father's oldest half-brother, who is a doctor, arrives by train in the evening, post-haste from Newcastle. Mummy used the Bridge House Hotel's office telephone to summon him urgently. He and Dr Mitchell discuss professionally, with our mother, what, in these distressing circumstances, would be the best course of action. The Twins are allowed, as though they too were grown-ups – which they nearly are – to join in the discussion. I am told to take care of Harvey, and to keep him, and myself, out of the way.

Afterwards Pam reports to me the verdict of the two doctors: Daddy, they agreed, has gone completely off his head, and he must therefore be put into a lunatic asylum. (This is known as *being sectioned*.) Whereupon Mummy declared indignantly that she wouldn't hear of such a thing – absolutely not! Her husband – Guthrie – a war hero, who was awarded the DSO for gallantry by His Majesty King George the Fifth, to be treated as if he were a lunatic, simply because he had lost his temper – good heavens! What ridiculous nonsense! It is her brother-in-law, Malcolm, said Mummy, who must be out of his mind even to consider recommending such a disgraceful solution.

At this point, the argument becoming heated and fit only for adults, the Twins were dismissed, and Pam can tell me no more, except that tomorrow we are to leave Porth, without our father, and return home to Crapstone. So the heaven-sent seaside holiday that was to have lasted for a fortnight, is to end after a mere four days, and the fourth day hasn't been heavenly at all; it's been pure hell.

The seaside holiday having collapsed in ruins, we must now by some means get ourselves home, returning without my father, of whose present whereabouts and future fate I know nothing.

Our big touring Austin has reappeared in Porth, kindly ferried over from Pentire and delivered to the door of the Bridge House Hotel by a young man called Pat Schneider, a friend of Jim's erstwhile Newquay friends, Bradford Johns and Oliver Jenkins and Peter Mitchell, who have all piled into our spacious automobile, seizing the chance to enjoy what for them is a jolly outing. They are eager to inform us that Pat Schneider, as well as being old enough, at eighteen, to drive, is also the proud and much envied possessor of a sporty little second-hand car of his own.

We are meeting this hero-figure of theirs for the first time today. A pimply-faced but extremely affable youth, he volunteers to act as the Hallsmiths' unpaid chauffeur, and at the wheel of our car convey us the considerable distance from Porth in Cornwall, across the windswept heights of Bodmin Moor, to the village of Crapstone in South Devon. No doubt the suggestion is again prompted by kindness, although I suspect that Pat Schneider is also hoping to prolong the pleasureable experience of handling a much bigger, more powerful vehicle than the one with which he is accustomed to impress his younger companions.

Mummy, however, declines his offer. Thank you, she says, but it won't be necessary, stating calmly, by way of explanation, that she is perfectly capable of driving the Austin – *her* Austin – home herself.

The particular emphasis that she surprisingly – even rather shockingly – places on her ownership is presumably to make clear to all of us listening, but chiefly to Uncle Malcolm, that the car is by rights her property: it belongs to her. And so, in actual fact, it does. Several years before we left Newquay our splendid tourer was extravagantly bought, spanking new, with a part of the inheritance – *the little windfall*, as Mummy likes to describe it – that had come to her on the death of her Uncle Stewart.

It was always our father who drove whatever car we happened to have, and always Mummy who sat, a docile passenger, alongside him. Which is why, until she now reminds us, we had quite forgotten that our mother, ages ago during the Great War, before learning to be an obedient wife, learnt how to drive a Red Cross ambulance; no mean feat in those days, for a woman. Having such a qualification under her belt, of course she can manage, Mummy says, to drive her family home in the Austin. Of *course* she can do it: driving is easy! Will everybody please stop fussing!

Perhaps the most astonishing aspect of this entire nightmare-ish real-life drama is what it has done to our mother. Undeniably the recent ordeal she suffered at the hands of her husband, Guthrie, was horrific, and might have been expected to crush her spirits utterly. Instead, it has had exactly the opposite effect. Her transformation is remarkable. No more tears! No more headaches and smelling salts! Brisk and resolute, she has taken decisive charge of our chaotic situation, implying that since everything is now fully under her control, all problems will be dealt with and resolved.

In twenty-four hours she has reverted miraculously to being the person who once, during that far-off period of the Great War, was not just able to drive an ambulance, but was Commandant, no less, of King Edward's Convalescent Hospital for wounded soldiers: a person of singular importance, obeyed by staff, nurses, doctors, patients – admired, adored; and finally, in Buckingham Palace, decorated by His Majesty King George for services rendered to a grateful country. Drive us back herself to Crapstone? Why, of course she can!

So it is that early on Friday morning we depart from Porth, travelling in convoy, our mother sitting majestically upright at the steering wheel of the Austin, Pam beside her, me with Harvey on the back seat, and Pat Schneider following behind in his rackety little sports car. He has insisted on escorting us, ostensibly to make sure we reach our destination safely, but really – in my opinion – for the sheer adventurous fun of it. Uncle Malcolm and Dr Mitchell, who are both equally dubious regarding Mummy's competence as a driver, have approved of what they term a precautionary measure. To me it seems that Pat Schneider's second-hand sports car, heavily overloaded with five boys – Jim having chosen to cram himself uncomfortably in amongst his boisterous friends – is a great deal more likely to break down halfway across Bodmin Moor than we are.

Not that the journey home is of any concern to me. My mind is wholly occupied by the agonising thought that I have a mad father, and the terrible shame of it. I don't see how I'm to endure the weight of this dark shameful secret. That it's bound to be kept a secret goes without saying. I can hardly tell the residents of Crapstone – can I? – or girls at school, that my father is a raving lunatic.

Almost the worst part of my anguish is the sense of there being nobody I can share it with. I don't know how much the Twins are troubled, or indeed if they are troubled at all, by the blight that has fallen on our family. I don't know what either of them is thinking. Pam has become uncommunicative, barely exchanging a sentence with me; Jim has deserted to the gang of his cheerful friends in the car behind us; and Harvey – Harvey is only six. I put my arms around him, hugging him tightly for comfort – my comfort, not his. He wriggles free.

'Don't, Ellie – you're squashing me –'

It's such a beautiful September day; the sky is blue, the sun shines. On Bodmin Moor the wind is blowing a scent of honey from the gorse bushes, still blazingly golden. And my heroic mother continues to conduct the big Austin without a moment's hesitation, steadily, slowly – as slowly as if she were driving a hearse in a funeral cortège – mile after mile, on and on.

I gaze at the back of her head, and the hairpins holding her bun in place, with a sense of total desolation. When we arrive home, as we soon shall, it will be impossible, I am wretchedly aware, for me to unburden myself to her, although this is what I yearn to do. Even if I could find the right words inside my brain, I wouldn't have the courage to speak them out aloud. It's not Mummy's fault, but she doesn't understand the feelings of other people. She would laugh at me – laugh kindly, but uncomprehendingly – and tell me not to be a silly duffer. Of the shame I'm being tormented by she wouldn't have the least idea; nor could I enlighten her.

No one can save me, nobody in the world, I realise, from facing up to what is the truth I must bear somehow by myself, on my own, alone: Daddy, my father, is mad. He is mad. Uncle Malcolm said that he should be sectioned. I have a MAD father.

* * *

It's November. I've moved up this winter term into Form 4, which has the school's lending library in it. We are allowed to borrow two books a week from the shelves on the wall behind our rows of desks. I've been reading the adventures of Sir Percy Blakeney, the Scarlet Pimpernel, written by Baroness Orczy, and a book by Jeffery Farnol called *The Broad Highway*; and I've discovered another author whose name is Dornford Yates.

At first it was intoxicating to have such a quantity of books, all so temptingly near and available for me to choose from every week. Novels galore! I could hardly believe my luck! But, for whatever reason – perhaps because I'm reading them greedily, gobbling them up like too much rich food, too fast – they're beginning, disappointingly soon, to pall, to lose their flavour, even to be slightly boring. I find, when I think about it, that I prefer the books Granny Hallsmith sends us as birthday and Christmas presents – *Moonfleet* and *Lorna Doone*, for example; and the collection of Nelson's Classics that were in the bookcase bought by my parents at a Newquay auction sale. These are stories I never get sick of, stories that linger in my memory, long after I've reached the final page. Pip, in *Great Expectations*, and David Copperfield, have the same reality for me as Laurence Brown, the boy who lives next door to us in Crapstone, and are consequently much more interesting than Sir Percy Blakeney and his dazzling exploits.

At the end of this month I pluck up enough courage to ask my mother if she will let me stop having ballet lessons. I was expecting her to be thoroughly exasperated, and to reproach me for the waste of money she has already paid in fees to my dance teacher. But I needn't have worried. Mummy isn't upset or cross; not a bit. What a relief!

'Oh,' she says, raising her eyebrows and sounding mildly surprised. 'I thought you *wanted* to learn ballet, Elspeth. Of course you can stop –' And that is *all* she says. Hurray! No more exhausting ballet lessons from sharp-tongued unfriendly Madame de Villiers, who never smiles.

I still catch a bus down into the town on Friday afternoons when school is over, but not so as to climb the stairs up to her dance academy above the butcher's shop. Instead, I make my way to the psychiatric nursing-home where my father is now a patient, to have tea with him. According to my mother's official version of events, Guthrie, her husband, has had a severe nervous breakdown, brought on by overwork, and will be staying here until he has made a full recovery.

Poor Daddy is ill, she says to us children, but with care and the right sort of nursing he will soon get better. She doesn't ever use the word which looms inside my own head so menacingly: *mad*! Nor does she visit him herself. I am sent along as her emissary, Daddy being, she says I must remember, especially fond of his younger daughter – me; I am his favourite, she says – and so I have to go.

But I dread, how I do dread, these regular compulsory visits every Friday to my father. We sit together in the nursing home's conservatory, surrounded by a forest of ferns and a potted palm tree, just the two of us, one on each side of a small table, drinking tepid tea and eating iced fairy cakes. Awkwardness prevails. I can't think of any subject suitable for talk, and my father, too, is at a loss for conversation. I try to avoid our eyes meeting. Daddy's eyes are strange, oddly unfocussed, but with something in them desperate; the desperation of a wild animal, trapped. They frighten me. He seems also to have become smaller: to have shrunk. I am thankful when the hour has ticked away, and I can stand up and leave. I force myself to kiss his cheek.

'Goodbye, Daddy. I'll see you again next week – next Friday,' I promise him.

'Goodbye,' he mumbles, nodding at me. And he repeats my name several times over, pronouncing it as he always does, and as only he does: *Elsa-beth*.

There is no denying that life at home, in the absence of our father, has changed completely. The whole atmosphere has lightened and brightened. It's as though, during the school holidays of December and January, a dank depressing fog lifted, evaporated, and we can breathe more freely; can at last, with Daddy away and Mummy in sole charge, invite friends back to the house, confident, which was never the case before, that they will be welcomed. Our mother is by nature, as our father is not, instinctively sociable.

Welcome them warmly she does, and they, our friends, encouraged by Mrs Hallsmith to come again whenever they like, do come again, dropping in at Melrose casually and often. The new conviviality is a pleasure for everyone, prompting Mummy to declare that it's high time the hospitality her children have received ever since our move to Crapstone was formally acknowledged. We will show our grateful appreciation, she announces to us at breakfast one Saturday morning, by giving a first-rate tip-top Christmas party. All the neighbouring boys and girls of our acquaintance – and when added together they amount to a good many – will be invited.

Having decided on her plan of action, Mummy immediately applies herself to making the necessary arrangements. She consults a calendar, settles on a date, writes out a list – writes out several lists – and the invitations are duly dispatched, some by post, and some, locally, on foot. Thus are we committed to an irrevocable step which causes me the most acute anxiety. Supposing the Hallsmiths' party, this ambitious project, is a failure, as in my heart of hearts I am convinced it will be – what then? How will we bear the

61

disgrace of our pathetic efforts being exposed to the mockery of public view?

But I'm wrong: quite wrong. The Christmas party isn't a failure. It's a resounding success!

When the fateful day dawns our ground-floor rooms appear almost unrecognisable, decorated lavishly with holly and mistletoe and multi-coloured paper chains and balloons. Furniture has been pushed against the walls, or removed entirely, banished to the garage outside. Log fires blaze and crackle in the grates. By five o'clock the dining-room table is loaded with quantities of the festive food and drink prepared by Mummy and Mary Northey. And on the stroke of six o'clock the guests arrive.

Here they come, as unfamiliar with their clean fingernails and tidy clothes as our rearranged partified sitting-rooms: Laurence Brown from next door, Sylvia Syson and her brother Michael, Charles and Sam Pyne, and a crowd of others, trooping through the porch to be greeted beyond it by a smiling Mrs Hallsmith, who remembers and pronounces correctly the name of each one as they sidle self-consciously past her.

Then, the company assembled, she claps her hands and informs them that the first item on the evening's agenda is Progressive Games, to be played competitively in couples with the pencils and notepads provided. Afterwards we shall have a buffet supper, followed by charades, and similar team activities. The two big front rooms of Melrose, being connected by sliding doors, are ideal for charades, and for any other sort of theatrical entertainment. From a sober start the pace accelerates rapidly: games and fun and food – more fun, more food. Crackers are pulled; balloons burst. The hours fly by. Every vestige of polite restraint has long ago vanished in the babble of loud voices and louder shouts and laughter.

Close to midnight, when it's over and the guests have all gone, fetched away by parents in cars, or venturing out, those who live near, on the slippery walk home under a frosty full moon, we Hallsmiths collapse into armchairs, drained and giddy with the magnitude of our triumph. It was, we agree, the best party we have ever been to, and guess what? – we gave it ourselves!

Our mother, it has tonight become abundantly clear, is a born organiser. She used to be the target of our father's critical, and sometimes cruel, scorn for knowing nothing about art or literature. I have heard him, in a fit of rage, accuse his wife, Janet, of having no eye and no ear – no artistic sense whatever. And perhaps he was right in his judgement, even if unkindly harsh. But what our mother can do, and she can do brilliantly, is organise. That is her natural flair, her genius. We, her four children, are proud of her.

The Twins and I have been asked by Terence Dewar to a dance – a dance! – at Dartmouth Royal Naval College, where he is being taught how to become an admiral, like his father.

I think it's nice of Terence Dewar to invite me. Pam and Jim are his age, seventeen, but I'm really too young. Dances are for grown-ups. They are quite different from parties. I've never been to one before, and I'm afraid it will show – afraid I shall look silly, out of place, a bit of a freak. I've had plenty of lessons in ballet, but none in ballroom dancing. How will I manage?

It's a worry, but a private worry. We've accepted anyway, all three of us, and Mummy is busy on her sewing machine, making us girls new dresses for the occasion. Besides being a first-rate organiser, our mother has always been first-rate at making clothes for me and Pam.

I was hoping I might have worn my golden taffeta bridesmaid's dress, but unfortunately I've grown so much since

Mildred Walker's wedding I can't any longer fit into it. So Mummy went off to Dingle's winter sale and bought yards and yards of a papery thin shot-silk material at the bargain price of sixpence per yard: blue-green for Pam – who has insisted on choosing her own pattern – and magenta-green for me.

I wish I could have had the blue-green shot-silk. My hair is a darkish red, a shade that clashes with magenta, but I try not to mind about that, or to mind that Mummy has given my dress a high neckline and a lace collar, the same as old ladies wear. I'm glad the skirt, at least, is full length, right down to my ankles, and I love its rustling sound when I move: the sound of leaves rustling when the wind blows through them.

Sylvia Syson's father is to drive the Twins and me and Sylvia to Dartmouth in his car. Presumably Michael Syson, Sylvia's brother, wasn't invited by Terence Dewar to the dance, or else he was invited and refused. In any case, he isn't coming, which is a pity, Michael being nearer to my age than are any of the others.

Mummy stands at the foot of the stairs when I'm at the top, holding a shawl ready to wrap around my shoulders. She looks up at me and says, laughing:

'Your poor little nose, Elspeth – it's bright red! What on earth have you been doing to it?'

I am absolutely mortified. How awful! I hadn't noticed my nose was red. It ruins everything. People are bound to stare at me, and laugh too, probably. I don't want to go to this beastly dance at all, not now, not with a red nose and my carroty red hair, and in a dress of a nasty ugly purpleish colour. But it's too late for me to say I'm feeling ill, that I've got a stomach ache. I have to go.

Things, though, as once again I discover, aren't always how you expect them to be. The evening at Dartmouth Royal

Naval College is more wonderful, in reality, than I could ever have imagined. Walking into the ballroom is like walking into a scene in a fairy-story: lights, music, decorations, and the floor crowded with boys and girls who look as if they're hardly older than me. The cadets, our hosts, are all in uniform: very smart! I have stopped worrying about my appearance – forgotten, even, to think of it. Just to be there, to be a part of the thrilling spectacle myself, is enough.

Terence Dewar asks me twice to be his partner, and it turns out he isn't any more used to ballroom dancing than I am. If anything, he's worse than me at knowing what we are meant to be doing. We shuffle around, keeping in time to the music as best we can, until he steps on the hem of my skirt, and rips it. Terence is aghast at his clumsiness, and terrifically apologetic, but I say:

'Oh, it doesn't matter – no, honestly Terence, it doesn't –'; which, as far as I'm concerned, is the truth. I hitch my skirt higher, tucking it into my knicker elastic at the waist, and instead of dancing we dodge off to the refreshment room and eat strawberry ice creams.

In the Sysons' car, on the way home, I decide I'm in love with Terence Dewar. To be in love with a real live boy is a great improvement on being in love with George Murphy and James Stewart, who are both American film stars, or with Rupert Brooke, who is dead. Their photographs are fixed inside the lid of my school desk with drawing pins. I don't suppose it will be possible to get hold of a photograph of Terence Dewar to pin inside the lid of my desk at school. I shall tell Jacquie Edelsten, who is my new best friend, that I'm in love with Terence, but I shan't tell anybody else.

I don't know what made Mr and Mrs Edelsten leave South Africa and come to live in England, but here they are in Crapstone with their three daughters: Peggy, who is twenty-one, and Betty, approximately the same age as our Twins, and Jacquie, the youngest, who is my age. They also have a dog, a snappy snarly unstrokeable dachshund.

Mr Edelsten, unlike his small dumpling of a wife and his two plumpish older daughters, is tall and bony and leathery skinned. He has a long sharp nose, and a habit of looking disdainfully over the heads of people, with much the same contemptuous air as that adopted by Miss Stewart, our games mistress. Jacquie, being tall and thin, takes after her father in appearance, but her manner is less discouraging.

Now that the Edelstens are living in the village, and Jacquie has begun to go to my school, Moorfields, we travel in and out together daily by bus, and so have become – automatically, as it were – best friends. I'm glad to have a local best friend, even if I'm not able to be as genuinely fond of Jacquie Edelsten as I was of Alice Winslow. I can't help admiring and secretly envying her reckless disregard for any authority she deems to be unjust or unnecessary, in spite of it causing me – obedient as I am by nature – a certain uneasiness. But I am made more than uneasy – profoundly dismayed – by Jacquie's lofty refusal at school to submit herself to practically all of our teachers' efforts to educate us: lessons bore her. She does, however, have a curiously obsessive passion for Shelley, the poet, invariably referring to him by his full name of *Percy Bysshe* Shelley, as if it demonstrates the closeness of her relationship with him. Rupert Brooke, my handsome hero, she despises, implying by her contempt for his poems – (*Stands the church clock at ten to three/ And is there honey still for tea . . .*) – that I, in praising them, am exhibiting my own inferiority. Actually, I don't believe Jacquie has read more of Shelley's poetry than his 'Ode to a Skylark', which she is forever quoting. I think her enthusiasm for Percy Bysshe Shelley is a sort of showing off.

But I am glad – thankful, indeed – to have a regular

companion on whom I can depend for our travelling to school together and back every day. Sometime before the advent of Jacquie Edelsten, I used to miss the Crapstone bus at the Mannamead stop in Plymouth, and then I was obliged to catch the next bus destined for Tavistock, dismounting at Yelverton to walk the two miles home across the moor – a walk I enjoyed except on those occasions when a sudden fog, swooping in and spreading with phenomenal swiftness, would obliterate every visible landmark, wrapping the whole wide area of moorland in a thick impenetrable blanket. This was when one of the convicts in the famously isolated Princetown Prison high up on Dartmoor might seize his opportunity to escape and make a run for it through the dripping ghostly shapes of stunted thorn trees and gorse bushes, rocks and heather. We inhabitants of the outside world would be warned that a dangerous felon was on the loose by the mournful muffled clang of the prison bell, tolling, tolling. *Then* the two miles between Yelverton and Crapstone would seem to be not so enjoyable, and I would hasten my steps, nervously jogging on as fast as I could, anxious to get clear as rapidly as possible of the cold grey curling coiling mist and be safe home by a cosy fire.

And once I had an experience infinitely more frightening than any imaginary encounter with an escaping prisoner. This was the day when I was trailed by a fat man in his big black expensive shiny car after I had clambered down from the Tavistock bus at Yelverton and set out walking homewards. He drove slowly, close behind me as I walked – walking quicker and quicker; but not until I had covered half the distance and was in the middle of nowhere – not until then did he put on a spurt and drawing alongside offer me a lift.

I shook my head at him, dumbly, speechless with terror. Whereupon he drove a few yards further, and stopped his car, and waited for me to reach it. As soon as he stopped driving, I stopped walking, and stood, rooted to the spot, not knowing what I should do or how I was to save myself.

Years ago in Newquay, when I was a little girl of seven, a stranger in rough ragged clothes had taken my hand and guided me into a cave already almost cut off by the incoming tide. But that was a different nightmare. The Great Western Beach had been crowded with summer holiday visitors, and the noise was deafening – children were shouting, dogs were barking, waves breaking – and I had been rescued by a search party in the nick of time.

Here there was no one to rescue me. The moor was deserted, a barren wasteland, and silent except for the whispering sound of the wind in my ears, and the loud hammering of my heart. What could I – must I do? Should I, like a desperate escaping convict, try to make a run for it? But where? And how? My weak and trembling legs were quite unable to run. I was alone; I was doomed. I was lost.

And then, at that precise moment, there appeared like a miracle, round the only bend in the entire length of the straight flat road, Miss Beevor at the wheel of her Baby Austin, with my mother sitting beside her.

'Mummy!' And as I rushed forward, sobbing as though I was again a very little girl, seven years old, the horrible fat man accelerated, and vanishing – like the Devil himself, but in a burst of speed, not a puff of smoke – was gone.

So I can forgive Jacquie Edelsten for scoffing at Rupert Brooke. It is a small enough price to pay for the reassurance of her bold, her utterly fearless company as we stand at the Mannamead bus stop together. Never mind if we do miss the Crapstone bus: I have Jacquie now to protect me.

Our father has ceased to be a patient in the Plymouth psychiatric nursing home where I had to go and visit him every

Friday afternoon of last year's winter term. Having, evidently, recovered from what Mummy always refers to as his nervous breakdown, he is now staying with his half-brother, our Uncle Malcolm, and Aunt Lilian, in Newcastle, which is miles and miles away, somewhere up in the north of England.

When I ask Mummy if Daddy will be coming home soon, she replies, calmly, that he won't be returning.

'What – never? Isn't he – isn't Daddy ever coming back?'

Mummy says she thinks probably not. She says the Midland Bank has promised that when he is completely better, her husband – our father – will be given the same job as he had before he was ill, but it won't be in Plymouth; it will be in an altogether different branch of the Bank, and wherever it is, that's where he will live and work in future, on his own, just as though he didn't have a family.

On hearing this astonishing piece of information I am conscious of an enormous weight, a black fear, lifting off my mind, evaporating.

'But won't he miss us, Mummy?' I ask her, feeling guilty at the immensity of my relief. 'Won't he feel lonely, all on his own?'

My mother tells me I'm not to worry. She herself sounds perfectly serene. What has happened is, of course, very sad, but it may perhaps turn out, in the end, to be for the best. Poor Daddy may really, she says, be happier living alone, without the nuisance of a wife and four children to get in his way and interfere with the painting he likes to do in his spare time.

It is undeniably true that *we* are happier without him; much happier. So far as the Twins and I, and even Harvey, are concerned, our lives are nowadays vastly improved: liberated. And for our mother, too, the catastrophe – as it certainly was when it occurred – has had a visibly beneficial consequence, enabling her to develop a small but companionable circle of what we, her children, were always plentifully supplied with, but she was not: local friends.

Mummy has become increasingly intimate with our near neighbours, the two elderly Miss Beevor sisters, whose hobby it is to breed Jack Russell terriers; and young Mrs Pilcher, wife of Commander Pilcher who gives Pam a lift into the Plymouth Art School every morning in his car, has requested Mummy, quite as a favour, to dispense with formality and call her Rosemary.

There are also, amongst those ladies who left their cards on our silver salver when we first arrived, others willing at last, it seems, to progress beyond the limits of polite acquaintanceship. In short, Mrs Hallsmith, unencumbered by the prickly presence of Mr Hallsmith, is beginning to be accepted by at least a few of the Crapstone residents as one of them.

As for me, I can relax, can let down my defences: they are not needed. I am no longer haunted by the bogey of that awful word, *madness*. In Newquay there would surely have been a considerable stir caused by the sudden disappearance of Mr Hallsmith. But here it isn't a subject for gossip. I overhear no whispers, detect no hushed voices. Nobody appears to be in the slightest bit interested, or to find it peculiar that we four Hallsmith children are reduced all at once to having a single parent. Illness serves as a sufficient explanation. The failure of our father to make an impression – more than a faint and a mildly disagreeable one – on Crapstone society, means that his abrupt removal from it is simply not noticed.

During the summer of what was to be – although we weren't aware of it then – our last year living in Newquay, Pam and I were sent on a long train journey from Cornwall to Surrey, to stay with our father's rich relations, Cousin Edith and her daughter Cousin Mildred Martin, for the Silver Jubilee of

King George and Queen Mary – an unforgettably colourful historical event, unlike anything we had experienced before.

When, eighteen months or so later, we heard that King George had died – the King we had ourselves witnessed riding through the streets of London in a splendid open glittering carriage – we were sorry, naturally, but not surprised. We remembered his white beard and his bent shoulders, and how old we had thought he looked: old and tired.

The young and popular Prince of Wales, who was next in line of succession to the throne, immediately became King Edward the Eighth. But then, before the ceremony of his coronation could take place, there was a tremendous fuss in the newspapers and on the wireless news bulletins, and we learnt that King Edward had abdicated. This was because of him being in love with Mrs Wallis Simpson, a twice-divorced American. To have a divorced person (and divorced, moreover, not once, but twice) as Queen of England was plainly out of the question. Consequently, King Edward had to choose: either he could be officially crowned the ruling British monarch, or else he could hold on to Mrs Simpson; and he chose to hold on to her.

This meant arranging at the very last minute for an entirely different coronation, with his younger brother stepping hurriedly into the breach. Which is the reason why now, in 1938, King George the Sixth, and his wife Elizabeth, and their two little princess daughters, are living in Buckingham Palace, while King Edward the Eighth – who was once the Prince of Wales – has been made into the Duke of Windsor and gone off to France to marry Mrs Simpson and change her into a Duchess. Except that she's middle-aged and not at all pretty, there are certain similarities, it strikes me, with the story of Cinderella.

Apart from such unavoidably noteworthy royal family upheavals, my attention has been so focussed in the last few

71

years on the momentous changes occurring within our own family that world affairs have rather passed me by. It's true I've overheard my brother Jim talking with boys of his age (they are nearly always boys) about the Spanish Civil War, and about the International Brigades – a name given to the bands of heroic men who, supported by nothing except their political convictions, volunteered to travel out to Spain and join in the battles because the British Government refused to have anything to do with foreigners fighting one another. But these were mere wisps of conversation, weightless as thistle-down floating past me on the breeze, unattached to reality.

Since the conflict was between Spaniards and Spaniards I tended to get muddled as to which – Republicans or Nationalists – was the good side, and which the bad. Jim did tell me I must hope that General Franco would lose the struggle: he is a Fascist. And Mussolini in Italy is also a Fascist, and so is Adolf Hitler in Germany; only the German Fascists are called Nazis, which makes it even more confusing. Nobody has explained to me what, exactly, Fascism is. Fundamentally, so I gather, it's *undemocratic* (but I don't really understand the meaning of democratic, either) and therefore a threat to everyone, even to us here in England.

This is the year when I shall change from being fourteen into being fifteen. As a matter of fact I've already changed a good deal. Until recently I was considered to be small for my age. Mummy used to call me a little shrimp, but she can't call me that any more. Everybody is astonished at how fast I'm growing – I'm surprised myself. And it isn't a question only of inches. Growing taller means I'm growing up. I've been slow to get started, but now that I have started all sorts of changes are happening – are bound to happen – the most important and pleasureable of which, I have come to the conclusion, is falling in love.

My sister Pam reached her full height, and people were falling in love with her, by the time she was twelve. Pam, though, was always extremely pretty, and I'm not; so I don't expect to be admired for my appearance, as she is for hers. Besides, it's me who does the falling in love – again and again: bouts of passionate adoration that never last, or remain fixed on the same person, for very long, and are seldom – actually, never – reciprocated. But to be in love with real live boys, or even *men*, even briefly, is so much better, so much more enjoyable, as Jacquie Edelsten and I agree, than being in love (our favourite topic at present) with film stars, or with someone who died, like beautiful Rupert Brooke (or, in her case, Percy Bysshe Shelley) before we were born. There's no comparison.

When Lewarne Hosking turns up unexpectedly in Crapstone one Friday morning in September, he doesn't at first mention our father, simply announcing breezily that he has driven here from Porth in Cornwall, the whole cross-country distance, for the purpose of taking us all – Mummy included – back with him to spend the weekend at his holiday bungalow by the sea. He will drive us home again, he says, on Sunday evening.

During the time we lived in Newquay, Lewarne Hosking was the eccentric generous Liverpool friend who came and went every summer; the holiday friend who played tennis with Daddy and who produced for us children a supply of treats and presents on a lavish scale. Since leaving Newquay and moving to Crapstone we haven't seen him; not until today. The reason for him appearing so suddenly, unheralded, and for his equally surprising proposal to whisk us off on an impromptu Cornish outing is especially, he declares, for us to have the tremendous fun of paddling his newly-acquired canoe on Porth estuary at high tide.

A canoe – but how marvellous! And how typical of Lewarne to think of conjuring up a magical canoe!

Almost at once, though, as we listen to him enthusiastically unfolding his plan to us, the vision, like a dream on waking, fades. Lewarne, we realise with consternation, has no idea – none – of the disastrous events which took place in the Bridge House Hotel, Porth's bed-and-breakfast establishment, the previous autumn. Hushed up as those events were, guarded from public view, he believes that our parents parted because of an unfortunate misunderstanding, a tiff of sorts, and our kind affectionate well-meaning friend has determined to heal the breach himself by bringing them together this weekend for a happy reunion under the roof of the Hoskings' holiday bungalow.

The scene has accordingly been set, and we now learn that Guthrie – Daddy – after staying for a while with Uncle Malcolm in Newcastle, then paid a brief call on Lewarne in Liverpool, and is at this very moment in Porth, awaiting the arrival of his long-lost family.

Meaningful glances are exchanged between the Hallsmiths. Clearly an explanation is required: an immediate spilling of the beans. Lewarne is led away by Mummy into the sitting room where, behind a discreetly closed door, she proceeds to give him – or we presume she does – an account of what actually did happen that awful night a year ago. Some version of it, at any rate, she must have felt obliged to tell him, for Lewarne emerges from their private conversation speechless and looking decidedly shaken: shocked, in fact.

Mummy, understandably, has declined the weekend invitation; and so has Jim. But there is nothing, she says, to stop the girls, Pam and Elspeth, from going, and taking little Harvey along as well. Lewarne, after all, was trying to be helpful, and we don't want to seem ungrateful. She urges the three of us to accept his offer.

Why, I wonder, does Mummy urge us to go? Is it perhaps in the hope of hearing news, a direct and up-to-date report from our lips, of how Guthrie, her banished husband, has been managing alone without the support of Janet, his wife?

Whether or not this is her motive, Pam and Harvey have no need of persuasion. For the anticipated pleasure of messing about in a real canoe at the seaside they are ready and willing to endure a certain amount of awkwardness, inevitable on meeting their disgraced father.

It is I who am filled with nervous dread at the prospect of coming face to face with Daddy again. Clutching tight hold of towel and bathing costume like a talisman to ward off evil, I climb into the back seat of the Lagonda, reminding myself, by way of comfort, that I am a year older than when I saw Daddy last in the Plymouth nursing home, and inches taller: growing up – fifteen! Besides, I shall have my sister close at hand if I need protection. Pam has never gone in fear of our father; or of anyone. When we were small I depended on her courage to shelter me: the courage I so dismally lacked. It's different now, of course; but still, I'm glad to think that Pam will be there.

I could have spared myself the worry. Daddy has, both figuratively and actually, shrunk. The shabby hunched individual we encounter in Lewarne Hosking's bungalow bears no resemblance to the monster I've been busily creating in my imagination. Bewildered, apparently, by our arrival, he seems hardly to recognise, much less to care, who we are.

The transformation in our father is truly astonishing. Can this be the same person, the parent who so darkened and dominated our childhood with his moods of ever deepening despair? Who inspired always an emotion of uneasiness, if not worse, in me, and often of terror in Jim? But instead of pity for today's poor, ignominious, inarticulate, shambling parody of the father we had known, I am conscious only of a sense of liberation, of the freedom gained by a burden being finally shed.

Do I feel no compassion, no compunction, no spark of gratitude in remembering how Daddy used to read poetry aloud to me, poems he wanted *El-sa-beth*, his favourite, to share with him? And what about the adventure stories he loved and recommended, and the interest he showed in my own puerile attempts at writing? No, I don't remember, here, now, in Porth, any of that. What I feel is relief, only relief.

By four o'clock the tide has flooded the entire estuary, changing it into a broad expanse of placid water. We carry Lewarne's latest expensive toy, his canoe – the description of which in Crapstone had proved an irresistible lure – down to the seashore, and launch it carefully, reverently, on to the gently lapping ripples of what looks like a vast lake. *This* is why we have come to Porth: for the delightful experience of learning how to paddle a canoe. Daddy has faded into insignificance.

The following morning, when the tide is out and too low for canoeing, I discover Frederick Hertzel. He is sitting in one of the many little secluded sandy coves, bare-legged and suntanned, wearing khaki shorts, his knees drawn up, reading a book. I too have a book – *The Tragedy of the Korosko* – so I sit down on the sand, a few yards from him, and pretend to be immersed in it. After five or six minutes he raises his head and asks me across the gap, speaking with a noticeably foreign accent, if the book I am reading is enjoyable, and what is its name, and who wrote it? I tell him. And by the time I've explained the plot, and sketched the characters, and answered, as best I can, his questions, it's as though we've been friends for years.

Frederick is a Swiss university student. His subject at

college, he informs me, is the English language, which he hopes, while on a walking tour of the Cornish coast, to improve by having conversations with anyone he may chance to meet – for instance, with me. At night he camps out on the grassy cliff-tops in a tent.

He is so handsome and smiling, Frederick, so very easy to talk to. We lie side by side on the beach, chatting away for hours and hours – for two hours, at least – about books, and my school, and me wanting to be a writer, and goodness knows what else. For the whole of Saturday morning he belongs to me. He is my exclusive possession: the treasure I found, the prize I captured, single-handed – *mine*!

But then – then, of course, inevitably I lose him.

This afternoon, when the tide is again high, and Lewarne and the rest of us are taking it in turns to paddle the canoe, Frederick Hertzel strolls up to our laughing, splashing group, and I have no alternative but to introduce him to the others. Whereupon he ceases to be just my friend, and becomes immediately everybody's friend; in particular Pam's.

Lewarne Hosking, our hospitable host, insists on the charming young foreign student joining us for supper at the bungalow. Frederick, likewise charmed, and practising his excellent English, helps to carry the canoe up from the beach, while I, trailing miserably along behind them, carry his jersey bundled in my arms: the nearest I can get to salvaging a bit of Frederick Hertzel for myself. When I bury my nose in the jersey's thick woolly folds, the smell of his dried sweat is almost unbearably poignant. I feel cheated, bereft. It isn't fair. Frederick was *my* friend.

Lying on the beach this morning, talking, talking, there had appeared to be no great difference in our ages. But I was wrong. It's obvious now that there is a crucial difference. Pam, at seventeen, is practically grown up, whereas I – it's true – haven't yet grown up. And apart from the matter of ages, I'm not – I know I'm not – remarkably pretty, which my sister Pam *is*. It was bound to happen.

On Sunday evening Lewarne drives the three of us, me and Pam and Harvey, back to Crapstone, as promised. Bidding goodbye to Daddy we forget to ask him where he means to go next – what are his future intentions? On the cross-country journey home my sorrowful thoughts are wholly occupied by the losing, not of Daddy, but of beautiful suntanned Frederick Hertzel.

It is the start of the winter term, and I am in the Fifth Form, appointed, to my amazement, one of the school's three prefects. Barbara Haley is the second of the trio, and Cynthia Winn combines being third prefect with occupying the most senior position of Head Girl. More amazing, however, than my new status is the total disappearance of Miss Bailey from the scene, a vanishing act for which I, and everyone else, was unprepared, but rejoice at wholeheartedly. No more Miss Bailey! Hurray!

Her place as Headmistress has been filled by Miss Ellen Pocock, the sister of tall stoopy droopy vague Miss Grace Pocock, who was until now Miss Bailey's ineffectual door-mat of a partner. Miss Ellen, as we have been instructed to call her, while not being as tall as her younger sister, is neither droopy nor vague, but the exact reverse. I'm attracted to her at once because of something about Miss Ellen Pocock that reminds me of Miss Howard, the person who gave Pam and me lessons when we lived in Newquay. Miss Ellen Pocock – like Miss Howard, but unlike Miss Bailey – has an air, instantly discernable, of being, above all else, an educational-ist: a born teacher. I find her presence, her calmly confident manner of steely but sympathetic authority, reassuring. With Miss Ellen Pocock I feel safe.

I've been entered for the Oxford and Cambridge Board's

leaving examination next summer, known as the School Certificate. My mother, on receiving a note from Miss Ellen Pocock requesting the favour of a meeting with her so as to have 'a little talk' about Elspeth, accordingly sets out one Saturday morning by bus for Plymouth, wearing her best hat and gloves, and serenely untroubled. It is I who am worried, not my mother. I hang around anxiously in the hall at home, waiting, and pounce on her the moment I hear the front door open.

'Why did Miss Ellen want to see you, Mummy? What did she *say* about me?'

My mother peels off her gloves with dramatic slowness, a triumphant gleam, which increases my anxiety, in her eye. 'Miss Pocock says –' An unsettling pause.

'Go on, Mummy – go *on*. *What* did she say?'

'She said that you are a clever child, Elspeth, naturally intelligent, and that you should do well in the June exam, provided –' Another, for me, agonising pause. '– *providing* you break off your association with Jacqueline Edelsten. She's a very bad influence on you, Elspeth – I've always thought so. Miss Pocock is quite right. She leads you astray, that wretched girl, Jacqueline.'

This – *ah ha!* – accounts for the gleam of triumph. My mother has indeed always disapproved of our friendship, and is glad to have been given official backing for her growing suspicion of Jacquie's flamboyantly anarchic attitude to the rules of behaviour generally accepted in polite society.

Although I'm convinced my mother's words are a fairly free translation of those used by Miss Ellen, there is nevertheless a grain of truth in them. Jacquie makes no secret of her scorn for Moorfields and for the entire school syllabus. My hopeful argument that with our new headmistress a new era has dawned she refuses even to contemplate.

I block my ears to Jacquie's remembered mockery,

beseeching my mother: 'Did she – Miss Ellen – did she *really* say that – that I'm brainy?'

'I've told you, Elspeth – yes, she did. She said you were clever – intelligently receptive, is how she put it – and that if you only work hard this coming year you stand an excellent chance of getting high marks in your School Certificate exam.'

I want so very much to believe what Mummy tells me Miss Ellen said, that I do succeed in believing it, and allow myself to glow with pride. *I'm not stupid* – I'm intelligently receptive! And to justify Miss Ellen's good opinion of me, I *will* work – I will. Because, after all, isn't this what I've always, deep down, wanted, longed for: to *learn*.

A frontier has been crossed: I feel I've entered that new era I had envisaged, had hoped for; a new world of exhilarating endeavour, and if Jacquie jeers at me – let her! I won't listen.

My brother Jim has also, simultaneously, crossed a frontier. He has reached the end of his time at Exeter School and, this term he goes up to Oxford University to read (meaning to study) Modern Languages. He has won an Exhibition (a sort of scholarship, I think) to St Edmund's Hall – or Teddy Hall, as they call it – the smallest of all the colleges, but ancient and distinguished, so Jim informs me.

Although my sister Pam and I have been drifting apart in recent years, Jim and I have drawn closer. I'm pleased and flattered that my older brother seems to enjoy having conversations with me, and likes to lend me books, and explain to me the political situation in Europe, which is very gloomy. There is an alarming rumour circulating of a possible – probable – war with our country and Germany. What will fighting a war actually mean, I wonder, to us? It sounds horrifying, and also incredible.

But then, luckily, our Prime Minister, Mr Neville Chamberlain, flies off to Berlin, the capital city of Germany, to see Herr Hitler, and returns waving a sheet of paper on the steps of his aeroplane, and announcing the wonderful news that he has achieved '*peace with honour*'. What a mercy! We can breathe again! And since there isn't, thankfully, going to be a beastly war, I can stop fretting, and concentrate my mind instead on the historical importance of the Industrial Revolution.

Every Sunday Harvey and I walk with Mummy downhill from Crapstone to the church in Buckland Monachorum for matins, the morning service. Pam comes with us on Christmas Day and Easter Day, but otherwise never. Jim, when he's home for the holidays, does occasionally, to please Mummy, join us on the Sunday church outing.

I like the walk there and back, and I like the church itself, which is old and small and snug, and I enjoy singing the hymns, but most of the prayers and the readings are dread-fully dull, and so, usually, is the sermon, a kindly and, with any luck, a brief lecture delivered to the congregation – including us in the front row – by the Rev. Lennard-Williams from the lofty eminence of his pulpit.

Once a month the eleven o'clock service has an extra bit, Holy Communion, tacked on at the end. I was confirmed this year by Bishop Dawkes in Plymouth Cathedral, so now, as though I were a full-blown adult Christian, I leave Harvey sitting alone in our pew, and follow my mother up to the altar rails where we kneel down, side by side, and I receive, when it's my turn, the biscuity wafer and a sip of the red wine.

Jacquie Edelsten did start off coming with me to the half-dozen religious instructions which were meant to prepare us for our solemn acceptance of the Christian faith, but she upset the vicar, interrupting and interrogating him so force-fully and to such an extent that he told her, after the second hour of instruction, not to come again. She was, he said, unready as yet, evidently, for the sacred rite of confirmation: a banning order that, of course, delighted Jacquie.

I'm not really sure if *I* should have been confirmed, either. During the administration of Holy Communion I ought to be feeling – oughtn't I? – something tremendous, uplifting, some sort of heavenly sensation; and I don't. My only feeling is nervousness, the fear of disgracing myself by dropping the biscuit or spilling the wine. And I worry that it's unforgivably bad of me – a form of cheating; even wicked, perhaps – to take Holy Communion without having the proper holy feeling inside. As I'm not able to explain my anxiety to Mummy, or to the Rev. Lennard-Williams, or to anyone (and certainly not to Jacquie), I shall have to go on suffering my sin in silence: I can't see any solution to the problem.

Daddy never went to church, except, like Pam, on Christmas Day. He didn't – doesn't – believe in God or Jesus Christ. It was one of the many disagreements between him and our mother. When Mummy was very young, before the Great War, she had been engaged to marry Basil McNeil, the son of a clergyman. Basil McNeil intended to be a clergyman too, and it was only because he died of TB that they didn't get married. I think if she had been a vicar's wife it would have suited Mummy extremely well. She would have been good at it.

Our mother appears to have adapted completely to a situation some people might have found awkward: that of being a married woman who has a husband alive but not living with her. Instead of skulking away shamefacedly, or behaving as if in mourning for a sudden sad bereavement, Mummy is resolutely cheerful and energetic, full of lively inventive plans to keep herself, and us, busy.

The confidence which for so long, like a life jacket floating on dark waters, had buoyed her up, she lost – losing it in the desolate stormy weeks and months before finally losing Guthrie – and without her necessary support was then left (as I remember clearly seeing her, one fearful afternoon) helpless and sinking. But now those days of desperation are past, and Mummy's native confidence, that vital attribute, is fully restored. Her spirited demeanour implies – insists – that there is no reason for Mrs Hallsmith to be viewed by the world as an object of pity: none whatever.

In the Christmas holidays she volunteers to organise and produce a festive entertainment in Buckland Monachorum village hall on behalf of the Mothers' Union of which she has become a member and a leading light. We are aghast at her audacity, predicting humiliating failure, but she pooh-poohs our concern. Nonsense! – it will be perfectly easy to arrange. And she assures us of having already once undertaken, and had acclaimed, a similar type of variety show with a group of her wounded wartime soldiers. We are to stop fussing and leave it to Mummy: she will manage everything, and all will be well!

So, stifling our misgivings, we do leave it to her. And as it turns out, in vindication of our mother's newly recovered self-confidence, all *is* well.

The evening's entertainment consists of a number of short – very short – amusing sketches, humorous incidents which are neither more nor less than jokes culled from the pages of ancient *Punch* magazines: slightly enlarged and embellished one-liners. Our mother's troupe of performers is composed simply of her family – Pam and Jim, me, Harvey, and herself – aided enthusiastically by Laurence Brown, the boy from next door, whose chief job is to pull the curtains back and forth, and be sharp about it.

Other than a chair or two, and a table, there is no scenery. The acting required is minimal; the dialogue likewise.

Costumes also are basic, a supply mainly of different hats and scarves. The only absolutely essential ingredient is a crackingly fast pace, and this, thanks to Laurence Brown, is maintained throughout. Our Buckland Monachorum audience roars with laughter, claps and cheers. Incredibly, for a single dizzy night, *The Hallsmith Hooligans* are a huge local success – as our mother had never for a moment doubted we should be.

The organisational ability of our mother is outstanding: a gift bestowed in her cradle. And her impulse, as guileless as a flower turning towards the sun, to exhibit herself dramatically, and provoke applause, is equally inborn and instinctive. Is it any wonder that in the initial years of marriage, before an overwhelming tide of despair blotted out their early optimistic hopes and dreams, Guthrie, her husband, grew increasingly resentful of his beautiful wife's never-failing star appeal, when what he wanted, and believed he deserved, was to be the star himself?

Every Wednesday morning since Christmas the two front sitting-rooms of Melrose – their intervening sliding doors pushed back to maximise the space available – have been converted into a temporary workshop, crammed with trestle tables and everything necessary in the business of tailoring. This weekly transformation is the consequence of our mother having read and responded to a printed notice pinned up in the post office window. Miss Higgins, an enterprising woman trained as a tailoress, earns her living by travelling around the countryside holding tailoring classes in the homes of her clients. Mummy and the six or seven Crapstone ladies she has persuaded to subscribe to the scheme, who have each paid three guineas in advance to Miss Higgins, are being taught by her how to tailor.

Our mother can claim, with justice, to be an accomplished

dressmaker. It was she who regularly chose the checked or flowery cotton material, and cut it out and sewed, on her Singer machine, the summer frocks worn by me and Pam when we were growing up in Newquay (nowadays my art-student sister prefers to design and create her own clothes, independently). But Mummy's dressmaking is a happy-go-lucky occupation compared to the rigorous discipline of Miss Higgins' professional tailoring, as she and her fellow pupils very soon discover.

Was it more for their sociability value that Mummy initiated these Wednesday morning meetings, rather than from a genuine wish to be taught – for example – the tiresome fiddly rule requiring lapels and collars to have a meticulously stitched canvas interlining? Does the whirr of sewing machines and the chatter of voices, the snip-snap of scissors and the chink of teacups fill an unacknowledged void in my brave mother's life, furnish her with a comforting illusion of being, for an hour or two, among friends?

Whatever was the real reason that gave rise to these Wednesday gatherings, they don't last. Enthusiasm for tailoring wanes. The novelty turns into a bore and then into a chore. Excuses are offered; attendance drops off. By Easter the only remaining survivors of Mummy's latest project are Rosemary Pilcher and the elderly Miss Beevors, whose motivation, I feel sure, in continuing doggedly to stick the course out, is an unselfish desire not to disappoint Mrs Hallsmith.

But at the conclusion they do together quietly decide that, although it undoubtedly is an advantage to have acquired, as they have done, the useful skills of perfecting buttonholes and set-in pockets, nevertheless one course of tailoring suffices.

Although the tailoring venture may have proved something of a damp squib, my mother is dauntless and refuses to be disheartened. She maintains that it was an experiment well worth attempting; as evidence of which she cites the fact that, thanks to the three guineas paid to Miss Higgins for her expert guidance, Elspeth now goes to church in a charming new green spring overcoat.

I'm grateful to Mummy for making me a new coat. It's very kind of her. But I'm sorry (I haven't said so) that it's green, instead of blue. It didn't occur to her to ask me beforehand what colour, or what shape, I'd like my coat to be. I can't help thinking the fitted waist and the flared skirt looks babyish. Mummy doesn't seem to realise that on my next birthday, in August, I shall be sixteen. She imagines I'm still a little girl, and I'm not.

She has, however, remembered and taken seriously what Miss Ellen Pocock said to her about the possibility of Elspeth getting good results in the School Certificate examination next term. Greta Gruber is the Swiss graduate whose photograph and qualifications Mummy found in the pages of an educational brochure, and settled on as a suitable young woman from whom I can receive intensive tutoring during the Easter holidays in French: an exam subject that could perhaps be given a much needed boost with a hasty bout of extra coaching.

Our mother has been abroad once only, and it was to Switzerland, very long ago, before the Great War, when Basil McNeil lay ill with TB in a sanitorium there. This might account for why she selects, as someone to teach me French, an inhabitant, not of France, but of Switzerland, which no doubt has for Mummy a reassuringly familiar ring about it. In any case, it is to Greta Gruber of Basel she addresses her letter, and Greta Gruber who, having responded, accepting Mrs Hallsmith's invitation, duly arrives in Crapstone.

She arrives in Crapstone, and, far from her being a damp squib, Greta Gruber is immediately perceived to be a live

wire. Suntanned and healthy, pretty, smiling, speaking fault-
less English and aged twenty-four, she and Mummy take to
each other at the very first glance. And we, also, take at once
– the Twins and me, and Harvey – without a moment's hesitation, to Greta Gruber. Made instantly welcome in the
Hallsmith household, she strikes us as being like the best sort
of an older sister: commonsensical and yet full of fun, ready
and willing to join in any of the outdoor activities we suggest
to her, no matter how strenuous.

Every day starts with the same routine. For three hours
after breakfast, from nine till twelve o'clock, she and I occupy
a corner of the sitting room and concentrate on my acquiring, under her inspired tutelage, a better knowledge than my
present feeble grasp of the French language. Why at school
did I dismiss it – (poor, tormented Mam'selle!) – as dull and
boring? It's nothing of the kind! Greta and I study grammar,
and as I commit to memory lists of verbs and their tenses I
revel in its precision, its logic. French is a beautiful language!
We read aloud the poetry of Baudelaire, and tales from
Lettres de Mon Moulin; and when she congratulates me on
my pronunciation I swell with pride. How amazing! I can
actually speak and be understood in French!

For the rest of the day Greta is free to have her company
enjoyed by the whole Hallsmith family, and by the numerous friends who dropping in, then remain, lingering on
captivated. Whatever it is we agree to do, Greta does it with
us. She plays hockey, and rounders, and kick-the-can;
borrows a bicycle and comes on picnics down to Denham
Bridge with us; tramps across the moors, and scrambles
ahead of us, laughing and agile, to the top of the nearest
rocky tor. At home, in the kitchen, she helps to prepare and
cook the meals, and she teaches Mummy how to make delicious *apfel strudel*.

Besides her inexhaustible energy and unfailing good

humour, Greta Gruber possesses the extra exotic charm of being a foreigner. We have seldom before, in our parochial existence, bumped into foreigners (members of any race not unmistakably British always had the effect of arousing Daddy's deepest suspicions), and we have certainly never until now had one of them staying as a guest in our house, actually sharing our daily lives. Bowled over, as we are, by Greta's frank engaging personality, she reciprocates the compliment, admitting that, ever since her childhood she has been a fervent admirer of England and the English. When the holidays are over, as they soon will be, and her Crapstone visit comes to an end, she would very much like, she says, to see more of our lovely country. But how can that be accomplished? How and where to begin?

Her enquiry is answered in the most fortuitous manner by the arrival on our doorstep of Frederick Hertzel, who has returned to England to complete his walking tour of the Cornish coastline, cut short last year due to the onset of winter. What in the world could be more timely? He is over-joyed by the happy chance of encountering under our roof a fellow Swiss citizen, and Greta, for her part, is equally delighted. What a lucky coincidence indeed! Frederick, by offering to take Greta with him – under his wing, as it were – on his travels, has at a stroke solved her problem. He guarantees that with him to escort and protect her, Greta Gruber will come to *no harm*.

We Hallsmiths are not exactly shocked, or scandalised, but we are a little dubious. Do the conventional rules of polite society allow, we wonder, for a young Swiss man and a young Swiss woman, who have only just met one another, to set off on a walking tour together? Perhaps the Swiss have different rules of behaviour?

'Dear Greta is a very sensible girl,' says Mummy, firmly, but frowning, as if not entirely convinced by Greta's assurance of the wisdom and the purely practical nature of the partnership. 'She's old enough to make up her own mind – it's her decision; and she is determined to go –' With an involuntary barely suppressed sigh of anxiety, Mummy adds: 'And she may be – yes, I daresay she's probably right. It really wouldn't have been wise for a girl, even a girl as sensible as Greta, to take the risk of going on a walking tour alone.'

As for Frederick, our mother judges him to be a thoroughly reliable young man. 'I'm sure he is; and absolutely trustworthy – honourable. He promised me – *promised* me – he would take good care of her; as good care as if, he said, he had been her brother.'

We shall see Greta again in a few weeks time when she stops by to pick up the suitcase left in our keeping. Meanwhile, we wave them off. A sturdy well-matched pair they look: each is shouldering a rucksack, and Greta is equipped in addition with her newly-bought lightweight camping tent, and stout walking boots.

'She's an adventurous young woman – a courageous girl,' says Mummy, rather wistfully, gazing after their disappearing figures. 'I couldn't have stopped her.'

Since the weekend in Porth when I found and befriended Frederick Hertzel, less than seven months have elapsed. It was I who found him. He was my discovery, my own particular friend, my hero – mine – and when I lost him to Pam and Lewarne Hosking I was miserable, torn by pangs of agonising jealousy. Yet now I'm able to stand in the road, calmly, and watch him striding off into the distance with Greta, and suffer not the faintest qualm. How can this be possible? I don't know how – I'm surprised myself – but that's the way it is.

Partly, I suppose, the adoration I felt in September for Frederick has evaporated because of me having recently fallen in love with Robert Winnicott, a boy Terence Dewar brought along to play in the Saturday hockey matches organised on the usual scrubby patch of moorland by Commander Burton. Robert is tall, handsome (*I* think), a year-and-a-half older than me, and a demon centre-forward. As he scores most, or all, of the goals for whichever side he's on, everyone, naturally, wants to be on the same side as him. So far he hasn't paid much attention to me, but according to Sam Pyne he's a tennis player too, which means that, with any luck, we'll meet again in the summer holidays.

Quite apart from Robert Winnicott, another reason why I no longer mind about Frederick is because I've become fired with an ambition to succeed in the School Certificate Leaving Examination, and falling-in-love thoughts are an emotional distraction I can't afford to indulge until it's over. I want, if I can, to get high marks in the English and Literature and History papers: these are my favourite subjects. And I might even – spurred on by Greta's praise – do well in French. I shall have to work hard, though – and I'm glad of that: I *want* to work hard.

This will be my final term at Moorfields, and on the first day back at school it's like stepping into a new and a rather exciting hothouse atmosphere. Not everybody in the Fifth Form is a candidate for School Cert., but those of us who are – Cynthia and Barbara, Brenda, Gillian, Joan Murray and me – will be having our lessons separately from now on. The room allocated to us for our exclusive use is remote and quiet, situated upstairs, on the further side of a door that divides the building in two, a frontier closing off and guarding its private elegantly furnished regions from any disturbance by the noisy swarming horde of inky pupils. None but staff would ever dare to cross that sacred threshold.

Now, for us, the rules of trespass are relaxed, and we, the

chosen few, have permission – have, indeed, instructions – to enter the forbidden territory. So impressed are we by the grandeur of our surroundings and the honour of our unique privilege that we mount and descend the wide soft-carpeted main staircase almost on tiptoe. The soundproof door is, we realise, a graphic symbol: in passing beyond it we have passed through a barrier of much greater significance to our lives.

We find that suddenly, here at school (home is a different country altogether), we are being taken seriously, treated as intelligent individuals, with powers of hidden, previously untapped initiative. Startled, but flattered, we respond by taking ourselves more seriously. If unknown, unseen university academics have deemed us worthy to be granted this test of scholarship, then we, put on our mettle, resolve to accept the challenge and to tackle it with gusto.

Day after day, heads bowed over old School Certificate papers, we try to get accustomed to the strangeness of their official printed appearance, so alarmingly unlike the blotchy purple-jelly handwritten stencilled copies normally distributed for our end-of-year exams. We struggle to familiarise ourselves with the format, the phrasing, and the type of questions asked; to learn how to pinpoint whatever is the central issue, and to deal with it swiftly and concisely, never for a moment forgetting the inflexible limits imposed on our efforts by the ticking of the clock. We read, we listen to our teacher, we scribble notes; we offer solutions, answers, are corrected, explained to, scribble again – day after day after day.

Miss Ellen supervises us for the set Scripture syllabus: St John's Gospel – short and exceedingly dramatic – and The Acts of the Apostles, also dramatic, in particular the description of St Paul's shipwreck. Then there is English as a written spoken language. Do we fully understand its grammatical structures? Can we parse, analyse, reduce to one brief succinct paragraph the rather stuffy essays of Charles Lamb and William Hazlitt? (A tiresome exercise that may, I presume, be useful training for anybody who has plans, as I have, to be a writer).

In comparison to the rigours of English grammar, English Literature is a glorious imaginative romp. I learn by heart, easily, the whole of 'The Rime of the Ancient Mariner' (*Fear not, fear not, thou Wedding Guest/ This body dropt not down*), and speech upon speech from *Macbeth* (*Infirm of purpose, give ME the dagger*). History is considerably more difficult: Disraeli and Gladstone, Home Rule and the Corn Laws – but enlivened by the Tolpuddle Martyrs and the Luddites. The subject of Geography is bound, I fear, to bring on me the shame of total failure, for which I blame fat smelly angry Miss Joplin and her insane insistence on the importance of the Trade Winds. As for Mathematics, if I can somehow manage to scrape by, even at the lowest level, it will be a miracle: numbers are my nightmare.

Thus the weeks of laborious preparation come and go, and the date we dread and look forward to in equal measure draws nearer and nearer, a creeping unstoppable tide that eventually reaches and engulfs us. The fateful day dawns when we six girls are to be incarcerated in our isolated upstairs room, as though infected with the plague. And here we must remain for a seemingly interminable fortnight of mornings and afternoons, until at last – yes, at last – we arrive at the end of the tunnel and emerge into daylight, exhausted but exultant, knowing that whether the results are good or bad, we did our best, and it's finished: it's over!

So also are my schooldays over. By the middle of July I have ceased to be a schoolgirl. What comes next? I wonder. What happens now?

* * *

It is the beginning of the summer holidays and Pam and I are again staying at Sanderstead with old Cousin Edith and her daughter, dear jolly Cousin Mildred, as we have done on several occasions previously. The third day we are here our visit – peaceful, if rather dull – is, without warning, interrupted, and brought to a sudden conclusion. We are swooped down upon and whisked off at five minutes' notice to spend the rest of our Surrey vacation with Granny Hallsmith and our Aunts Dorothy and Rosemary, Daddy's two sisters, who live in Warlingham, a village not many miles away from the Martins' residence.

This is our first visit to their home, although why we haven't been before is a mystery; as great a mystery as why on earth our father's relations, the Hallsmiths and the Martins, living as they do at such close quarters, normally avoid, so it seems, having any social contact with one another.

Until now we have seldom met, and scarcely know, Aunt Dorothy and Aunt Rosemary. But Granny Hallsmith is by no means a stranger. Every August, as regular as clockwork, she used to visit us in Newquay. She came because she wanted, as we instinctively understood, to keep in touch with us, her grandchildren – her only grandchildren: the Twins and me, and, in due course, Harvey. Each year we looked forward to the day when we would see her familiar figure step down briskly from the train in the station, would hear her soft Scottish accent, her musical laugh, and be given the books she invariably unpacked from her suitcase for us; meanwhile observing, and puzzling over, the absence of affection, thinly disguised by a veneer of mutual civility, between the Granny we loved and our parents. What reasons could there possibly be to account for the coldness? We were left unenlightened. Parents, in our experience, do not speak openly to their offspring about the complicated emotions of adults. On the contrary, they are at pains to conceal.

This particular summer, Granny Hallsmith, having learnt by chance that Pam and Elspeth – *her* grandchildren – were staying once again with those Martins, was so indignant she resolved to act immediately and put an end to a situation blatantly unjust. It was outrageous that old Edith Martin – not even a blood relation, but connected merely by marriage (she is the widow of Granny's first cousin, Alec Martin) – should repeatedly be trusted to provide hospitality for the girls, and yet their own grandmother be denied their company. It was too bad! – insulting, unfair, and, in short, not to be borne!

Precisely what methods were employed for the successful kidnapping of me and Pam remain unclear. We think there must have been an almighty row, with sharp words exchanged, and feelings ruffled unforgiveably; but for us the upshot, however it was contrived, is totally delightful.

Fond as we are of good-natured Cousin Mildred – who used also to be a regular Newquay visitor – we find her old-fashioned elderly mother, Cousin Edith, somewhat awe-inspiring, and are constantly aware in her presence of the rigid rules of behaviour we must be careful not to transgress for fear of arousing disapproval. In Granny's modern bungalow there is no such formality. The little house resounds with jokes and laughter, and Pam and I can stop worrying the whole time, as we were having to do, about our manners and being polite: here, we quickly realise, anything goes! Whew! What a relief!

Aunt Dorothy, who is very tall, and her much younger, shorter, plumper, prettier sister, Aunt Rosemary, both embrace us as warmly as if we were long-lost lambs happily rescued from the wilderness. We are treated by them, moreover, not as children, but simply as young people of no particular age, and made unreservedly welcome. Might this cheerful, spontaneous behaviour, this lack of restraint, altogether different

94

from the restrictive atmosphere prevailing under Cousin Edith's roof – might it be enough, we wonder, to explain why the Warlingham Hallsmiths and the Sanderstead Martins are divided by what amounts to a state of downright hostility? Or is there more to it than appears on the surface – secrets that are thought to be unfit for our ears?

We do know Aunt Dorothy has a surname which isn't Hallsmith. She is called, officially, Mrs Henderson, because of having once been married. And we know, too, that her husband wasn't killed in the Great War, like her older brother Martin; nor did he die in the 'flu epidemic, which is what happened to Harvey, her younger brother. In fact, Aunt Dorothy and Captain Henderson were divorced, and whereas death, although sad, is an honourable fate, to be suffered with pride, divorce is unspeakably shocking. This could perhaps be the real reason for the mysterious family estrangement; but since we don't venture to enquire, we shall never be sure whether or not our guess is correct.

Granny's next-door neighbours have a grass tennis court that our Aunts Dorothy and Rosemary are allowed to play on whenever they want. They lend us a racquet each, and one afternoon we are joined there by Ronald and Bobbie Barnett, two gorgeous young men who are said to be so immensely rich they even possess their own private aeroplane and can pilot it themselves. Goodness, what sophisticated glamour! We are dazzled. Aunt Rosemary has been taken up in their aeroplane, she tells us, by Ronnie, for a flip. She refers to Ronnie as her boy-friend. (Our parents consider the phrase *boy-friend* a vulgar Americanism, and have forbidden us to use it.)

After supper we all (excepting, of course, Granny) decide to go for an evening spin under a full harvest moon in the Barnetts' expensive car that has an unpronounceable Italian name. The hood is folded flat, and Ronnie, with Rosemary beside him, drives us faster and faster on a straight open stretch of country road, singing loudly. Soon everyone starts to sing. Laughing, singing, shouting, we rocket along.

When Bobbie Barnett stands up, having been squashed behind uncomfortably between Aunt Dorothy and me and Pam, I also stand up, steadying myself by clutching the top of the seat in front, and feeling the night wind rush wildly through my hair. How unreal it is! How wonderful, extraordinary! A dream! Then Bobbie Barnett's left hand falls out of the darkness and covers my hand. Nobody else can see what he's done, which isn't – I'm certain it's not – by mistake, but on purpose. And this moment is, without a doubt, the most ecstatically thrilling moment of my entire life.

It doesn't matter that Pam and I have to return to Crapstone by train the following morning. What I take with me is the memory of Bobbie Barnett's hand on mine. Bobbie Barnett has thick wavy blonde hair, the same exactly as Rupert Brooke's hair in the photograph fixed with drawing pins to the inside of my school desk; but Bobbie is a living, breathing young man, a young god, and he held my hand in the moonlight. He *did*! Oh joy! Oh the glory of being fourteen (nearly fifteen) and in love!

Our house, Melrose, feels oddly draughty without my sister Pam. She's taken a summer job waitressing in the restaurant that Lewarne Hosking and Enid, his sister, have just opened in Newquay, and is staying with them, and with Nancy, Lewarne's wife, in their Porth bungalow. Lucky Pam!

I miss watching her, as I used to do – enviously – while she was getting ready for the dance held every Saturday evening in the ballroom of the Moorland Links Hotel. The dance had become a regular social event in Pam's calendar, a fixture. At eight o'clock punctually she would be picked up by Sub-Lieutenant Marco Morris, resplendent in uniform, driving an open-top sports car, in which he then whirled her off to the hotel ballroom, there to join a group of his fellow officers from Keyham, the Royal Naval Engineering College at Devonport, Plymouth. And since Pam's acquaintance with these young men was brought about by friendship with Josephine Pipon, and since Josephine's naval pedigree is impeccable – father a serving commander, uncle an admiral – our mother had had no hesitation in bestowing her blessing on the weekly revels.

Pam's two dance dresses were both made by herself, from material sold at bargain price in a Dingle's sale, and she wore them on alternate Saturdays. I thought the taffeta dress, vertically striped in brilliant multi-colours, was absolutely stunning, but Mummy pursed her lips: according to her taste it a good deal *too* brilliant – rather gaudy, in fact – an opinion that, if expressed aloud, would have incurred her older daughter's withering scorn. So Mummy, sensibly, held her tongue; but it was perfectly obvious to me what she was thinking.

My sister's absence has its compensations. Chiefly, it enables me to enjoy more of my brother Jim's company. Anybody who meets Jim today would never guess that not many years ago he was a puny sickly frightened little boy, with flat feet and a stammer. Now nearly nineteen, a robust good-looking Oxford undergraduate, more than six foot tall and still growing, he is welcomed by everyone (except for Josephine Pipon), everywhere he goes. I am proud to be seen alongside this witty, animated, boldly opinionated brother of mine, proud of his popularity. Although he doesn't care for dancing (his feet, he says, are so big they get in the way and he's deaf to music), nevertheless he will, on occasion, agree to escort Christine Johnson – currently the girl in favour – to a Saturday night dance at the Moorland Links Hotel, if only because it's what the girls round here expect as a public demonstration of allegiance.

I'm not yet old enough to go to these dances. I soon shall be old enough, but I don't know any person who would be willing to take me. Robert Winnicott wouldn't – of that I can be certain – not after the Tavistock Tennis Tournament fiasco. When Robert asked me to be his partner in the junior mixed doubles, I was in heaven. It was a dream come true! By chance he had caught sight of me when I happened to be playing exceptionally well, as I sometimes can. But if I do, it's a fluke. I'm just as likely next time to play badly, especially if I'm nervous. On the day of the Tavistock Tournament I played worse than I ever had before. All my serves were double-faults, and all my volleys went either out of court or landed in the net. Not merely did we lose every single match, we lost them catastrophically. Robert turned his back and walked away, stiff-legged, without saying a word to me, and I hid behind the pavilion to weep unseen.

As far as I'm concerned, this 1939 summer is a peculiar sort of an interval, neither one thing nor another. I've left school, but I'm not grown up: I'm in-between. And it isn't just me; the holidays too have a funny in-between feeling about them. We carry on the same as we always have done, playing tennis, bathing down at Denham Bridge or in the Moorland Links Hotel swimming pool (an occasional sophisticated summer morning treat). And one fine warm August evening we are invited by Commander and Mrs Burton, a whole crowd of us (what they call *youngsters*), to a huge supper party in their wild overgrown garden, with an outdoor fire for cooking potatoes and sausages.

It is the greatest fun. But even so, no matter what picnics or bicycle rides we go on, what parties we have or games we play, we are conscious of a vague persistent uneasiness in the air which no amount of our frolicking and fun can dispel. Over everything we do there hovers a disturbing sense of impermanence – and a sense, as well, of expectation, without us being sure, precisely, what it is we expect, or when.

The Spanish war has ended, and General Franco wasn't the loser: he won it. Why Jim, and most of his friends – though not all of them – view General Franco's victory as catastrophic and profoundly ominous, I'm not sure. But in any gathering, whether large or small, the talk will sooner or later, as though magnetically drawn there, revert to the likelihood of war with Germany. I thought all that had been settled last year by Mr Chamberlain when he met Adolf Hitler; but apparently not. The country everybody was speaking of then was Czechoslovakia; now it's Poland.

Often at tennis parties, or perhaps when we are bathing and lounging, a group of us, in and around the Moorland Links Hotel swimming pool, listening, as I do, to a variety of opinions being aired – the arguments growing sometimes quite heated regarding the rights and wrongs of Fascism, Communism, Herr Hitler, Sir Oswald Mosley, the Russians, General Franco – it's difficult for me to take their talk seriously, hard to believe any real danger lurking overseas could ever possibly come close to us in Crapstone; could touch our carefree village lives, be able to cast a shadow, blot out the sunshine, interrupt our games of tennis, our supper picnics, our fun. Surely not!

But I hear them saying, these boys, with an irrepressible undercurrent of excitement, that trouble, without a doubt, is brewing in Europe, a witches' cauldron boiling up across the English Channel, not so very far away, and that Germany is to blame for it.

I'm grateful to my brother Jim for recognising – as nobody else does – that I'm not a child any more. He has taken an interest in my political education and lent me a book by John Strachey: *An Introduction to Socialism*. I've read it from cover to cover, as slowly and methodically as if I were going to sit a School Certificate exam paper on it, and as a result, convinced by as much of the logic and theory as I can understand, and fired by enthusiasm, I've decided to become a socialist. I tell Jim of my conversion, and he, of course, is pleased, and congratulates me on my intelligence.

Socialism strikes me as being a worthwhile cause, a flag I can enlist under with confidence. I'm not so sure, however, that I want to be, as my brother declares he is, a pacifist. It's a question I shall have to consider. Jim has heated arguments with Josephine Pipon (who is visiting us while her parents are away in Scotland), on the topic of wars being either – depending on which of them is talking – justifiably necessary and honourable, or imperialistically wicked and wasteful. Josephine says Jim is unpatriotic. She says he is a coward, and that in the Great War conscientious objectors were presented with white feathers, and so should he be. Jim dismisses her reasoning in terms of lofty disdain as infantile; asserting, more rudely, that she is a fool.

I listen to their furious disagreements, keeping quiet in the background and not interrupting. They will never agree. Which of them is right?

As well as to socialism, my brother Jim has introduced me to what has had an even greater revolutionary impact on my life than politics: modern poetry. I am overwhelmed by the joyous discovery of a flourishing fertile landscape I had had no idea existed.

Not that I am a stranger to poetry. I owe it to my father that he shared with me, at a time when I was very young, and he had no one else to share it with, the poetry he himself loved, extracting for our mutual entertainment gems, already familiar to him, from the pages of *The Golden Treasury*; encouraging me to linger over the mysterious and bewitchingly illustrated verse of Omar Khayyam; reciting Masefield's

100

rollicking 'Sea Fever' – and more, much more – until, with the heroic stanzas written by Rudyard Kipling, poetry, in my father's view, came to a full stop. Enthralled as I was by all of the poems Daddy chose, they left me with the impression, confirmed at school, that poetry, glorious though it is, belongs to the realms of antiquity.

What an astonishment, then, to hear voices speaking to me, loud and clear, not from the past, but *now*! So *this* is what poetry can be – a communication direct and powerful, intensely vibrant, like a pulse beating in my own veins. I'm hearing what for me is a totally new poetic language, re-invented, made adventurous, immediate: *I sang as one who on a tilting deck sings/ To keep their courage up* . . . The feeling I have while reading it, as I do, voraciously, again and again, is of walking from the shadowy interior of a shuttered house out into a blaze of sunshine.

Messrs Faber & Faber have published a selection of the works of living poets in slender prettily pastel-coloured volumes, priced at half-a-crown each, and Jim has let me borrow five of them: poems by Cecil Day-Lewis, Stephen Spender, W.H. Auden, Laurie Lee, and Louis MacNeice. A line from one of Louis MacNeice's poems lodges in my brain and echoes, echoes, like the distant thud of an axe ringing across a valley: *They are cutting down the trees on Primrose Hill* – words, I don't know why, that haunt me, thrillingly ominous. I can't get them out of my head: *They are cutting down the trees* . . .

The results of last term's School Certificate examination have been advertised. I learn of my abysmal failure in Geography (is it a record, I wonder, to be allotted marks of 3 per cent?). In every other subject I have passed, gaining a credit in English Literature, and also, surprisingly, in Scripture.

But the School Certificate, once of such major importance to me, has lately dwindled into insignificance, due to the darkly foreboding clouds looming up on our horizon. However much we try not to notice them, they can't be ignored. And then, one day, we are forced to acknowledge the reality of the storm these clouds herald, by what is the equivalent of a first warning flash of lightning.

Lise, an Austrian schoolgirl, has been staying for several weeks as the guest of Colonel and Mrs Batson, with the avowed intention of improving her English. She is the grand-daughter of an old army friend of the Colonel's (a friendship dating from the beginning of the century), and everybody here likes her – everybody thinks, indeed, that she is charming, and we have gladly included her in all of our activities. Sam Pyne is head over heels in love with Lise. (He falls in love frequently; as do I.)

Sam, and his younger brother Charles, and the Sysons, and the Hallsmiths, and a host of other young people, were invited by the Batsons to a party they had planned to give in the Moorland Links Hotel as a celebration of Lise's sixteenth birthday. Her mother had sent from Vienna to Crapstone, by special delivery, a ravishingly pretty pink chiffon dress made on purpose for the gala evening. I was present a few days ago when Lise, flushed with excitement, lifted the lovely fairy-story dress clear of layers of tissue-paper wrappings, and tried it on in front of a mirror.

Then we are told: there will be no party at the Moorland Links Hotel – the event has been cancelled. Lise is in tears. Dear kind old Colonel Batson has received an urgent tele-gram dispatched by her father, who is a serving general in the German army, summoning his daughter home to Austria. She is to leave *at once*, without delay: tomorrow.

It is the sudden cancellation of Lise's birthday party, and her tearful farewell, that shocks us into realising something momentous and terrible is about to occur. This, it seems, is what the rumours, the uneasiness, the faint thunderous rumblings throughout the months of June, July, August, have been leading up to: here it is.

On Sunday, September the third, Mummy, Harvey and I walk in sober silence downhill to Buckland Monachorum church. The weather is windless and calm; peaceful, summery. I am wearing the new hat Mummy has bought me for winter church-going. It is a very ugly hat, and it makes me look ugly too. A chocolate-brown felt monstrosity, it has a high backward-sloping crown, decorated with a row of matching brown felt bows. I *hate* this hat.

We sit in a pew close to the pulpit, and when the vicar, the Reverend Lennard-Williams, climbs up into it, instead of delivering a sermon he repeats for the congregation the announcement broadcast this morning on the wireless by our Prime Minister, Mr Chamberlain. Hitler has broken his promise and invaded Poland, and the consequence is that Britain and France are now at war with Germany.

PART TWO

DURING

We know we are in a state of war, because we have been told we are, but if we hadn't been told, except for the gas masks, and the ration books, and the black-out regulations, we might not have known. To our relief, but rather to our surprise, little has happened in Crapstone to make any difference to the life we lived before September the third.

Every day we listen without fail – everybody does – to the six o'clock news on the wireless, which is how we learn that our army, or what is called the BEF (short for British Expeditionary Force), has been shipped over the Channel to join up with the French army, France being our ally in this fight to the finish against Hitler and the Nazis. That we shall defeat the Germans, and probably quite quickly, is thanks to the very thorough measures taken in preparation: these consist of, chiefly, the Maginot Line and the Siegfried Line, underground fortifications, guaranteed impregnable, built right across the frontiers of France, and most of Belgium, to prevent the enemy's invasion of a sovereign territory, which is what Germany treacherously did when it marched into Poland.

For us here in Crapstone there are, of course, some obvious indications of a war we can't see – a war far away and out of sight. The gas masks we've been issued with have a terrifying appearance. They make people wearing them look inhuman, like creatures in a nightmare. We must, by law, carry them with us wherever we go, because of not knowing when a gas attack might suddenly happen. Each mask is kept in a cardboard box, and the box has a webbing strap attached, so that it can be slung around the neck, or dangled from a shoulder.

The ration books are because we live on an island, and if the war continues beyond this winter, into next year, the food supply may start to run short. But we are forbidden to hoard food. Hoarding food would be selfish – it would be wrong; and also unnecessary. Our ration books will, if need be, ensure that we shall have plenty to eat – more than enough.

Another Governmental directive, the latest and the strictest, is that we must on no account allow even a glimmer of light from our houses to be seen outside in the street after dark; which is why Mummy is busy lining all our curtains with yards and yards of thick heavy black material bought from Dingle's upholstery department. I think she likes to feel that by obeying promptly and without question (as would a soldier) the Government's black-out order, she is doing something absolutely necessary for winning the war. Everyone wants, like my mother, to help, but it isn't always easy to know how.

I lend a hand, and Jacquie Edelsten does too, getting in a second harvest – the blessing of a providentially abundant season – with the younger son of Mr Fosbury, a local farmer, his older son having enlisted in the navy on the morning after war was declared.

Bob Fosbury is almost the same age as me and Jacquie. Riding to and fro, high up on top of the hay cart, the sky blue and the sun shining, is tremendously enjoyable, which worries me a bit: if there hadn't been a war declared, we shouldn't be having such fun.

Mr Crooke of the post office, wearing an armband with *Air Raid Warden* printed on it, bicycles round the village, blowing a whistle. There is no air raid in progress, but he is demonstrating how we may expect to be alerted if there should be one.

Pam is back from Porth. The Hoskings' restaurant in Newquay, so recently opened, has had to close down: it wasn't a lucky year for Lewarne and Enid to have taken the gamble of embarking on a business venture. Pam tells us how the hotels emptied overnight. In the last week of August, and the beginning of September, they were full to capacity, and then, twenty-four hours after the news of war was broadcast, all the visitors had packed their bags and, in a mass exodus, were gone. It was amazing, she says, the speed of their departure. She describes the strangeness of walking by herself, alone, on beaches that had been crowded, suddenly deserted. She says it was eerie. She says she's glad to be home.

Not that she intends to stay at home. Anyone aged eighteen, boy or girl, is old enough to volunteer for the army, navy, or air force. Josephine Pipon, our guest, who is eighteen, the same age as the Twins (they will be nineteen in October), naturally means to follow in the footsteps of her naval family and join the WRNS – which is the women's branch of the Royal Navy – and my sister Pam decides to join with her.

Having discussed it briefly and made up their minds, they at once, not wanting to waste another day, catch a bus into Plymouth. But when, aglow with patriotic zeal, they arrive at the door of the WRNS' recruiting office, they find it most disappointingly shut. On the other side of the road, however, and temptingly open, is the recruiting office for the Women's Auxiliary Air Force. Taking this to be a sign from heaven, the two girls change tack instantly, cross the street, and

109

enlist for war service, not with the navy, but instead with the air force.

There! They've done it! They return to Melrose triumphant at the audacity of this last-minute switching of their plans. The die being cast, they must now wait impatiently for their calling-up papers to arrive through the post.

Jim, meanwhile, true to his declared principles of declining to play an active part in this or any war, and unmoved by the scorn that Josephine continues to heap upon him, has registered as a conscientious objector. He has written to inform his Teddy Hall tutor that he is terminating his studies for a degree in Modern Languages, and won't, therefore, be returning in the autumn term to Oxford University. Until, at least, the date of his tribunal – in front of which panel of judges he will presently be required to defend the sincerity of his awkward beliefs – Jim has applied for permission to work at St Hugh's Settlement, a farming community run by and for dedicated pacifists.

And what, I am wondering, does Mummy think of the behaviour of her twins, her son and her daughter, each of them motivated by such differing views, and starting off in diametrically opposite directions? She, our mother, a decorated heroine of the Great War, and married to a hero who was awarded the DSO in that inferno of death and destruction – what is she thinking now? She hasn't, I notice, offered advice, either to Pam or to Jim, or attempted to dissuade them from their chosen paths. What could she say?

She says nothing; except once only, when she overhears Josephine's undisguisedly contemptuous reference to Jim, and then she does speak, in a tone that is affronted and sharply reproachful: 'I forbid you, Josephine, to use that word in my house again about Jim. He isn't a coward. No, Josephine, he is not! He is being very courageous – indeed he is. It's going to be hard for him, poor lad – poor lad – very hard; very, very difficult.'

I am struck as much by the quiver of anguish in my mother's voice as by the unusualness of her remarks. Mummy has many admirable qualities, but appreciation of other people's inner emotions is not one of them. What she feels herself, she expects others to feel. She is, in fact, always convinced that her own reaction is certain to be theirs as well, without ever having to enquire further. It isn't, I know, my mother's fault that she lacks the gift of perception, and I don't blame her for what is missing, any more than I should have blamed her had she suffered from the handicap of being born physically short-sighted.

But now it has apparently dawned on Mummy what Jim, her son – *poor lad* – is letting himself in for, and although not fully grasping *why* he is determined to sow this dangerous wind, she nevertheless can recognise courage when she sees it, and is bound to, and does, respect him for the bravery of his stand, while trembling at the prospect of the whirlwind he will inevitably reap: a world of Josephine Pipons, all, in their thousands, condemning him for cowardice.

He is the son she has learnt, over the years, to be proud of, the boy who has grown into a fine young man: tall, good-looking, who reads books she couldn't possibly begin to comprehend, who is clever – and who will come, she greatly fears, to grief, her grief and his, through making the unpopular unwise decision not to put on a uniform (as his twin sister, Pam, is doing) and sally forth to fight for his country.

Josephine, quelled by Mrs Hallsmith's uncharacteristic outburst, apologises to Mummy, her admired and respected hostess; she doesn't, however, apologise to Jim.

Everybody except me knows what he or she is going to do, and is going off and doing it. My problem is that at sixteen I'm too young to join any of the Armed Forces, and the war will be over long before I'm eighteen. So how shall I occupy myself throughout the pointless boring weeks and months in front of me?

It is Miss Pitts, headmistress and owner of the small prestigious junior school in Yelverton attended by my little brother, Harvey, who rescues me from this dilemma. For Miss Pitts also has a problem: shortage of staff – the younger of her two teachers having hastened away immediately on the outbreak of war to join the ATS, the women's branch of the army. When Miss Pitts hears that one of her pupils, eight-year-old Harvey Hallsmith, has a sister, Elspeth, who has just left Moorfields and is at a loose end, she invites me to tea.

Miss Pitts is large, grey-haired, bespectacled and, at first sight, a rather alarming figure. She quizzes me closely on the results of my School Certificate examination and, undeterred by the dismal Geography marks that I am obliged, shamefacedly, to reveal, offers me there and then, the position of assistant to her sole remaining teacher, Miss Daisy Milligan. If I accept, says Miss Pitts, eyeing me sternly, she will, as a starting wage, pay me ten shillings a week.

Of course I accept! – it sounds too good to be true. I have a job! I am being employed, like a real grown-up person – I am even going to be paid!

Afterwards though, thinking it over, my euphoria dissolves into a panic of doubt. What do I know about giving lessons to a mixed class of boys and girls between the ages of five and eleven? Absolutely nothing at all! They will see at once that I'm not very much older than they are, and can't possibly, therefore, be a proper teacher. Why should they take any notice of what I say? They won't. They'll simply sit and laugh at me.

My hair is too short to be screwed into a bun, like my mother's. I scrape it back and tie it, tightly, at the nape of my neck with a ribbon, but the face that stares out from my mirror is still the worried face of a sixteen-year-old ex-school-girl. How on earth am I to manage?

My salvation turns out to be the blessed Miss Daisy Milligan. Although in her thirties – ancient! – my new colleague welcomes me warmly and treats me, without a hint of condescension, as an equal, a partner in fun. Nimble, wiry, brimful of jokes, Miss Daisy Milligan is, I find, a delightfully frivolous ally, exhibiting, whenever we happen to be on our own in the kitchen – the classroom doors closed and Miss Pitts, our employer, safely elswhere – an irrepressible gift for clowning and mimicry.

Before I'm considered fit to be let loose alone on a class I absorb, at her side and by her enlightened example, the art of making lessons for little children seem as enjoyable as playing games with them; a pleasure to be shared. A pleasure which has, in my case, one humiliating exception: mental arithmetic. My quick-witted pupils always arrive at the correct answers to the shopping-list sums I invent as a test for their mathematical agility while I'm still frantically adding up and subtracting shillings and pence on my fingers under the table.

But otherwise all goes well. Together we act out the drama of dozy King Alfred burning the cakes. Together we chant, in joyous unison: *Matilda told such dreadful lies/ It made one gasp and stretch one's eyes* ... And an introduction to the rudiments of a French vocabulary is rendered painless with a dolly's tea set and a pretence tea party: *Regardez, mes enfants – ici le lait – le sucre – une tartine* ...

Harvey, who had been as anxious as I was beforehand, has become proud of me; proud that every morning I cease to be his sister and am metamorphosed, as if by magic, into his teacher. He is punctilious in remembering to call me *Miss Hallsmith* and not *Ellie*. Every morning – the Orr-Ewing family and their convenient lift-supplying car

113

having departed from Crapstone – Harvey and I catch a bus into Yelverton. The school day begins at nine o'clock with prayers read aloud by Miss Pitts, followed by the daily ritual of nose-blowing.

'Handkerchiefs out, children. Are you ready? – *blow*!'

And blow we must, Miss Pitts, Miss Daisy Milligan and me included, whether there is anything to blow, or not. A child who fails to produce a clean handkerchief is reprimanded, and never forgets a second time to have it in his or her pocket, awaiting the command.

At twelve-thirty school finishes; but Harvey and I remain behind for another quarter of an hour, helping to tidy the classrooms. Then – once more reunited as a brother and sister – we scamper home along the two miles of windy moorland road to Melrose and the hot nourishing meal that Mummy, we know, aided by Mary Northey, will have been cooking for us.

Miss Pitts is pleased with me. Elspeth, she confides to my mother, shows unusual promise – more than that: a true vocation for teaching. So much so, indeed, that she, Miss Pitts, can even envisage handing the school on to Elspeth as her eventual successor when, in approximately fifteen years from now, she retires.

My mother returns from this tête-à-tête with Miss Pitts exceedingly gratified, both by the commendation and by a proposal that offers young Elspeth, in an uncertain world, the prospect of a steady rewarding future career. Manna from heaven, is how Mummy views it. But I – I am appalled!

To teach in Miss Pitts's school during the term ahead, and the next term, and perhaps the next, is fine – but for *ever*? No, no, NO! The very uncertainty of the world, the huge wonderful world out there waiting to be discovered, is what makes it so exciting. As soon as we've won the war with Germany, and I'm grown up and free, I mean to set off travelling, exploring, having adventures. Surely my mother must understand that I don't want to be stuck here in Crapstone for the rest of my life? Emphatically NOT!

The period leading up to and over Christmas has acquired an air of pleasantly settled routine, undisturbed by any disagreeable interruptions. War? – what war? No reports reach us of bloody gladiatorial battles in France. There continues to be a reassuring silence, expressive of stalemate. Week by week we buy our modest allowance of rations, using the stamp-like coupons in our ration books. When evening comes we dutifully draw our black-out curtains. Jim writes to us regularly from the farming community, St Hugh's, with graphic descriptions of his exploits driving a tractor. Pam writes from Somewhere in England, an anonymous location at which my sister and Josephine Pipon are being drilled into becoming good officer material for the Women's Auxiliary Air Force. And we lay members of the great British public listen to a light entertainment programme, *Music While You Work*, broadcast daily on the wireless with its cheerful idiotic songs that are intended to raise our spirits by conveying, absurdly but comfortingly, the continuing static situation abroad: *We're going to hang out our washing on the Siegfried Line/ Have you any dirty washing, mother dear?* ...

Somewhere in France, somewhere unspecified, our troops, the BEF, are snugly encamped behind the security of the Siegfried Line and the Maginot Line, keeping ceaseless guard to make certain that no harm can come to those who depend on them, the trusting obedient population back here in Britain.

Secrecy is now the nation's watchword. Signposts have been removed so that if a wicked marauding German should stray by chance into our country he will have no idea where

115

he is, and be quickly captured. And then there is the hazard of spies – traitors! Posters have everywhere been pasted up warning us to be wary of what we say, and to whom we say it: *Careless Talk Costs Lives; Be Like Dad – Keep Mum.* Other posters exhort us to *Join the Land Army*, to *Dig for Victory*. But were it not for the proliferation of these posters, we in Crapstone might almost forget that we have an enemy, and that he could be lurking round the next corner, or sitting beside us on the bus. He is invisible, this enemy of ours; and having adjusted ourselves to the imposition of gas masks and black-out, we carry on through the autumn and winter months of 1939 calmly and peacefully.

Then, at the beginning of the New Year, in January, *the letter* arrives: a letter written to Mummy from Delhi, by Sir Maurice Gwyer, Lord Chief Justice of India, which has the effect, for me, of changing my entire existence.

Sir Maurice Gwyer is the tall old man with the bushy black eyebrows who took an interest in me when I was twelve and a bridesmaid in Finchley, London, at the wedding of Mrs Bazin's grand-daughter, Mildred Walker. Since then he has written to me, off and on, from Delhi, and I have replied.

During the Great War Mummy missed by a week, the merest whisker, marrying Geoffrey Bazin, the son of Sir Maurice's dear friends, and thus becoming the Bazins' daughter-in-law; which, I suppose, is really the reason why Sir Maurice Gwyer is taking an interest in the one child of hers from a later marriage that he has ever actually met – me.

He writes now saying that in these difficult and troubling times he would like to make himself responsible for Elspeth acquiring some sort of a qualification which would allow her, in due course, to stand on her own feet and be financially independent. He suggests in his letter that a secretarial training would probably provide the best general insurance against the unforseeable vagaries of fortune. A proficient secretary, he writes, can always be assured of earning a decent respectable living. If, therefore, Mrs Hallsmith (although he must presumably have known Mummy as *Janet* when she was unmarried, long ago, Sir Maurice addresses her with the utmost formality) – if she agrees to his suggestion, he will leave it to her to make all the necessary arrangements, and to have the bills for whatever costs are incurred sent on to him.

The letter is quite short, quite dry, but there it is, in his own spidery pen-and-ink writing on thin blue airmail paper, wafted thousands of miles from the city of Delhi, and delivered to us here in Crapstone, mixed with the usual morning's post on the breakfast table, as if it were the most ordinary of letters.

But could any letter be, in fact, more extraordinary? It is the tangible evidence, the proof of a magician's wand being waved far off in another continent on my behalf. An elderly personage of unique eminence, the Lord Chief Justice of India, no less, somebody I met only once, has decided, on a whim, to appoint himself my fairy godfather, and is presenting me with – not a pumpkin coach or a ballgown – (what use would they be?) but a pair of glittering wings. For this is how my benefactor's inexplicable generosity appears to me: the means by which, as soon as the war has been won, I shall be able to fly up, up, up and away to – well, to *somewhere* – to India, perhaps – as free as a bird. Liberty is what Sir Maurice is giving me: a passport to anywhere in the world.

My new address is Clarence Lodge, Englefield Green, Egham, Surrey. Queen's Secretarial College has recently moved here from Kensington, London, as a far-sighted precaution against involvement in any possible future urban warfare. My mother chose Queen's College out of a pile of competing brochures mainly because of it being the most expensive on offer, and she trusted that the highness of its fees were indication of a corresponding high standard of tuition.

Clarence Lodge – the building – bears no resemblance to what had been my idea of a college. It is a charming sprawling unpretentious country house, painted a creamy white, with big windows, and verandas, set amongst lawns and trees and flower beds: the typical home, one might imagine, of a large well-off English family. What were previously the ground-floor reception rooms have been turned into impromptu classrooms, furnished with typewriters and blackboards, giving the general impression of a house vacated hurriedly by its former residents to allow for the sudden influx of strangers: namely, secretarial students, like me, and our teachers. Essentially it remains unaltered. Such a make-shift haphazard conversion implies that the occupation is intended to be of a temporary nature, and rather as though it were some sort of amusing charade, without the need for strictly binding regulations.

I am sharing an attic bedroom on the second floor with Eve Griffin and Paula Mason, who are the same age as me, and we have become at once an inseparable trio. Our low-ceilinged room has chintz curtains, one armchair, a table, a cupboard, a small chest of drawers, and three squeezed-in single beds. Snug and cosy as a nest, we consider it to be absolute perfection. Not only is it *ours* – our private unassailable retreat – but, best of all, we are able to climb out through the dormer window on to the roof. If there is a rule forbidding this unorthodox activity, it's a rule we haven't been told about.

The weather is warm for late spring: summery. We lie, safely hidden from view, in the valley between two sloping roofs, our backs propped against the sun-heated slates, our feet in the intervening gulley, listening with half an ear to the soft swooning music of Victor Silvester's dance band being broadcast on Eve's battery-powered wireless (*I'll See You in My Dreams . . .*), meanwhile applying ourselves, lazily, either – as we should be doing – to the practise of shorthand exercises, or else, in my case, reading the next chapter of *Black Mischief* by Evelyn Waugh, a Penguin copy of which has been lent to me by Paula. *Black Mischief* is the most sophisticated, hilariously funny novel I have ever come across. We share the jokes in it. We pass round a precious packet of biscuits. We are in heaven.

Eve and Paula have each brought a bicycle with them to Clarence Lodge, and so I write home to Mummy asking her please to send me my bicycle, which she does, by way of the Great Western Railway service, and it duly lands up, with a label attached to it, in Staines railway station's goods department. Being now equipped, like the Three Musketeers, with a steed apiece, we plan mightily daring exploratory expeditions for our spare time: to the shops and cafés of nearby Windsor, or, even more adventurously, to the swimming pool of the Blue Lagoon Hotel in Virginia Water.

Jostling for space in front of the mirror, we experiment with lipsticks, with powder, mascara, eyeshadow. What on earth, we wonder, giggling, would our mothers say if they could see us, their daughters, painted like so many Jezebels? Mine would undoubtedly be horrified. Seized by guilt, I wash my face, rubbing and scrubbing it clean of any speck of depravity (as indeed we all do) before appearing in public.

Life in Clarence Lodge isn't the least bit the same as being at school. We don't wear a uniform; there are no punishments; even the lessons aren't compulsory. It's for the students themselves to decide on whether or not they will work sufficiently hard to obtain those diplomas which, at the completion

119

of the course, will fit them (quoting from the brochure) to enter the job market with confidence, aware of the superior advantage bestowed by their having had a Queen's Secretarial College training.

And as to working hard – surely it's more like fun than work to set about mastering the coded language invented years ago by clever Mr Pitman? More fun than work to sit in rows, bolt upright, at the immensely heavy office type-writers, our hands concealed beneath a metal screen, picking out by touch, and according to the visible printed guide placed alongside our machine, the invisible lettered keys; all the while keeping in time to the regular rhythm of 'Colonel Bogey's March', played by a brass band and relayed to us loudly and solemnly – tumpety-tumpety-tum – on a gramophone record? Miss Patterson, our big-boned slow-spoken placid Irish typing teacher, winds up the gram-ophone again and again. Typists must learn to have a light but a firm touch, and to strike the keys rhythmically. Can the acquisition of such a skill possibly be described as work? Is it not, in fact, the greatest pleasure – an entirely enjoyable sort of game?

Only one disagreeable incident mars the otherwise idyllic happiness of my life at Clarence Lodge. I hadn't expected the episode to be disagreeable – although it's true, I would actu-ally rather have spent Saturday bicycling over to Virginia Water with Eve and Paula than travelling by train, boringly, up to Paddington Station where Lewarne Hosking meets me, as promised. He had written, inviting me to have lunch with him in London. Bother! – but I stifle the irritation. How kind of him!

We go by taxi to some restaurant or other. And it is there, sitting at a table near the window, that I see the face of my father peering in through the glass at me.

Daddy! *Here*? Impossible! I must be hallucinating. It *can't* be Daddy. But it is. I convey the alarming news to Lewarne.

'Oh, good! Excellent!' he says, unsurprised. And then, smiling and nodding, adds an explanation: 'Your father – Guthrie – is going to join us for lunch.'

'You didn't tell me –'

'No – I'm sorry; perhaps I should have done. But I thought you'd be pleased,' says Lewarne, cheerily unrepentant. 'Your father mentioned how glad he'd be of a chance to see you, Elspeth, and this seemed like a splendid opportunity.'

So that's what it is: a plot, arranged by well-meaning blundering Lewarne who used to play tennis with my father in far-off Newquay days, and for whom a friend, once made, is a friend for ever and has, consequently, to be offered help in any domestic crisis, if such help appears to be needed. He *is* well-meaning, Lewarne – I know he is – but he *doesn't understand*. I feel deceived and upset; I feel very upset indeed.

Lunch is a painful affair, stilted and awkward. Lewarne gallantly attempts to keep up a flow of jolly conversation by pretending to have a lively interest in Queen's Secretarial College, but I – although trying to respond – answer his enquiries distractedly, at random. And I can think of nothing at all to say to Daddy, who, for his part, remains almost completely silent throughout.

When the uncomfortable meal does at last come to an end, I refuse Lewarne's suggestion of a visit to the Royal Academy, or to anywhere else, telling him in desperation that I want to – that I *have* to – return immediately to Clarence Lodge; murmuring excuses: homework – shorthand exercises that must be finished before tomorrow.

'Goodbye, Daddy,' I say, giving my speechless father a kiss: a quick peck on the cheek.

Lewarne takes me by taxi to Paddington, and puts me into

a train. I thank him; but he realises, dear kind Lewarne, that he has made a mistake. It wasn't a success, his lunch party. It was a fiasco.

Delightful as our daily existence continues to be, it is becoming increasingly obvious to the three of us, Eve and me and Paula, that it lacks a very important element.

After treating ourselves to a movie in Staines – *Snow White and the Seven Dwarfs* – we toil back up the steep hill from Egham to Englefield Green, pushing our bikes and carolling lustily in chorus: *One day my prince will come/ One day I'll find my love* . . . But a sentimental song is no substitute for the real thing. These princes – where are they? And *how* do we find them? Only females undertake secretarial courses, and the management of Virginia Water's Blue Lagoon Hotel is inclined to extend a frosty reception to three young girls on bicycles, who arrive armed with bathing costumes, but minus male escorts.

Windsor is a better bet. And as it happens, this is the Saturday afternoon when we alight upon just what we are seeking: a group of three – no, four – young army officers, drifting aimlessly about the streets of Windsor, pausing in front of shops with – it's easy to tell – no particular object in view. They appear, what's more, to be scarcely older than we are: boys, merely, disguised as men by their smart khaki uniforms, and undoubtedly intended by Fate for us.

We trail them: not too close, but close enough for them quite soon to grow aware that they are being trailed, and to exhibit – we are fairly certain – signs of encouragement. But what comes next? We can't just approach them, bold as brass, and say *Hullo!* What are we to do?

They wander into Woolworths. We follow. And then Eve – brilliantly inventive – drops her purse, and the coins (mostly pennies) scatter and roll on the floor in every direction. The boys are all down on their knees in a flash, picking the money up, returning it. And the deed is done!

'Oh, how *sweet* of you,' cries Eve. 'Thank you – oh, thank you so *much*!'

Eve is by far the prettiest of us three. She really is very pretty, and her smile is irresistible. The four boys don't attempt to resist it. In a matter of minutes we are sitting together round a café table, with tea and cakes ordered, exchanging names and laughing like the warmest of old friends. They are called Johnnie and Clive and Freddie and Arthur, and their manners are perfect: they are neither too forward, nor yet too shy – exactly, in short, what we had been hoping for; and Johnnie and Clive and Arthur and Freddie make us feel that we are just exactly what *they* had been hoping for. Goodness, how lucky!

From the café we move on to a riverside pub. Eve and Paula ask for and are given glasses of cider, but I think it safer to stick to ginger beer, which sounds alcoholic, but isn't. Before parting, the boys invite us to meet them tomorrow, Sunday, at the same pub, for lunch, and we, of course, accept. Well, of course we do!

Pedalling back to Clarence Lodge, cock-a-hoop, through the gathering spring twilight, we sing Snow White's wistful song triumphantly, at the top of our lungs. Today, for us, it has come true: today – glory be! – we found our princes!

But then – then the blow falls.

At eleven o'clock on Sunday morning we are ready to go. We have dressed with painstaking care; applied, daringly, the tiniest touch of lipstick; powdered – why not? – our shiny noses; and are on the verge of departure when a maid taps at our door and Eve is told that she is wanted *at once* in Miss Simmons' office downstairs.

Miss Simmons, the elderly Principal of Queen's Secretarial

College, doesn't teach a subject. She is more like a superintendent; and so we seldom see her. Severely lame, she leads a solitary existence in her ground-floor apartment, alone except for the snuffly shaggy little dog which is always tucked up under her left arm when, at intervals, leaning on a silver-headed stick, she emerges. Not herself a smiler, she has the effect of discouraging smiles in others. Her staff, although friendly enough to us, are not, it would seem, on intimate terms with their Principal, and whenever Miss Simmons, after having completed a formal tour of inspection, again disappears inside her fortress, there is a widespread sense of relief.

So why now, we wonder anxiously, is Miss Simmons, a sort of dragon-lady, sending urgently for Eve? Are we in for a wigging? – a reprimand, or worse, because of our discovered Windsor escapade?

In a matter of minutes Eve, breathless, tearful, distraught, is back upstairs. And yes! – it is worse, a great deal worse, but not on account of the dreaded interview with Miss Simmons, who had displayed, apparently, instead of wrath, a total indifference to the spare time exploits of us, her students.

'Johnnie – it was Johnnie on the phone –' Clarence Lodge's only telephone is in Miss Simmons' office. 'He says it's off – all off. Cancelled! Our meeting, lunch, everything –'

We gaze at Eve, uncomprehendingly. 'Cancelled? But why? What did he say?'

'He said it's off because *they're* off – they've been ordered abroad – his regiment. He didn't say *where* abroad – he probably shouldn't have said even that. He didn't say much – hardly anything – he was in a tearing hurry. There was a queue, Johnnie said, for the phone. He said he'd write – and that he was sorry about it. But he sounded excited –'

We sit on our three beds, dressed in our needless finery,

utterly deflated. The beautiful dream we had is over. We did find our princes, but the very next day – we lost them.

That Sunday morning's disappointment, so intensely bitter at the time, didn't last. The pain of it faded, diminished, and soon was quite forgotten. For subsequent events have rendered our Windsor adventure unimportant, a triviality, not worth remembering.

In the days, and then the weeks afterwards, our ears have been filled and our thoughts darkened, to the exclusion of all else, by the sheer awfulness of the news, the frequently issued Government bulletins, filtering through on Eve's wireless, to which, at first, my reaction was the same as when I saw my father's face peering at me through the window of a London restaurant: total disbelief. *It can't be true!*

But it is, it is! It's dreadfully true. The war that wasn't a war has ended, and the real war has begun.

Nothing unpleasant having happened since the previous September, we were lulled into regarding this as how things would continue to be, with nothing unpleasant ever happening. How wrong we were! Those Germans, who we had grown accustomed to thinking of as much like harmless pet dogs, snoozing quietly away on a far-off hearthrug, have awakened, and they are not pet dogs at all: they are ravening tigers, fierce and furious beasts, attacking Belgium, sweeping across the French countryside, an unstoppable enemy, taking by horrid surprise the Belgian, British and French armies; pouring, at phenomenal speed, on and on; overwhelming villages, towns, not pausing, until they have entered, conquered, Paris itself.

What about the Maginot and the Siegfried Lines that were meant to have been our impregnable defences? What about that silly song we sang: *We're going to hang out our washing on the Siegfried Line . . . ?* It *was* a silly song: oh, silly, silly!

Did our experts not realise that aeroplanes, carrying deadly bombs, can easily fly above trenches built underground? That tanks with machine guns can bypass them in a few hours? Alas, we are done for, defeated! The news on the wireless is horrifying. We have lost the struggle, the war waged against wicked Adolf Hitler, and the consequence is inevitable: ignominiously beaten, we are – we surely must be – doomed.

But a change in outlook has become apparent with the appointment of a different Prime Minister. He has taken the place of Mr Neville Chamberlain who was wrong about everything – and we hear our new leader, Mr Winston Churchill, declare in a broadcast to the nation that all is *not* lost; that if Hitler dares to invade Britain, the British people will fight him, and fight him, and go on fighting him: '*We will NEVER surrender.*'

And as though to prove he could be right, our soldiers, hundreds and thousands of them, exhausted, wounded, but alive, are fetched back across the English Channel from the beaches of Dunkirk by an immense armada of boats – vessels of every shape and size, from naval frigates to fishing smacks, and even Thames barges. We are shown on our cinema screens Pathé newsreel pictures of the incredible enormous rescue operation, with the sea as calm as a millpond. It's hailed as a miracle; and perhaps it is. But if Hitler decides to pursue our once armed, now disarmed Forces over the water, and to invade this country, as everybody says he will do – what's to stop him?

The idea of it terrifies me. I am so frightened, I feel sick with fear. I don't want to have to fight on the beaches; I wouldn't know how to. I, who only recently was in a fever of impatience to cut loose from Crapstone and my mother's apron strings; who had prided myself on being as good as grown up – nearly seventeen – I have reverted, pathetically, idiotically, to the mindless panic of a child. If the Germans are going to invade us, then I want to be invaded when I'm at home, with Mummy.

I tell Miss Simmons that my mother has sent for me; and Miss Simmons – too much occupied with matters more pressing than a need to check my story – unlocks her cash box and hands me a sufficient amount to pay for my train fare, saying merely that it will be added on to the bill.

And so I pack my suitcase, and flee headlong – fleeing, as many millions of other Europeans are doing, but with considerably less reason than theirs, from the terror of approaching Germans.

Besides my mother and Harvey, I find, when I get home, that Mrs Brendon and the youngest of her sons, Jeff, are there also, staying in Melrose on a temporary footing as PGs (which means Paying Guests) while deciding what should be their next move. We used to know the Brendon family when we lived in Newquay and they were regular summer holiday visitors to the seaside. Now, having been advised that a naval port and its adjoining docks are bound to be top of Hitler's list for imminent bombing raids, they've closed and left their Plymouth house in a hurry, and sought refuge with us in Crapstone village.

Jeff's three older brothers are all at present serving in the wartime army, but he, although nineteen, is exempt from doing any sort of national service because of ill health. He is a chronic invalid, pale and delicate as gossamer, and his fate, poor Jeff, is sealed. He will spend the rest of his life being the sole companion of his mournful widowed mother, a position he wouldn't have chosen, but must endure. Jeff's own companion is an ancient brown-and-white spaniel that answers to the name and description of Flabby. Jeff Brendon, so frail in physique, has, by way of self-preservation, a mordant sense of humour.

127

It wasn't until I got back to Crapstone that I realised how strange, how ghostly it would seem to me. There is an emptiness about it. All those girls and boys with whom, not long ago, I was picnicking, bathing, playing tennis – they're none of them here. They've gone, vanished. All of them are now in uniform of one kind or another; whereas I, at the first whiff of danger, panicked. I feel ashamed of myself; more and more I feel ashamed.

Charles Turner hasn't yet put on uniform. He's only just left school, and on his eighteenth birthday he bought a car for fifteen pounds, a Baby Austin. Together, one afternoon, we motor up to Hey Tor, and Charles, trustingly, lets me sit behind the wheel; teaches me how to switch on the engine, manage the gears, the steering, the braking – not on the road, which would be illegal, but accelerating across an open space of bumpy tussocky grass. With the sun shining and the sky blue, it ought to be the greatest fun. But fun, nowadays, has a hollow ring to it. Next week Charles Turner is joining the air force, and then even he will have vanished.

We know from the news on the wireless that squadrons of our fighter planes, Hurricanes and Spitfires, have been swooping about in the sunny summery skies over the white cliffs of Kent throughout August and these last weeks of September and October. Many of them are piloted by boys no older than Charles Turner, young men who perform fantastically acrobatic feats of bravery, meeting and shooting down dozens, if not hundreds, of incoming enemy aircraft, and being themselves – although, mercifully, in lesser numbers – shot down. It is they we have to thank for saving us from the expected invasion of our shores, and who, by their heroic deeds, oblige Adolf Hitler to think of an alternative plan for winning the war, as he is still, it seems, intent on doing.

I go for walks on the moor, short slow walks with Jeff Brendon and Flabby, and laugh at Jeff's wry unhappy jokes.

One Friday Eve Griffin comes for the weekend, a quick visit before she starts work as a fully qualified secretary in a branch of the War Office which has been evacuated from London to the comparative safety of Oxford. That's what I could be doing too, if only I had stayed on, as Eve did, at Clarence Lodge; if I had only not run away.

Hitler's readjusted plan of attack is soon made atrociously clear: *bombing*; but in the night-time, instead of during daylight hours, and on a massive scale. Towns and cities, ports, docklands, factories, ordinary streets and the people living in them, ordinary houses, shops – all, without exception, are targets now for the clusters of lethal bombs, high explosives and incendiaries, dropped from above. By such a strategy, Hitler reckons, the British people, deprived of the spirit to resist, will do what Mr Churchill said we never would do: surrender.

Everywhere is being bombed. This, we are learning, is what war, real war, means. My brother Jim has also had, as have I, had second thoughts. Recognised by an official tribunal as a genuine conscientious objector – which he is – and allowed, therefore, to accept employment on a farm, immediately France was invaded by the Germans he swapped his driving of a tractor for driving an ambulance with the FAU, a Quaker peace organisation. So when we turn on the six o'clock news and hear of the nightly bombing raids on Bristol, we know that he, Jim – brother, son – is in the thick of them.

Plymouth and Devonport, as the Brendons were warned would happen, are undergoing repeated pulverising bombardments. Sam Pyne, a lieutenant in the army now, and home on leave, stands after dark with me on the edge of Dartmoor, and side by side we watch the ghastly bonfire glow of Plymouth, ten miles away, going up in flames. The night sky is criss-crossed by beams of restless roving

129

searchlights. We can hear the ominous drone of enemy aircraft, and the sickening sound of explosions; every explosion, although dulled by distance, signifying further devastating ruin.

At sea, the German submarines – U-boats – are forever prowling to and fro, torpedoing the merchant navy vessels laden with food supplies being sent to us from America, sinking the ships in mid-Atlantic, drowning their crews. I can hardly bear to listen to wireless announcements broadcasting disaster following disaster; and yet I *have* to listen.

Then one morning Phoebe Brown thumps on the partition wall, shouting that Pam is on the phone, ringing Mummy from the RAF station outside Newcastle where she and Josephine Pipon were posted once their initial training was done.

'Pam wants to speak to you, Mrs Hallsmith – urgently –'

We squeeze through the gap in the fence, and Mummy snatches up the Browns' telephone. 'Yes, Pam – yes! What is it?'

On a faint and crackly line Pam tells us that Josephine had succeeded in wangling a special pass which gave her forty-eight hours leave; time enough to travel the long journey by rail down to Portsmouth on the south coast, and be present as godmother at the christening of an ex-schoolfriend's newly born baby. That night – last night – the air-raid shelter they were all sleeping in received a direct hit, and everyone in the shelter, including the baby and Josephine, was instantly killed. Josephine Pipon – tall, beautiful, opinionated, laughing Josephine, aged nineteen, is dead: impossible to believe – *impossible*! But it is true.

This hideous war; this toll of death and destruction – will it never end? And why am I skulking here in the shameful security of Crapstone? Why did I cut and run as I did? How cowardly of me, how disgraceful. How could I have been so craven?

130

What I must do, I realise, is return at once to Clarence Lodge – tomorrow – so as to complete the secretarial course I left half-finished: better late than never. Only when I've acquired my shorthand and typing diplomas, only then shall I be prepared and ready, fit to take part, like Eve Griffin, like everybody else today, in this nightmare life-or-death struggle for survival.

It's odd to be back again at Clarence Lodge. Nothing is quite the same as it was. Eve Griffin and Paula Mason are missing, and I don't think any of the girls here at present will become special friends of mine. Being the middle of the current term, they are all thoroughly settled in already. They seem to me also, not exactly unfriendly, but a bit stand-offish: rather older and rather grander than the frivolous bunch of students, fresh out of school, who were at Clarence Lodge when I first came. The change of atmosphere is due, partly, I suppose, to a change in the times, which are no longer frivolous. And I'm older, too. I'm seventeen now.

I find my bicycle leaning up in the garage shed, precisely where I left it. The railway label that has my name on it is still tied to the handlebars. But I don't feel inclined to set off on my own, riding around the countryside, or into Staines or Windsor: I shouldn't enjoy it by myself. And besides, it isn't spring or summer any more. It's winter, and outside the weather is cold and rainy. I mean to concentrate instead on improving my speeds in shorthand and typing, so as to gain my final diplomas as quickly as possible, and be able to apply for a job. Having just restarted attending the typing sessions, and struggling with Pitman's exercises, I regret the approaching five-day Christmas break. I would prefer to keep going – but it can't be helped: it's only for five days.

My mother didn't attempt to dissuade me – as I had feared she might do – from returning to Clarence Lodge. In the

131

summer, when I arrived back in Crapstone unexpectedly, she assumed that I, in a national emergency, had judged it right to hasten home on purpose to render what support and comfort I could to her and my little brother, Harvey. And when I declared my intention of resuming the course, she agreed at once, self-sacrificingly, to let me go: it was, to her, a simple matter of doing one's duty, and so not a decision to be questioned.

Mummy herself, indomitably courageous, has always been strong on obeying the call of duty. At the beginning of the Great War, Will Lawrence, to whom she was then engaged, asked her whether he should continue to pursue his vocation of missionary out in India, or stay on in England and fight for his country; and when she advised him where, in her opinion, his duty clearly lay, he enlisted in the RFC and was almost immediately, fatally, shot down over the battlefields of France. Mrs Lawrence, Will's mother, blamed, and has never forgiven, Janet – *my* mother – for the death of her eldest son.

Just as I'm about to leave Clarence Lodge to catch a train home for Christmas, I'm told that my mother, miles away in Crapstone, wants to speak to me on the telephone in Miss Simmons' office.

'Elspeth? – I thought I should warn you so that you'd be prepared. Your father is here – yes, here. He turned up on the doorstep last night, unannounced – and I'm afraid he's not at all well. It's because of the bombing raids in London – they've upset him, poor Daddy. He's had a sort of a minor relapse, but there's nothing for you to worry about. Dr Ferguson is looking after him, and he'll be better – quite better – quite recovered, very soon.'

My mother and Harvey were not, I'm glad to say, entirely alone in Melrose when Daddy turned up unexpectedly at

Crapstone. With them was my dear and favourite Aunt Molly. She had taken the place of Mrs Brendon and Jeff shortly after they departed, more than a month ago, for Scotland.

Aunt Molly, following the deaths of, first, my Granny Laurie, and then my Aunt Margaret, had decided, rather than selling the little terraced house in Oxford where the three of them had lived together for years and years (and where I well remember visiting them on several past occasions), to let it out, fully furnished, to respectable tenants. This being accomplished, and finding herself at a loose end, she had volunteered to aid her younger sister, Janet, with the many arduous tasks of house clearance preliminary to my mother's final removal from Melrose.

The present lease of Melrose is due to expire in the New Year, and, instead of renewing it, my mother means to shake the dust of Crapstone off her feet for good, and resettle in a place of her own choosing – somewhere, she says, near to the sea. She has never felt wholly accepted as a member of this local village community. We exchanged Newquay for Crapstone in 1935 on account of the Midland Bank transferring Guthrie, her husband, to its larger Plymouth branch – a reason for being here that has now ceased to exist. While she made the best she could of a bad job, Mummy, I know, will be thankful to put behind her what amounts to, all in all, a sorry period of prolonged and dismal failure, and to begin afresh on a completely new chapter of her life. The experience of failure is foreign to my mother's naturally self-confident character. She always expects to be successful, and generally is, in whatever she undertakes.

The practical preparations for a future thus optimistically envisaged were proceeding briskly until yesterday, when they were brought to a sudden halt, and thrown into utter confusion, by the startling arrival on the scene of my father – ex-head of the family. His reappearance, just at this moment, could hardly have been more disorientating had he risen from the grave.

Here he is, though – a presence to which we must grow accustomed: a disconcerting, disturbing figure, snooping silently round rooms piled high with boxes and packing cases; his garments in a peculiar state of neglectful disarray, wearing gym shoes so that nobody hears him approaching; picking things up, inspecting them, staring at people, making Mary Northey nervous – making *me* nervous; setting *everyone's* nerves on edge, because, in spite of Dr Ferguson's visits and pills and reassurances, we aren't certain how to deal with him – how we ought to behave.

Mummy informs me in a hushed voice that he, Daddy, during one of the worst air raids over London, switched on all the lights in the building where he lodged and went upstairs to stand at the top, actually on the roof, and was arrested by the police.

Is this really what happened? I don't know if it's true, or who told her; but this is what Mummy tells me, and what she believes.

'I don't blame your father,' she says to me. 'Poor Daddy – it's not his fault. I blame the Bank. After his last illness, when he recovered from it, they should have had more sense than to give him a London posting. What he needed, instead of being imprisoned in a stuffy London office, was to be in some sort of countrified surroundings, or by the seaside – where he could paint his pictures. He needs to have healthy air to breathe; to be out of doors, poor man –'

And in this instance, Mummy, who so seldom understands the feelings of others, is absolutely right. She was once, after all, Commandant of a convalescent hospital for soldiers who had suffered and been grievously wounded in the Great War.

Throughout my parents' inharmonious, difficult, and finally despairing marriage, their one point of total agreement – the single passionate desire they shared equally – was a longing to be out of doors. And it is a desire, a longing, I have inherited from both of them. I have the same yearning to feel the wind in my hair, the sun or the rain – I don't care which – on my face; to have sand under my feet, and waves lapping round my ankles: to be *outside*!

Christmas Day has become a blur in my memory, overtaken and submerged by the greater blur of what followed it, directly afterwards. Who would have guessed that something as ridiculous as a pain in the big toe of my left foot could have led so rapidly to such a catastrophe?

When I casually mention having a pain in my toe to Mummy, she in turn mentions it to Dr Ferguson. Whereupon he promptly, and most alarmingly, diagnoses this apparently minor affliction as a first symptom of deadly crippling rheumatic fever; for which, however, he hastens to reassure us, there is now an infallible cure – but only, that's to say, if the disease is recognised and dealt with in its early stages.

Immediate salvation, we are thankful to learn, is available in the form of a drug, known as M & B, developed recently by an American pharmaceutical company, and just, providentially, put on the market.

Dr Ferguson is an ancient Scotsman (not unlike Mr Edelsten in stature: tall and thin and dessicated) who wears the same type of unfashionable, stiffly-starched high white collar as Mr Chamberlain. His diagnosis of the sickness which I have somehow mysteriously contracted, and his prescription for its cure, my mother accepts without hesitation: despite him being as old as the hills, and altogether devoid of charm, he is a doctor.

The useful early warning symptom provided by the pain in my big toe wasn't, perhaps, quite early enough to enable the miracle American drug to perform its act of healing.

Can this be the reason why, within a very few hours of having it administered to me, I become exceedingly ill? – so ill that I lose my hold on reality and sink into a feverish world of near delirium.

For how long do I remain stretched out on the mattress of a low narrow divan, pulled up close to the double bed in my mother's bedroom that used to be shared, but isn't anymore, by both my parents? I haven't the least idea how long it is. Time has no meaning for me, no borders. I exist in a perpetual twilit zone. The table lamp, when I wake in what may be the middle of the night, is heavily shaded, and all day the windows have their curtains partly drawn. In this dim surreal environment, my mother – my nurse – is a presence never far away from me. She gives me my medicine, my pills; reads often, with pursed lips, my temperature registered on a thermometer; replaces daily – or even twice daily – the sweat-soaked sheets with others clean and dry; bathes my hot brow with a cool wet flannel cloth. Whenever I surface briefly from a muddle of grotesquely distorted dreams, Mummy is always there, close by, raising me up to sip water from a tumbler, speaking in a gentle soothing voice that lulls me back to sleep.

And so the nights, the days pass, the fever subsides, and gradually I mend. I lie perfectly still, lacking the strength or the wish to move an inch; but restored. And – amazingly! – I have an appetite again. What I want to eat – all that I do want to eat – are brown-bread-and-butter sardine sandwiches, produced for me endlessly, devotedly, by my good mother. Lying idle, contented, untroubled, I suppose vaguely that Aunt Molly must be somewhere about, in charge of Harvey and the household.

Then one morning, when Mummy is kneeling on the floor preparing to change my nightdress, I open my eyes and see my father standing immobile at the foot of the divan, wordless, watching.

136

'Daddy? –'

My mother glances up sharply across her shoulder and, at the sight of Daddy, hurriedly grabs a blanket to throw over my nakedly exposed body. I close my eyes, hearing her cry out at the sudden shocking apparition of her husband:

'What are you *doing* here, Guthrie? Go away! Now – at once! Go!'

And I hear Daddy answering, loudly and angrily, in a furious revitalised flash of those past embittered uncontrollable rages that her scornful dismissal of him has aroused:

'Why shouldn't I be here, Janet? Why shouldn't I look at Elsa-beth if I choose to? She's my daughter too, isn't she? – mine, as well as yours –'

'Go! Go, Guthrie – go!' My mother, sounding increasingly agitated, almost incoherent, keeps repeating the single word: '*Go! – go! –*'

I open my eyes, and he's gone, disappearing as noiselessly as he has come. Later I wonder if the whole episode was simply another feverish dream – an illusion: if I'd imagined it all.

The delayed removal from Crapstone has finally been effected: the furniture put into storage, bags packed, farewells made to Mary Northey and such friends and neighbours – not very many – who will notice our absence and miss us. And here we are, temporarily resident in a hotel on the seafront of Exmouth while the next step is being decided upon.

Aunt Molly has left us to visit another Laurie sister, Aunt Nancy, who lives alone in the Devonshire village of Ottery St Mary. Her vacant place has been filled by Aunt Lilian, the wife of Uncle Malcolm.

I don't know whether Aunt Lilian is joining us because she needs a respite from the constant bombing raids on Newcastle, or whether it's because her sister-in-law, Janet, is in need of support; both, probably. In any case, to have the stalwart and dignified presence of Aunt Lilian interposed as a buffer between my parents is distinctly a comfort. Travelling by rail, she arrived ahead of us and was already installed in the Regency Hotel when we got here. Daddy also came by train, from Plymouth; while Harvey and I, and Harvey's little dog, Roo, plus a mountain of luggage, were driven from Crapstone to Exmouth by our capable mother in the big old maroon-coloured Austin tourer.

My brother Harvey is considered, as a child, young enough still to share a spacious bedroom with me and Mummy (and Roo) on the first floor. Our father has had a separate room booked for him on an upper landing. We all meet for meals, a group ostensibly united, sitting round the same table reserved for the five of us in the hotel restaurant. But within a matter of hours it has become obvious that an awkward family situation isn't merely awkward: it is impossible.

Daddy's violent outburst of temper a week or two previously in Mummy's Melrose bedroom appears to have been a sort of trigger, blowing the lid off a veritable cauldron of passionate resentments which must have continued to simmer away unseen ever since his initial breakdown, and subsequent recovery, in 1937; and which now, when stirred, can bring on a fit of ungovernable rage.

We are having breakfast: Harvey and I eating as fast as we can so as to escape as soon as we can, aware, in a state of nervous dread, that there may at any moment be a repetition of yesterday evening's excruciating scene. Luckily the restaurant was fairly empty during supper, but even so it was indescribably embarassing and shameful to have to witness our father taunting Mummy openly, calling her rude names, ranting and raving at her until, after what had seemed like an eternity of horror, he finally flung down his knife and fork with a clatter, and stormed out of the dining room.

At nine-fifteen this morning every table is occupied. Mummy and Aunt Lilian are striving to maintain an artificially bright exchange of chit-chat, to which Daddy is paying ominously close attention. We have reached the stage of toast and marmalade safely when the dam of his brooding silence breaks and out it pours, at full volume, in public, a flood of pent-up venom.

'You are a *fool*, Janet! Only a fool could utter such absolute inanities – drivelling on as you do. Why can't you learn to keep your mouth *shut*?'

'Hush, Guthrie – hush! Not *now*, dear – you're forgetting where we are –' Mummy lays a beseeching hand on her husband's arm. He shakes it off angrily.

Guests at the other tables glance at us covertly, and whisper. The one elderly waiter and the waitresses, clustered in a bunch, are staring in our direction, wondering if they ought to intervene.

'I won't hush – why should I hush?' His eyes are blazing. 'Who do you think you are, to give orders to me?'

'Daddy – stop,' I say, pushing back my chair, standing up. Yesterday he called my mother much worse names than *fool*. They will get worse again – vile accusations – and I can't bear to hear them. 'Stop, *stop*, STOP!'

Then, with my head lowered, so as not to catch the eye of anyone, I march across the crowded restaurant, and straight across the hotel foyer, and out through the swing doors, and across the road to the esplanade, where I dump myself down on a slatted wooden bench, and gaze at the sea; not blinking, not crying, only fixedly gazing and gazing at the placid grey and silver sea, glittering in the wintry sunshine, and at its far horizon.

As early as this in the morning there is practically nobody strolling along the front. I'm alone, and I resolve to stay where I am, all day, alone; but after five minutes I'm not alone anymore. Somebody – Daddy – has very quietly sat himself down at the other end of my bench. Between us there is a space. For a while we say nothing. I wait for my father to speak, and at last he does.

'A fine kettle of fish we're in – eh, Elsa-beth? What do you think I ought to do about it?'

I survey him with astonishment. But his eyes, half-closed – not blazing any longer – are fixed, as mine were, on the sparkling waves. My father is asking me – *me*! – for advice. Amazing! It must, I suppose, be because he has nobody else to ask. I'm bound to answer him, to say something – but what?

So I say, in a panic, for fear it's the wrong thing to say: 'We aren't really managing – are we, Daddy? I mean, it isn't working, is it? –' Floundering, I rack my brains for inspiration. 'I mean – wouldn't you really be better on your own? – without any of us to bother you?' And then inspiration does come to my aid. I recollect, mistily, my mother's remarks regarding Daddy when I arrived home the day before Christmas. 'Painting is what you like doing most of all, Daddy, isn't it? – painting pictures. I expect it's a good deal easier to paint them when you're by yourself, isn't it?'

'You think I ought to go away?'

I take a deep breath: *say it*! – *say it*! 'Yes – yes, Daddy, I do. Don't you?'

He doesn't reply.

'Where would you go?' I ask him, speaking more boldly, gaining courage. No response.

An impulse, an inexplicable yearning, seizes me to reverse our roles, to make him, Daddy, my confidant instead of me his; to confess to my father what I've pondered over, worried about, but not mentioned to anyone before:

'I don't believe,' I blurt out, 'that it was rheumatic fever I

140

had. Actually, I'm quite sure I *didn't* have rheumatic fever. I daresay my toe hurt because I banged it. I think it was the new American drug which Dr Ferguson – stupid old Dr Ferguson – prescribed that made me ill. That's what I think.'

'Very likely,' says my father, nodding in agreement. 'Some doctors are blithering idiots. Not all of them, of course. My brother Malcolm – he's a doctor, and he's tophole at his job. I'll probably spend a bit more time up in Newcastle with him. Yes! – I've always rubbed along well enough with Malcolm – with my sister Rosemary too, as a matter of fact –'

'Might you go and stay with her – with Aunt Rosemary?' I ask. I'm pleased at how smoothly our talk is progressing, rather proud of how harmonious it is. I feel we are two adults conversing as equals: planning reasonably, sensibly.

'Oh no, no – that wouldn't do. I can't put my feet up with Rosemary – more's the pity. Dorothy's the trouble there. She and Rosemary live together, you see, and I can't stick her at any price – never could. My sister Dorothy is one of those bossy order-you-about women, like – like –'

I don't want to hear Daddy say *like your mother* and so I interrupt him quickly: 'Well, what I think, Daddy, is – you shouldn't go on staying here with us. It will be better for everyone if we aren't – you know – part of the same family any more.'

'Perhaps,' he says, reflectively, nodding, 'perhaps you're right, Elsa-beth.' And he repeats: '*Not part of the same family.* You may have put your finger on it – clever girl! Best if I push off – eh? Yes – by thunder – you're right!'

And so it is that I presently find I'm the only person sitting on the bench. For the remainder of this morning I wander to and fro on the pebbly shore, penned in behind huge impenetrable rolls of anti-invasion barbed wire, listening to the splash-splash of waves. When the incoming tide forces me back up the steps on to the promenade, and I return to our hotel for lunch, Daddy – my father – has already left.

Sam Pyne drives over from Crapstone to the Regency Hotel in Exmouth on purpose to see me, which is a great surprise because, although Sam has always been in love with different girls, I was never one of them. It's true we held hands when we were watching Plymouth being bombed and on fire, but holding hands was as far as it went. I'm accustomed to Sam Pyne counting me as unimportant – the younger sister of the Hallsmith Twins: that's all. But now Sam is on embarkation leave, and he presumably hasn't got a current special girl, so he's come to say goodbye to me.

It can only be a short visit. He motors us up on to Dartmoor in his rackety Ford saloon, bought as a bargain, he says, from a fellow officer who has already gone overseas, and we ramble about for half-an-hour amongst the gorse bushes and heather. It's windy, and rather cold, and Sam keeps looking at his watch. He has a camera, and takes a photograph of me; and then I take a photograph of him.

We are standing by the car before getting in it to drive back to Exmouth when Sam says: 'Will you write to me, Ellie? – if I write to you?'

'Why, Sam', I say, 'of course I will. Of course I'll write to you if you write to me.'

'Promise you will?'

'Yes – yes, I promise.'

This is when he kisses me. It's the first time a boy has kissed me: my very first kiss! Whenever I've thought of it since – and I keep thinking of it – I feel dizzy. It's an extremely agreeable sort of dizziness. I can remember and repeat as often as I want, inside my head, exactly the sensation of having Sam's lips – his very soft lips – pressed against mine for several seconds: just once – but it's unforgettable.

I thought perhaps that when Sam drops me off at the hotel, he might kiss me again, but he doesn't. There are people passing who would see.

'Goodbye, Ellie,' he says.

'Goodbye, Sam. And thank you for – for the drive. It was a lovely afternoon.'

His regiment is being sent out to India. Probably Sam shouldn't have told me, but he did. I know why he's going to want to write letters to me, and why he wants me to write letters to him. It's because we've played tennis on the Batsons' court together, and hockey in the Easter holidays with Commander Burton and bathed and picnicked together down at Denham Bridge. I understand that what Sam needs is to be absolutely certain of having somebody, when he's thousands of miles away in a foreign land, who will represent for him Crapstone pre-war: remind him of home as it used to be. And when he kissed me up on Dartmoor it was so as to seal and make sure that I wouldn't forget my promise.

I shan't forget – of course I shan't – either to write to Sam Pyne, or – how could I forget it? – the first ecstatically thrilling kiss I've ever had.

I've had an operation to chop out my tonsils and adenoids which an Exmouth doctor (recommended by the hotel manager) said were completely rotten and must be removed without delay before they poisoned the rest of my system. It happened very suddenly – an emergency – and although I was convinced the rheumatic fever had been a mere figment of Dr Ferguson's imagination, I believed wholeheartedly in the rotten state of my tonsils and adenoids if only because the soreness of my throat meant that to swallow anything except ice cream and barley water was acutely painful.

Mummy is at her best in an emergency, especially if it's medical. Without wasting a moment she arranged for me to have the operation done in a private nursing home evacuated from Plymouth to a vacant house in Crapstone, conveniently next door to where our friends and ex-neighbours, Commander and Mrs Pilcher, live. She drove me over in the Austin, leaving Aunt Lilian in charge of Harvey, and after I'd had the operation, and had then spent a week convalescing with the Pilchers – which I very much enjoyed – she fetched me away.

Aunt Lilian has returned to Uncle Malcolm (and perhaps to Daddy, too) in Newcastle, and Harvey and I and our mother (and Roo) are now staying some miles outside Exmouth in the village of Otterton. Here Mummy has rented rooms for six months with a young married woman, Mrs Bowen, so as to provide us with a secure base while she sets about energetically scouring the locality in search of a suitable house to buy.

Young thin white-faced Mrs Bowen has a year-old baby, George, and a husband who was once upon a time a market gardener and is nowadays a soldier fighting on the north coast of Africa. I think she's glad to have us as her lodgers, not so much on account of the money we bring in as for our company.

This isn't how I had planned to, or thought I should, be spending the summer. I am assailed again by feelings of nagging guilt. Otterton is a drowsy Devonshire village: secluded. Except for the daily news bulletins on the wireless, and Mrs Bowen's permanently anxious eyes, and the bristling unsightly rolls of barbed wire which render out-of-bounds the greater part of the steeply sloping shingle in nearby Ladram Cove – except for these indications, there is no sign of a war being bloodily and continuously fought elsewhere.

An opening has been left between the Ladram Cove barbed-wire barricades in order that bathers, when the weather gets warm enough, may be able to reach the sea. From Mondays to Fridays it's usually only my brother

Harvey and I who have the leisure to take advantage of this benefit, but on Sundays the small beach – reduced by its fortifications to an even smaller size – and the designated patch of water beyond, are crowded with local families: men, women and children in a determinedly holiday mood. On such a Sunday as this an incident occurs in Ladram Cove that makes a profound impression on me.

My sister Pam has joined us from her RAF fighter station for a few days' leave. She and I, having had a swim, are standing together at the top of the slope, idly watching the various amusements being pursued on a lower level, when my attention is caught by what no one else appears to have noticed. The limited area of sea, its boundaries marked by red flags, is teeming with splashing flailing arms and legs, amongst which – no! – surely not? I must be mistaken.

'Pam – look!' I exclaim, aghast, pointing. '– that little boy in the middle of those bathers there – look at him – he's drowning –'

And he is. But while I remain rooted to the spot, paralysed by horror, my sister has already streaked off down the shingle and into the noisily breaking waves, up to her chest; has grabbed hold of the child and hauled him on to dry land; has turned him upside down, and shaken the sea water out of his gasping spluttering mouth, and handed him back to the care of his hysterical mother.

The whole drama is over in a matter of seconds, but I am awed by Pam's heroic promptitude. If this is how she instinctively behaves in a crisis, with speedy life-saving action, no wonder she has been elevated to the rank of WAAF cipher-officer. How useless, by comparison, am I. My sense of inferiority increases. What is the point of me lounging about here on the beach in the sunshine with my schoolboy brother while the war, the horrible war, goes on and on?

* * *

145

Next month I shall have my eighteenth birthday. At eighteen every able-bodied person, male or female, is obliged by law to contribute in one way or another to the defence of the realm: meaning, put plainly, to the protection of our beleaguered country. All my friends, all of my contemporaries, are, or were, involved in the struggle; some, including Josephine Pipon and Robert Langley, the boy who taught us how to play kick-the-can, have been killed. Robert Langley's mother, widowed in the Great War, has now, in the Second World War, lost her only child.

The four sons of Otterton's vicar, Mr Grimaldi, are in uniform. Martin, the youngest of the four, is half-a-dozen months older than me. With mounting dismay I overhear Mummy confiding to Mrs Grimaldi details of my recent illness and my operation for TB infected adenoids and tonsils which will debar me, she says, from enlisting in any of the Services. She describes me as 'delicate'. Elspeth, my mother murmurs in Mrs Grimaldi's ear, will have to be kept at home under close supervision until her health is fully restored.

I am stunned. My mother may believe what she says, but it isn't true. I didn't have rheumatic fever – I had a pain in my toe; and the poisonous tonsils and adenoids were successfully got rid of by that operation. There's nothing wrong with me now. I don't need to have my strength built up. I *am* strong. I am perfectly fit and well.

Like a warning ghost the memory of Jeff Brendon haunts me. Poor Jeff – *he* was delicate: he really *was*. But I am *not*. I shudder at the idea of becoming my mother's Jeff Brendon; of being made a prisoner for life on the false assumption of ill health. If I am ever to win free, I realise, my healthiness has to be established, and insisted upon; and at once.

I confront my mother and announce to her, as a statement of fact, that I am now fully recovered, and therefore the secretarial training, twice begun and twice interrupted, must, absolutely *must* be resumed, and this time completed. Only when I've achieved my diploma shall I be qualified to take on some sort of essential war-work, the same as everybody else. I introduce the sacred concept of duty into my argument; and, after much persuasion, it does the trick. Eventually, reluctantly, Mummy – my dear devoted mother – agrees to let me go. Not immediately, she says, but – yes! – she gives me her word: very soon.

I am saved!

Things, I've discovered, very seldom turn out to be just as you expected. If they do, you are lucky. I have been lucky.

It's 1942; I'm eighteen, living in Oxford, a qualified secretary, employed in the same branch of the War Office, MI5, as Eve Griffin. This is the future I had hoped for, and had counted on in Otterton last summer, but it nearly didn't happen.

My mother kept her promise, and I returned, for a third time, to Clarence Lodge, and for a third time made friends, but no intimate friends, with a fresh batch of students. I was desperate to work my way through all the Pitman's exercises as quickly as possible, to reach the required speeds and accuracy in shorthand and typing, to pass the exams at the end of term and be rewarded with the precious Queen's Secretarial College diploma that would prove my secretarial worth. And as soon as I was – at last! – in possession of this vital document I applied for and was granted an interview with an eagle-eyed but sympathetic woman on the Appointments Board of the War Office, who questioned me closely, seeming, nevertheless, to have prior knowledge of, and to lay particular store by, my father's DSO.

Two days later I learnt that I had been thought suitable and accepted, and was instructed, therefore, to present myself at Keble College, Oxford, on the first of February to start my new job. So far, so good.

But these preliminary hurdles having been successfully conquered, now came the most critical of them, one that I was afraid would scupper me. For I couldn't any longer post-pone revealing the secret malaise I'd been hiding from everybody: a growing throbbing pain on the left side of my neck, and its accompanying unsightly bulge that was begin-ning to be visible if I shook my hair back. How was I to convince my mother that a bulgy neck was of no more importance, and could be as easily dealt with, as infected adenoids and tonsils?

During the weeks when I was obsessively occupied at Clarence Lodge, Mummy's house-hunting activities had borne fruit. She had found and, with Harvey and Roo, had moved into a charmingly picturesque thatched cottage built at right-angles halfway up a steep, a very steep, hill which runs a few hundred yards inland from, and parallel to, the coastal road between Dawlish and Teignmouth. This precipi-tous hill climbs its way past the handful of modest white-washed dwellings that form Holcombe, a hamlet too small to be termed a village, with a dairy farm nestling at the bottom, a tiny chapel-sized church in the middle, and a pub, The Castle, splendidly crowning its top. Holcombe also boasts a minute general stores, doubling as a post office, and is five minutes' walking distance from Smugglers' Cove and the sea. What more could anybody want?

Moreover, our new home, St Bernard's Cottage, with its thatched roof and its Trafalgar windows, and its big south-facing garden, is no mere rented accommodation, as was previously the case. It has been bought outright, paid for by a chunk of the inheritance Mummy's Uncle Stewart left for her when he died in 1930, and so it actually does, now and for ever, *belong* to us. It really is *ours*.

Having belatedly admitted to the traitorous bulge in my neck, and undergone a medical investigation of it, I was

immediately operated on, with maximum celerity and minimum fuss, in Dawlish Hospital. The deed being done, I then
prepared myself for a mammoth contest of wills, but the
veto I had feared and anticipated from my mother was not
forthcoming. She raised, surprisingly, no objection to me
going ahead as planned – after a slight delay – with the War
Office job: a post which she regards as a sort of honour
bestowed, and thus not to be lightly rejected. Even so, I
can't help wondering at her unexpected compliance; at the
ease of my victory.

Teignmouth's chatty, sociable Dr Courtenay (a character
very different from Dr Ferguson) proved to be an invaluable
supporter of my claim, pronouncing me, once the stitches
were out, *as fit as a fiddle, and ready for anything*: my view
precisely.

Also, by a curious coincidence, Pam had had an operation,
when she was a child, identical to mine. Did our mother
reason, perhaps, that if Pam, after the removal of TB glands
from *her* neck, subsequently flourished, why not Elspeth
likewise?

Chiefly, though, I think the state of independence I
currently rejoice in is due to my mother's overwhelming
relief at having finally – as it were – reached harbour and
dropped anchor in the safe haven of her own idyllic property. Behind her is the difficult, not to say dangerous,
navigation of a stormy uncertain passage, during which
time she was obliged, as captain of her craft, to keep a tight
grip on the tiller. But with the discovery and ownership of
St Bernard's Cottage, my courageous mother can afford,
thankfully, to loosen her hold and draw a deep breath, and
allow herself once again the indulgence of being guided by
her natural optimism.

Be that as it may, and whatever the true explanation for
this welcome leniency, here I am, in spite of many trials and

tribulations, living on the outskirts of Oxford, and earning my keep – a proper salary – as one of a team of three girls dedicated to fulfilling the secretarial needs of our masters, three army officers. The moral of which tale surely is: never give up hope!

Keble College has been requisitioned by the War Office to house its multitude of young ladies employed, as I am, in a secretarial capacity. Being full to bursting it has no space left for a newcomer. I was told it was up to me to find my own accommodation, as Eve Griffin, arriving some months previously, had succeeded in doing. For me to join Eve and the group of four other girls cosily installed in St John's Street was disappointingly out of the question, their land-lady declaring the plain impossibility of squeezing in more than the five extra inhabitants she already had under her roof. So this is why, having no alternative solution in sight, instead of living, as I should have much preferred, at the invigorating heart of a university city, I am a reluctant resident of 57 Victoria Road, Summertown, on Oxford's quiet respectable outskirts.

It's an address I'm extremely familiar with. One of my earliest memories is of staying here. Many a blotched home-made Christmas card or calendar, or scrawled note of thanks for birthday presents received, have been posted, over the years, to my Granny Laurie at 57 Victoria Road. For it is here she spent her long sorrowful widowhood after my grandfather was drowned in Southampton Water, and where, eventually, she died. From this house, ages and ages ago, my mother used to set off daily to Oxford Girls High School. Now my Aunt Molly has rented it furnished to a Major and Mrs Thompson, and they have agreed to provide me with bed and board. I am their lodger.

My mother considers that I have fallen on my feet; she

thinks that for Elspeth, her daughter, to have been taken in by the Thompsons, Molly's tenants, is the most tremendous stroke of good fortune, a veritable gift from the gods; and at first, when all my efforts to find myself quarters were unavailing, I thought so too. Not any more.

Major Thompson is no wartime soldier. He is a regular officer in the British Army. A small man, with ginger hair and a peppery temper, he orders his taller, sweet-natured obedient wife about, as of right, and bullies his nervous but bravely defiant fifteen-year-old son, David. Occasionally an older Thompson son, also in the regular army, turns up. Except for being junior in rank, he is more or less a carbon copy of his father. David, though, with whom I've developed a teasing brotherly-sisterly relationship, I'm glad to say resembles his nice mother, both in looks and in personality.

The Major isn't always at home: he comes and goes. Where he goes when he's away, and what he does there, I haven't enquired, and wouldn't most probably be told if I did. During his absence the household of 57 Victoria Road relaxes, and at his reappearance automatically stiffens to attention. Towards me, his lodger, he is unfailingly affable, and I, ever a coward and wishing at whatever hypocritical cost to preserve the peace, smile and nod in a pretended conspiracy of mutual appreciation.

Every morning, a few minutes before eight o'clock, swallowing a last hasty mouthful of breakfast, I rush to the end of of our road, where I'm picked up by either the first or else the second of the two special War Office coaches that drive out from Oxford to the village of Woodstock. Here, on arrival, they swerve in between the guarded, splendidly ornamental entrance gates of Blenheim Palace: this is my place of work.

I don't work in the Palace itself, but in one of the innumerable flimsy huts that have sprung up, like a toy town, to cover its extensive forecourt. Each hut's interior is divided in half. The semi-partitioned inner sanctum of my particular hut is the office shared by Colonel Waring, Major Deacon, and Captain Scott-Vaisey, the immediate overlords of Rosemary, Veronica and me.

Colonel Waring is a dear old bumbler, anybody's favourite elderly uncle. Major Deacon, paunchy – verging on fat – wears heavy horn-rimmed spectacles, is pompous, verbose and fanatically keen on precision in punctuation and spelling (details about which I am inclined to be vague). As to poor young Captain Scott-Vaisey, he suffers from a shyness so painfully acute – blushing uncontrollably – that he can't bring himself to dictate by word of mouth to a female secretary, but has to use a machine, a dictaphone, as intermediary. For this device I am heartily thankful, since the main stumbling block in the career I've embarked upon is an unfortunate difficulty – sometimes a downright inability – to decipher my own panicky shorthand.

Captain Scott-Vaisey's handicap allows me a further benefit, for which I am also grateful. Approximately once a week he sends me off across the forecourt with a bundle of his completed dictaphone rolls to be swapped for a new supply from a storeroom in the Palace basement.

I try to spin out these missions, liberating as they are, by a policy of deliberate dawdling. The route I choose to follow between the huts is a leisurely zigzag. On reaching the graceful flight of shallow steps that lead upwards to a splendid portico, I ascend them slowly, slowly. At the top I pause to survey the scene spread beneath me; and only then enter, unhurriedly, the majestic vastness of historic Blenheim Palace. When I retrace my journey it is at the same lingering pace. But no matter how shamelessly I loiter to and fro, the freedom gained from my stuffy prison never amounts to more than the briefest breath of fresh air, enlivened by a fleeting glimpse of palatial glory. It isn't much; not nearly enough to compensate for the boredom of before and after.

Because when, at the end of each day, I climb down from and am left behind by a crowded Oxford-bound coach, the evenings that await me are devoid of interest, as colourless and uninspiring as those preceding hours of monotonous drudgery. Wouldn't any girl of eighteen hanker, as I do, for entertainment more socially exciting than a game of rummy with David Thompson?

But worse than the lack of fun, worse than feeling myself cut off completely from events in the big world, most depressing of all when I've got through the day's work is my growing sense of the actual work I do being utterly worthless; and me with it. The letters I type, morning and afternoon, and lay dutifully in front of the Colonel, the Major, or the Captain to be signed and dispatched – I ask myself: are they helping, these boring *boring* letters, in the smallest slightest degree to win the war? *I don't think so.*

Every day our coaches pass by an airfield where we see huge transport gliders practising take-off and landing. They will be used to carry our troops over the Channel to France when the time for retaliatory invasion comes; as come – we are informed and believe – it ultimately will. In Africa Rommel, the German General, is being defeated by our General Montgomery, and forced to retreat. My sister Pam, in the WAAF, plots the heroic death-defying deeds of our fighter pilots. My brother Jim, realising that this war against Hitler and the Nazis is altogether different from the 1914–18 war, has stopped driving an ambulance and enlisted instead in the RAF to train as a bomber pilot.

And I? What am I contributing? It seems to me *nothing* – nothing of the least importance. Besides which, I hate, hate, *hate* being shut up all day, every day in a beastly fuggy hermetically sealed little wooden box. I *long* – as I always do long – to be out of doors.

Queuing with my tray in the canteen I have made a new friend, a girl named, exotically, Damaris de Boulay, who apparently has the same yearning as me for fresh air. If we eat sparingly, and then walk fast, we can just manage to circle on foot Blenheim Palace's fabulously beautiful lake in our lunch hour. But the energy required to maintain this regular daily exercise, while it expands our lungs, also fuels our impatience at the pointless tedium of our lives.

Eve, too, is restless. We are all three dissatisfied and wanting more and more desperately to be doing something we can assure ourselves is directly involved in the war effort. Something – yes; but what?

It is Eve Griffin who spots the fairly obscure paragraph in a newspaper; a short article reporting the fact that canals (it doesn't specify which canals), needing urgently to increase the traffic of vital cargoes from dockside to factories, have instigated a scheme for employing women on their waterways.

Canals! What a brilliant idea! Not one of us has any knowledge, none at all, regarding canals. Our ignorance in respect of them is total. But we are positive, at once, that this is exactly the job we have been hoping for, are suited for, and are destined to do.

From a handbook on British canals we copy out the particulars of six, and write to each of them expressing our interest in learning more about their scheme for employing women, as reported in the press. Time enough, we think, to select which of the six to settle on after getting their answers. But since we receive only one reply – from a Mr Kempton, office manager of the Grand Union Canal Carrying Company Ltd – we are spared the anxiety of having to make a choice.

154

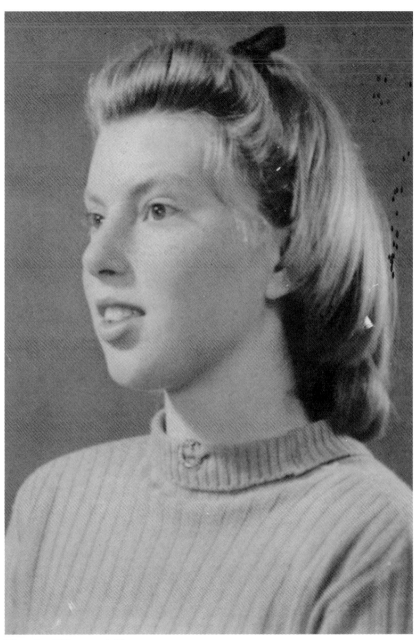

Elspeth – Ellie – aged fifteen, 1939.

Summer picnic at Denham Bridge, River Tavy, 1937. *Left to right*: Sam Pyne, Daphne, Jim, Robert Langley, Mummy, Harvey, Pam, Aunt Dorothy, half of me!

The estuary at high tide during a weekend in Lewarne Hosking's holiday bungalow, Porth, Cornwall, 1938. Harvey in canoe; Pam, me and Daddy alongside.

While staying with our Granny Hallsmith in Warlington, 1939, Pam and I attended a tennis party in the garden of the next-door neighbours. Me, *standing left. Back row*: Bobbie Barnett, *second from left*, Pam and Aunt Rosemary, *right. Seated centre*: the neighbouring hosts and Aunt Dorothy, *right*.

Jim, 1939.

Pam, *c.*1941.

Harvey, 1939.

St Bernard's Cottage. Holcombe, Devon.

Mummy (Mrs Hallsmith, née Janet Laurie), c.1942.

Jim, *left*, with the crew of a Lancaster bomber in the RAF, *c.*1945.

Harvey, with Roo, in St Bernard's Cottage garden, *c.*1943.

Pam, in WAAF uniform (except for straw hat!) on leave, *c.*1943.

Me in St Bernard's Cottage garden, on leave from the Grand Union Canal, 1943.

Ministry of Transport publicity photograph of Trainees. Kitty Gayford, trainer, on left, 1944.

Harvey and me, having just won the three-legged race during Holcombe village's VE-day celebrations, 1945.

Me at my Greenpark Documentary Film Production desk
in Guild House, Upper St Martin's Lane, London, 1945.

Aboard the *Andes*, en route to India, 1946.

Filming in Assam, India.

Ralph (Bunny) Keene, in Assam.

An overnight stop in Karachi, on return from India, February, 1947.

Summer in Paris, working on *The Far Cry* and keeping cool by the Seine during a heatwave, 1948.

Pam's wedding day in Holcombe, 1948. Me, as bridesmaid, adding the finishing touches.

Pam and David Pearce – married!

Picture Post, 29 April, 1950

A Young Publisher Gives His Most Successful Author an Introduction to His River

Emma Smith's publisher, James MacGibbon, keeps an old boat on the river, not far from where she lives. But this is her first trip, and she brought anti-seasickness pills, just in case. She is a sailor of only an hour or two's experience, not counting her wartime trips, working as a bargee on canal barges, which gave her the subject for her first book. But already she has made the boat and the river all her own.

Emma Smith's experiences of working in the war as a bargee on canals, and travelling in India and Assam when she was with a documentary film company, gave her some of what I call the mental furniture for her books. But mental furniture is like wooden furniture in the sense that the interesting point is : After you've set up house, what then?

For instance, we took Emma Smith for a day's sail down one of those wide muddy rivers of the east coast, where she is in fact setting up house. Emma went in for sailing like a puppy with a bone between its teeth. Emma, having got a hand on the helm, could not let go. The memory of the rest of the day is of Emma picking up the technical terms and the tricks of sailing; Emma gurgling like a bath-plug every time we came about; Emma

excited by the pull of the sheet and the rudder; Emma totally absorbed. This is a gift rather rarer than you might expect. I think it is a necessary part of Emma Smith's talent.

Some reviewer remarked Emma Smith has a name like a Jane Austen character : a nice point and a hint perhaps of what to expect, though I am not sure it might not be misleading. One of Jane Austen's talents was sitting still. I am not sure it may not be Emma Smith's style to get out and about, always a little farther afield.

Meanwhile, she is setting up house. There has been discussion recently about that traditional place, the writer's cottage. In the days of *Georgian Poetry* it was a thing authors believed in. Certainly, with the five-bob cottage, pump water, outside sanitation,

kitchen garden and six hens, a writer could conceiv able say, "I care for nobody, no not I, and write exactly what I like." There is something to be said on both sides. The Jolly Miller had his limitations Writing is not only a rural sport. In any case, the question is academic, since to all intents and pur poses the cheap country cottage has disappeared.

Emma Smith is just moving into one. It stands by the church in the village of Stoke-by-Nayland one of three, the other two being let at a total ren p.a., as the bill of sale said, of £7 13s.

Emma Smith should by now be installed. Ther has been a bustle of repairs, a fireplace put in, sink with a cold tap—the new occupier has the ambi tion to put in a bath one day, but that can wai Outside sanitation, but electricity for heat, light an

Picture Post, 29 April, 1950

keeping its family ties fresh and warm, collecting family albums as if this feeling of being rooted in many other people was a need.

Emma lives at present with her married sister, brother-in-law, and their Daniel, aged one. Her sister Pam, who lives two miles away, bought the cottages, two with tenants, so that Emma could have the third. The old family car, Pam driving, provides transport for going to auction sales all over the county. When she gets to her cottage, Emma is going to have the loan of Pamela's bicycle, for the time being.

Loan? For the time being? That sense of living provisionally is not unusual with writers who live to write, more than they write to live. If the way of life gets in the way of the writing—scrap the way of life.

Young talent that is recognised and sure of itself is simple, modest and quite ruthless. Emma Smith talking about her own style can stand back from it, can examine her way of thinking and writing, objectively. If necessary she will take it to pieces and put it together again differently, a process so drastic that setting up house for the first time or the twentieth is nothing to it. It's usually the way with writers. You're never sure when you've got them. They seldom settle down. A good thing, too.

MONTAGU SLATER.

The Cottage Sister Bought Her
Now, she is almost ready to move in—the last job of distempering nearly done.

Auctions are the Thing
She collects catalogues, marks the nice cheap lots with little drawings of chairs.

...oking. She will be comfortable. Gardening ...esn't interest her, so it is just as well the patch at ... back is small. I don't think she will keep six ...ns.

...Architecturally, the cottage is as traditional as a ...ristmas card. It has an eighteenth-century front ...or, but the beams look older. There are stone ...ors below : upstairs, the wide and crooked ...orboards go up and down like waves.

...When we were there, it had all the atmosphere ... a house nearly ready for life. The sofa from the ...ction sale stood about exhibiting its lot number, ...d unsure if this was the room. The unconnected ...le stuck a forlorn end from the fuse-box, the torn ...per of a cement bag flapped at the corners, and ...mma washed her distemper brush and sat on the ...erstep in the sun to wonder. What will it be like ...ing here?

...I have noticed before a habit in young talent of

This Was a Good Bid
She bought this in a sale, too. She has found that writer's cottage people dream about.

What Will it be Like?
Living here alone—sister two miles off— nice cottage. Can I really write here?

41

A double page spread in *Picture Post* magazine, from a feature in April 1950. I am pictured (*main photo, right*) sailing with my publisher James MacGibbon and (*right*) setting up my new home in Stoke-by-Nayland, Suffolk.

Having a drink outside a pub by the Grand Union Canal, post-publication of *Maidens' Trip*, 1948.

Beech cottages, Stoke-by-Nayland, Suffolk, 1949. The first home of my own.

Cheltenham's first literary festival, 1949. Me, jubilant after giving my first-ever public talk.

Emma Smith and Richard Stewart-Jones – married! February, 1951.

Mr Kempton doesn't appear to have grasped that what we are doing is putting out a tentative feeler: seeking information. In a few curtly businesslike sentences he confirms that the GUCCC does have such a scheme, and proposes a date a fortnight ahead when we should come to the depot at Hayes, Middlesex, for an interview.

Instead of rejoicing at this answer, we are thoroughly flustered by it. We had been asking, not for an immediate interview, but – as we thought, sensibly – for a brochure to study at our leisure. The GUCCC manager's brisk assumption of our readiness to take on the canal job without further preliminaries engenders a crisis of confidence, a turmoil of doubt and hesitation. What might we be letting ourselves in for? To have a total stranger, someone called Mr Kempton, make our minds up for us, and in so great a hurry – to be catapulted by him into the unknown – is this really what we wanted?

It isn't what Damaris de Boulay wants. Her enthusiasm for canals waning, she changes direction and decides to apply instead for admission to the Wrens. Eve and I, however, resolve to persevere with what we've already begun; at least by going for the interview. It won't, we tell each other, commit us in any way. If we don't care for what's on offer, we can simply decline it.

One damp dark Saturday morning we set off boldly, the two of us, having not the faintest idea of what we shall find on reaching the rather dreary sounding Hayes Depot, our destination. It's only on arrival that the reality of the step we've been blithely contemplating hits us, and we become fully aware, suddenly, shockingly, of the stark contrast between where we have come from – Oxford, Keble College, Blenheim Palace – and where we are now standing. So this is a canal!

Moored side by side to the cold grey stone wharf is a row

155

of immensely long narrow brightly-painted boats, a kind of water-borne street, the inhabitants of which all seem to be waiting expectantly, as though for news of some sort. They eye us in a disconcerting silence as we walk self-consciously by. What they may be thinking of us we can't guess, but our first impression of them is of encountering a foreign tribe, so completely different are they from any people we have met and mingled with before. Can it be possible, we wonder, that entire families, men, women, children, and their dogs, live, not in houses, but crammed hugger-mugger down inside those tiny cabins glimpsed as we pass? We too, presumably, would be obliged to live aboard such a boat, in such a cabin.

The shock, though, for me, is the shock of instant delighted conviction. When the sun bursts out from behind a bank of clouds, and the brass rings on the smoking black cabin-top chimneys sparkle as if made of gold, and a dark-skinned woman with dangling earrings, leaning in the hatches of her gaudy boat, nods at me, I know absolutely, with a huge sense of relief and excitement, a lifting of the heart, that my future, which I couldn't ever clearly envisage, but had dreamed of, yearned for – it is *here*.

On being pointed – silently, still – towards an inconspic-uous ground-floor office, we join the tail-end of a queue of unshaven roughly-dressed men wearing heavy boots and knotted neckerchiefs who are blocking its open doorway. Not wanting to seem presumptiously pushy, we hover uncertainly outside in the chill wind, until noticed by – as we rightly suppose – the manager, Mr Kempton. Busy tele-phoning behind his cluttered desk, he beckons to us impatiently, and when we shove our way in, murmuring apologies, he tells us we don't have to feel guilty at jumping the queue. The boaters, he says (we must remember that terminology: *boaters*, not *bargees*) are waiting to be given their loading orders before setting off for the docks, and an extra five minutes of hanging about will have no adverse effect on their pay-slips.

Five minutes? Is that as much time as it will take the efficient Mr Kempton to deal with and dispose of us two girls?

Apparently so. He looks at Eve, and then at me, summing up our potential in a single sharp comprehensive glance; makes a note of our names and ages, informs us of the need to provide a doctor's health certificate, and to obtain permission from the Labour Exchange, and the interview, lasting scarcely a moment more than the predicted five minutes, is concluded. Dazed by the speed of it, we thrust our way back through the crowded entrance, as good as employed!

Well – not quite. There remain various obstacles that must be surmounted. Under the prevailing rules and regulations of a country at war, a person can't just change jobs on the mere promptings of a whim. Permission has to be sought from the authorities, and a sufficiently persuasive reason given for needing to make the change.

Dr Courtenay, my willing accomplice, arms me with a letter in which he states the medical advisability of his patient, Miss Elspeth Hallsmith, who has recently undergone a surgical operation to remove tubercular-infected glands from her neck, working out of doors instead of, as at present, confined within the four walls of an office.

I forget what sort of a compelling argument Eve submits, she not having the benefit – like me – of genuine TB glands to support her claim, but whatever was her story we are both successful in being swiftly released, and with none of the difficulties we had anticipated, from our War Office contracts of employment.

Thus it is that almost exactly one year after I first arrived in Oxford, supposedly qualified by Queen's College to set forth on a secretarial career, I say goodbye to dear old

Colonel Waring, to Major Deacon, to Captain Scott-Vaisey, and to my fellow wage-slaves, Veronica and Rosemary, who can't imagine why I should want to leave them and the peaceful beautiful surroundings of Blenheim Palace.

It's farewell, in 57 Victoria Road, to my peppery host, Major Thompson, and to his gentle sweet wife, and to poor sorrowful David, now to be deprived of those interminable evenings we shared, he and I together, playing games of rummy. And because Damaris de Boulay, staunch companion of countless lakeside marathons, has chosen the Wrens in preference to the GUC, I have also to say goodbye to her – and this I do indeed regret; but it is my only regret. I depart from Oxford otherwise without a single pang. How wonderful that in future there will be no more deadly dull letters to type; no more daily struggling to decipher my own disgraceful shorthand; no more wasted hours and hours of imprisonment in a stuffy little hut deprived of the inspirational vagaries of weather: wind and rain and sunshine.

I've escaped! I am free, free, FREE!

Here we are again, Eve Griffin and I, at Hayes Depot, but accepted now as genuine GUC Carrying Company Trainees, and appropriately dressed, we hope, to do battle with the elements and the unknown hazards ahead of us. Aiming for maximum warmth and a general standard of toughness, our garments have been mostly either donated or stolen from brothers: cricketing flannels dyed brown to conceal what they were initially meant for, thick home-knitted jerseys, knee-high football socks, woolly scarves. Only my boots are new. Being boys' boots they require, as do all clothes for children, fewer precious coupons than clothes for adults.

The GUCCC's trainee crews work in teams of three. Since – alas – Damaris de Boulay isn't with us to complete the trio, we are introduced at the lay-by (the correct name, we take note, for the quay where boats moor while waiting in between trips) to a very nervous, very young, practically speechless girl, Anne Avery, whose dejected air seems to indicate a growing realisation on her part of having made a dreadful mistake.

If we two ex-War Office secretaries had also been harbouring secret doubts, they vanish as soon as we meet our trainer, Kitty Gayford. Not by birth a boat-woman – far from it – Kitty (as we in due course learn) has previously, and up to several years before the outbreak of hostilities, pursued a varied and a colourful career on land. Her commitment, heart and soul, to the Cut (a new word for us) is relatively recent.

Small and agile, trim, thin, of indeterminate age (thirty-five? – forty-five? who can say?), there is about her something bird-like, a resemblance enhanced by the peak of a navy-blue skiing cap jutting sharply forwards above a beaky nose. She's wearing tight-fitting navy-blue bell-bottom sailor's trousers. But better even, much better, than her obvious reassuring efficiency is the welcoming smile, and the good-humoured, breezy, playful manner of her greeting. What a relief! Two, at least, of the Trainees are thankful to feel, in a flash, that life with Kitty is going to be fun.

We sit in the blistering heat of her motor boat cabin, drinking mugfuls of hot strong tea, and sweating profusely. Eve and I, and Anne Avery, are squeezed together in a row on the narrow side-locker, facing the stove a few inches in front of us, which is blazing away like a miniature blast furnace. Our teacher, Kitty, wasting no time on idle chit-chat, begins immediately the education of her new pupils. Perched, mug in hand, at the top of the steps leading down from the hatches, she outlines for us, briefly but entertainingly, the journey that will start early tomorrow morning when we steer the *Battersea* and the *Uttoxeter*, Kitty's pair of empty boats (remember: *boats* not *barges*), towards London's East End and the Regent's Canal docks (in boaters' language, *Lime'us*) to pick up a cargo, most probably of steel billets.

Once loaded, we'll return the way we came, retracing, more slowly now, the miles back to the Depot. Passing the lay-by, and Mr Kempton's office, passing the canteen, the engineer-ing-, carpentry-, and paint-sheds without stopping, we shall continue steadily north-westwards, travelling on and on, day after day, negotiating the uphill and downhill flights of innu-merable locks, until we finally reach Birmingham – *Brum* – where, at Tyseley Wharf, our cargo will be unloaded.

Then, the boats empty again and riding high in the water, we shall proceed by a route known as the Bottom Road, to Coventry, taking on board there a second and different cargo, not of steel but of coal for delivery to one or another factory in the south, close to Hayes Depot, our original starting point. The whole round trip, Kitty informs us, will last approximately three weeks, to be followed immediately by another trip, at the end of which initiation we will have acquired enough knowl-edge and competence to be put in charge of our own pair of boats, and given our loading orders, and told to get on with it.

Good heavens! – *really*? After only two trips – a mere six weeks' practice – we girls will be expected to manage, on our own, two of these gigantic seventy-foot-long canal boats? To manoeuver them in and out of *locks*? Of *docks*? How terrifying!

'Don't worry,' says Kitty, laughing at our dismay. 'One trip is really enough – by the time we're back here, believe me, you'll be old hands at the game – proper boaters. You will – I promise you will.'

Anne's face wears an expression of sheer panic. But Eve and I resolve, on the spot, that if Kitty Gayford promises to make us, in just six weeks, fit to operate a pair of GUC canal boats, then fit, in six weeks' time, we will be.

* * *

Nine days later we reach Birmingham, tired but triumphant, and in the waning light of a drizzly chill afternoon tie up the *Battersea* and the *Uttoxeter* at Tyseley Wharf, ready for eight o'clock tomorrow morning when their cargo of steel billets will be unloaded.

We are here, actually here in Brum, having steered our pair of huge, heavily laden craft – the motor boat towing its engineless butty – over miles and miles and *miles* of winding waterway, through pitch-black tunnels, up and down flight after flight of locks (those marvels of engineering ingenuity), to complete, without any irretrievable disaster, the initial stage of this, our maiden voyage. *We got here!* And we are boastfully convinced, Eve and I, that it has taken little more than one back-breaking, arduous, amazing week for us to have become the tough old hands Kitty had sworn we would be by the end of the entire trip.

Of the trio of greenhorns who set out from the Hayes Depot at Bulls' Bridge – an age, as it now seems, ago – we two are the survivors. The third Trainee, Anne Avery, packed her bag on the journey down to Lime'us and jumped ship, apologetic and tearful, the moment we arrived in London's docks.

Kitty took her departure philosophically. 'Poor child – it wasn't her fault. She was interviewed, the same as everybody is, by Mr Kempton. He's the person to blame, for signing her on. He ought to have known better. I could see, as soon as I laid eyes on Anne Avery, that she wouldn't do.'

We heard with some anxiety this unequivocal judgement uttered by our trainer. What then, we had asked her, about *us*? Should *we* do?

Kitty told us cheerfully not to worry. Eve and I, she said, were exactly the sort of capable self-reliant intrepid girls the GUC Carrying Company was aiming to recruit for its newly inaugurated scheme.

Intrepid? What, *us*? Could this really be the impression we gave? Alone at night in the privacy of our shared butty cabin we had promised each other, whispering, that henceforth we would strain every muscle, exert every ounce of self-control, to merit her undeservedly good opinion. We would complain about nothing, flinch at nothing, not even the dismaying possibility of bedbugs; would contrive to appear unconcerned and be quite at our ease when obliged, in the greasy cramped engine-hole, to use a bucket as a lavatory. It was the bucket which had represented for Anne, we were sure, the final straw.

We had noted how fearfully our companion edged along the inches-wide gunwale, clinging at every step to the cabin-top; how she refused to venture so much as a foot on the line of single planks which, by spanning the gaping void of the boats' empty holds beneath, provided a temporary bridge between stern and bows – planks we ourselves had run across at full speed, rejoicing in their jolly bounciness and the acrobatic balancing skills they consequently required. It wasn't, though, these minor trials of courage, daunting as they clearly were for poor timid Anne Avery, but the bucket in the engine-hole that – understandably – had finished her off.

Now, in Brum, with a free evening ahead of us, we two remaining Trainees are introduced by Kitty to the Municipal Public Baths where we luxuriate, for next to no money, in our first hot-water soak since leaving home. What heavenly bliss! And then comes the further treat of supper – fish and chips – eaten, instead of aboard the boats, in a café which, we learn, must in future be pronounced as a *caff*.

Oh yes! there is a great deal for us to learn in our new life on the Cut; and we are learning fast.

The distance from Birmingham to Coventry, if drawn as a straight line from place to place, isn't actually very far, but when toiled over on the so-called Bottom Road it lengthens into a trial of endurance that seems to last for ever.

Travelling northwards after leaving the London area we passed through country that was a constantly changing vista of rural beauty. Not so the Bottom Road. Nobody could describe the surroundings where we now find ourselves as beautiful, or as anything but an unlovely barren wasteland, with a depressing atmosphere of industrialised neglect. And whereas our boats, operating in pairs, can lie side by side in the spacious GUC locks to which we have become accustomed, this stretch of waterway was constructed for the purpose of facilitating a local traffic in the transportation of coal, and the locks, built as they were to allow the passage of one horse-drawn coal boat at a time, are correspondingly narrow.

When, therefore, we reach a lock, or a flight of locks, with the *Battersea* towing the *Uttoxeter*, the motor boat has to forge on ahead, casting the butty adrift and waiting, whether above or below, for its mate to catch up. Eve and I, following behind, take turns to raise or drop the paddles, filling or emptying, as need be, each separate lock, before dragging the butty, at the end of a cotton-line, in and out and in and out: a slow and increasingly wearisome task.

The coal-boat skippers we encounter on the Bottom Road are a breed of person altogether new in our experience. Although occasionally aided by a teenage daughter, or, even more rarely, by a small boy, a son, their families aren't usually involved in the arduous business of earning a weekly wage. Independent in character, voluble, cheery, these hard-working men don't live aboard their vessels, as we, and all proper boaters born to the water, do, but instead, plying a day-to-day trade, have houses ashore, homes they return to sleep in at night, the same as Thames bargemen. Being neither wholly the one thing nor the other, we have some difficulty in knowing how, rightly, to label them.

They are not, these coal-boat owners, ill-disposed towards us – we foreign interlopers from the south, who invade their territory – but they are in a perpetual relentless hurry, and their horses, skinny skittish creatures, cover the miles of dirty towpath at a tremendously fast walking-pace, which never quite breaks into a trot, being urged on meanwhile with hellishly loud cries of encouragement – or possibly threats – by the steersman at his tiller; so that again and again the bow-wave of a speeding coal-boat washes our helpless floundering butty on to the mud, from where, with aching arms, it has to be shafted free. We don't hate the good-humoured indefatigable coal-boat men – how could we? – but we have grown to hate their Bottom Road.

The GUC boaters, ourselves included, have been instructed to use the shorter Bottom Road to Coventry so as to save water – that vital element, on a plentiful supply of which depends the functioning of the whole canal system.

One evening in a pub we are told, with relish, the story of a rebellious boater who refused, point-blank, to obey his Company's orders, insisting stubbornly on going from Brummagem's Tyseley Wharf to Coventry's coalfields by way of the two longer water-wasting sides of the triangle, rather than taking the designated quicker route of the Bottom Road.

'I married my wife,' he is reported as having said, 'to be a wife, not a bloody 'orse.'

Our cargo of coal, destined for Nash's Paper Mill way down south, isn't stowed on the boats neatly in those tidy sacks delivered to householders, as we had optimistically hoped, but pours aboard in a loose gravelly choking stream from the wide-open mouth of an overhead chute.

Wading knee-deep in the black engulfing tide, and struggling with shovels to maintain a level distribution of it, we now understand why Kitty advised us to wear our oilskins when it isn't raining: we are almost instantly enveloped in swirling suffocating clouds of coal dust. And we realise now, also, the practical advantage of Kitty's curiously anachronistic skiing cap, which entirely hides her hair and ears, while its peak, to some extent, protects her eyes. We too, we vow, once back in London, will each procure from Lillywhites, the Piccadilly sports shop, an identical article of headgear.

At Lime'us Basin we watched, but took no part in the slow careful loading of steel billets. Here, in Coventry, it is a different matter altogether. We are involved unavoidably in the hurried and dirty process of loading coal. As soon as the dizzy noisy rattling inrush has ceased, and both boats have received a sufficient amount of cargo, we summon up what remains of our strength in order to fling haphazardly over the top-planks a provisional covering of the huge heavy awkward tarpaulin sheets, leaving them to be dealt with properly later. Clothing-up is a job that can't be skimped – every stiff crease must be smoothed flat, every cotton-line made absolutely taut, every knot secure – but the immediate priority is to seek purification for our unrecognisably grimy selves. And so, abandoning a half-hearted attempt at rinsing clean our filthy oilskins in the unclean water of the Cut, we hasten off, exhausted but jubilant, to the heavenly bliss of a neighbouring public bath-house.

Travelling south we shall have to remember, Kitty warns us, day by day to keep a vigilant watch on our present cargo, and have shovels ready for action. Loose coal is a shifting commodity that can all too easily unbalance a boat, tipping it out of true, and causing the steering to be troublesome, or even worse – a disaster, even. Coal is treacherous, not to be trusted.

We listen, and pay heed – as we always do – to what our teacher tells us, and assure her that we won't forget her words of wisdom. We will remember, we promise – yes, yes, we *will*! – to be constantly watchful. But our spirits are soaring. If the new cargo we carry proves to be worrisome, who cares? At last the *Battersea* and the *Uttoxeter* have their bows pointing towards Bulls' Bridge, which, while it isn't *home* exactly, does count for us as the next best thing: a sort of home port. On arrival at the Depot we shall have completed our first ever trip, from beginning to end, on the Grand Union Canal. Worth a celebration!

Following the second of our training trips with Kitty Gayford, we shall be allowed a breathing space of three days before a further two trips: these undertaken, frighteningly, on our own, with just another Trainee girl, but without our guardian angel. How on earth, deprived of Kitty, are we going to survive? Goodness only knows; but manage to survive, somehow, we must. And our reward for winning through will be *six* clear days of leave: long enough for me to catch a train down to Dawlish, Devon, and then a bus on to the village of Holcombe, where, safely ensconced beneath the thatched roof of my mother's cottage, I shall entertain her and young Harvey with exaggeratedly adventurous tales of life on the Cut.

It's all I'm able to think about at present. My horizon is occupied exclusively by boats: canal boats. The dreadful war of death and destruction, waged by others, elsewhere, has dwindled to become no more than faintly heard noises in the distance. Boats predominate.

The next trip, which follows directly after the first one, will complete our training, and for it a third member, replacing the missing Anne, has been added to Kitty's crew. Eve and I regard Nina Heseldine, the Scheme's latest recruit, in dismay. Surely this roly-poly girl, small and plump, with her pink-and-white complexion and her upper-class accent, is yet another of Mr Kempton's mistakes? We imagine how horrified she will be – as horrified as Anne Avery was – when she discovers what is expected of her and the conditions that she is going to have to endure.

But we are wrong. Appearances, we learn, can be deceptive. Nina takes everything – or nearly everything – in her short little stride. She doesn't flinch, we note, on being told the reason for a bucket in the engine-hole. She negotiates gamely, step by careful step, giggling a bit, arms outstretched, the hazardous bouncy top-planks. She persists, and succeeds, in her strenuous efforts to wind up, unaided, the heavy lockside paddles. We watch, critically, keeping aloof, while she props her chubby shoulders against the massive beams and with feet scrabbling for purchase on slippery flagstones, continues to shove and strain backwards until, inch by inch, the huge beams respond and the gigantic gates begin to swing slowly open. Doggedly determined and unquenchably cheerful, Nina accepts and triumphs over every challenge, bar one.

A full working day in her company suffices for us experienced old hands to have quite revised our opinion of this greenhorn, who has amply demonstrated her worth as a future shipmate. Consequently – reaching Lime'us Basin too late to be loaded with a fresh consignment of billets before the morning – by way of indicating our approval and friendship, we whisk her off on a bus ride the whole length of Commercial Road to the big multi-storied Aldgate outfitters known as Gardiners' Corner that Kitty introduced us to several weeks – an age! – ago. Here, at the cost of many clothing coupons but not much money, we had obtained the warm navy-blue duffel coats which the Council issues to its rubbish collectors and street cleaners and other similarly employed manual labourers. We had also, at the same time, invested (on Kitty's advice) in the tough navy-blue weather-resistant sweaters worn by seamen.

Nina is so flatteringly ready and willing to copy us, agreeing to our every suggestion, that Eve and I, conscious of superior knowledge, can't resist rather showing off to a naive newcomer – boasting, in fact. But later on, sitting in the saloon bar of the famous *Prospect of Whitby*, overlooking the Thames, the revelation that Nina is no stranger – as were we – to the taste of beer comes as a surprise. And it dawns on us that Nina Heseldine, despite her childish dimples and innocent blue eyes, may very likely be, in some ways, more sophisticated than we are.

Although she takes to life on the Canal with the enthusiasm and alacrity of a duck to water, there is, however, one requirement with which Nina adamantly refuses to comply. If the lock we have emptied is deep, and our boats are about to move forwards out of it, she will not, absolutely *will not* jump down on to the cabin-roof of the unmanned butty below: an inflexible resolve she expressed at the end of what had been her first afternoon, when we were returning to Bulls' Bridge after Kitty's customary local trial run for new Trainees. As soon would she chuck herself off the summit of Mount Everest, she then declared, as throw herself into the dark dankly dripping abyss of Denham Lock, deepest of all the locks on the GUC.

'Don't worry,' Kitty had urged her, 'just remember to *keep your knees bent* as you're landing, and you'll be fine –'

But Nina wouldn't even try. She studied the awful suicidal drop from above, and shook her head. 'No fear! – not me!'

These misgivings of Nina's I secretly share, especially when, as is sometimes unavoidable, I have to force myself to make that horrid stomach-churning leap, (remembering always the vital importance of *keeping the knees bent* on landing).

We two spend our free days – Friday, Saturday and Sunday – staying in London with Mrs Griffin, Eve's mother, in her shabby untidy convenient ground-floor Earl's Court flat. The weekend has a curious air for us of being unattached to reality. We wake, from habit, at 5.30 a.m. But having savoured the treat of not being obliged, at once, to roll out of bed, we thankfully close our eyes, turn over, and go to sleep again.

Saturday's breakfast merges imperceptibly into the midday meal. Lounging around in pyjamas, chatting, yawning, dozing, we don't even bother to get properly dressed. At six o'clock we listen, as everybody does, to the news on the wireless, but find it hard to visualise or relate to far-off battles, whether victories or defeats; a failing enhanced by our dismal grasp of geography.

Eve's mother – vague, hospitable, chain-smoking Mrs Griffin – produces an early supper for us: corned beef shepherd's pie, and a pudding to follow of tinned peaches and Bird's custard. And when it's all been eaten, the table cleared, the dishes washed, what we crave, more than anything else, with renewed yawns, is the luxury of a snug bed and hours of uninterrupted sleep.

On Sunday I do get properly dressed. It seems very strange, but very pleasureable, to be putting on silk stockings (the only pair I possess), and a suspender belt, and wearing a frock! I've been invited by my sister Pam to have an expensive lunch, together with her Canadian air-force friend, Ricky, in a smart restaurant off Regent's Street.

As soon as we've met and greeted each other, Ricky holds out Pam's left hand in order to show me the ring on her engagement finger.

'Goodness gracious,' I say, amazed and delighted, '– you're engaged, you and Pam! You're going to be – are you? – actually going to be *married*?'

'We sure are,' says Ricky, smiling broadly. 'Isn't that right, Pam?'

I've met Ricky before. He's a fighter pilot on the same

station as Pam's, young and handsome: a dear. How romantic!

But when I glance up and see the expression on my sister's face, I'm startled. It's the fond amused look of an adult indulging the passing whim of a small boy; as though, I think, the pearl-and-sapphire ring, and what it signifies – marriage – is merely part of a game she's playing to please this nice young man.

Confused, I feel a shiver of apprehension, and with it the chill touch of a wider anxiety. Can nothing nowadays, in wartime, be taken seriously? – nothing be relied upon as the simple truth? Do we all have to, like my sister Pam, pretend? Is pretending a sort of necessary protective shield? And if so, a shield against what, exactly?

Back at the Depot, Eve and I find that for our third trip we have been allotted as crew, aboard the *Ascot* and *Crater*, to Cecily, a Trainee some years older than us and already experienced in skippering a pair of boats.

We learn from Mr Kempton that she is a New Zealander. From Cecily herself we learn nothing of her personal history. She isn't by nature chatty. Indeed, she is singularly lacking in conversation of any sort. After the sociability we enjoyed with Kitty and Nina we are disconcerted by Cecily's stand-offishness. Doesn't she like us? Have we inadvertently offended her? What is it we said or did to antagonise this tall stiff-legged uncommunicative older person? But then, in the privacy of our butty cabin, we come to the conclusion, whispering, that we can't be blamed, Eve and I, for Cecily's upsetting silence: *it's not our fault*. She simply has a melancholy disposition. Or perhaps it's a case of homesickness – New Zealand being, we remind one another, a very long way away, quite on the far side of the world.

Or perhaps, worse, she may recently have lost somebody

especially dear to her – all too sadly frequent in wartime – and is grief-stricken. How dreadful! But is it really true, we wonder? Not knowing for certain if it is, and afraid to ask outright, we feel at a loss, inhibited from offering either sympathy or comfort. She persists in keeping herself to herself, and us at arm's length, and the consequent inexplicably chilly gap defeats our best efforts to bridge it, creating an awkwardness that continues throughout our trip with Cecily; a trip which almost at once deteriorates into an unrewarding daily slog, a grim test of endurance, devoid of pleasure.

The weeks we spent in Kitty Gayford's exhilarating company taught us a great deal more than how to manoeuver canal boats in and out of locks. We learnt that because the three members of every GUC Trainee crew have to work for so many long hard hours in such close co-operation, a bond of tolerant understanding is as essential to survival as the hurried meals we share at the beginning and end of each exhausting day.

Some of the girls, Kitty told us – Audrey and Anne and Evelyn, for instance – have been together and stayed together amicably for trip after trip; and so have Bridget, Rosheen and Jill. Since we are always on the move there is no chance of us getting acquainted and making friends with these lucky Trainee girls, but when we meet their boats and pass them by on the water, going in opposite directions, it's obvious to see, even when exchanging mere waves and shouted greetings, how enviably harmonious is their team relationship – exactly, in fact, what Eve and I had hoped for in our life on the canal. Instead of which, here we are, doomed to be stuck, apparently for ever, with poor depressed and depressing Cecily. Unbearable! Something, we vow, must, absolutely *must* be done about it. Yes – but *what*?

Late on a Friday morning, our cargo of coal duly discharged to Nash's Paper Mill wharf, we reach the Depot, and moor the now empty *Ascot* and *Crater* side by side in the lay-by. Cecily is left, as captain, to visit the office, report our safe arrival, hand over the trip-card, and pick up the next loading orders that will enable us to set off again first thing tomorrow for Lime'us Basin. Meanwhile, we two, free at last, hasten to catch a bus into Hayes for a café treat of fish and chips and some necessary shopping.

Little do we imagine that in an absence of less than a couple of hours the nagging problem regarding our present unhappy situation will – most surprisingly – be resolved. Cecily, we discover on our return to the lay-by, has vanished. Without saying a word of goodbye or giving us any indication of her intended departure, she has cleared her cabin, packed her bag, and gone; gone for good! Mr Kempton, in his tiny cluttered office, is tight-lipped. Why, or where our captain has gone he won't tell us. Perhaps, like us, he doesn't know.

Alas, poor Cecily! We try to be sorry for her, but our overwhelming emotion is of relief. A kindly Fate has intervened on our behalf, and we can only rejoice!

We don't have to hang about in a state of uncertainty for long. On Saturday evening we witness through the dusk a pair of strung-out boats approaching, homeward-bound, from the direction of Denham Lock, and see as they get closer, standing on the cabin-top of the leading vessel with a shaft in her hands, poised for action, the unmistakably familiar figure of Kitty Gayford: our own dear Kitty. At the tiller, scarcely less welcome and familiar, is little dumpy Nina Heseldine, completing, even as we watch, her second training trip, and so being now qualified instantly to join us – by forfeiting a few days leave – as the third member of our crew. What could be more fortuitous?

Kitty's two newest pupils, about whose suitability she has

yet to make up her mind, are packed off to their homes in an accessible London suburb for the night, while the rest of us crowd into *Uttoxeter's* cabin to swap tales of the preceding weeks we've spent apart, our reunion celebrated by slabs of bread and strawberry jam and endless mugs of tea.

They nearly caught us up, it seems, in Coventry, and have been hard on our heels ever since we left the coal-dumps, hearing repeatedly, as they chased us southwards, colourful stories from the mouths of Kitty's numerous boating friends travelling north: anecdotes, related with chuckles, of the difficulties encountered by *that Cecily* and her hapless young Trainees.

This is how news is made known, aired and shared on the Cut: bawled aloud across a widening space during brief moments of passing proximity, or over the rattle of descending paddles. As long as daylight lasts the pressure on boating families to keep going, *keep going*, is relentless, prohibiting anything except these hurried snatches of conversation. But later on after dark in a lockside pub there will be plenty of leisure for talk – for argument, contradiction, embellishment.

Owing to the astonishing speed with which gossip is transmitted and circulated, Cecily's act of jumping ship, abandoning her boats and her crew for no given reason, had already reached the ears of Kitty and Nina, who were thus fully prepared to find Eve and me on our own at the lay-by, skipperless: a purely temporary handicap, Kitty assures us, and one that will prove a blessing in disguise as soon as she has officially – to our jubilant satisfaction – arranged matters with Mr K.

In summer there can surely be no more beautiful stretch of the English countryside than Tring Summit. Indeed, the landscape through which we journey on the Grand Union Canal between London and Birmingham and Coventry is incomparably lovely, and also, of course, deceptively peaceful. For me, with my passionate desire to be out of doors in all kinds of weather, these months from May to October are a source of continual delight – a delight that is tinged with guilt. For at the back of my mind is the reproachful knowledge that while I am at liberty, a free spirit, almost everybody else in the world is entangled one way or another in a horrible war. What right have I to enjoy myself?

I don't see them, I don't hear them, but I can never quite manage to forget the countless men and women – children as well – who are somewhere each moment facing destruction and death, perhaps courageously or perhaps in terror, and who must yearn, those millions of my fellow human beings, for what I every morning have surrounding me like a blessing: leafy trees, blue skies, the song of birds.

To be brave is not required of me. I am not, presently, at risk of bullets and bombs. I have simply to keep going, keep going, in imitation of the boating fraternity, and the resulting state of nightly exhaustion is a price I willingly pay, because it serves to stifle that discomfitting murmur inside me: *Why should you, Ellie Hallsmith, be so lucky?*

Consciousness of undeserved good fortune, however, isn't enough, in spite of guilty pangs, to prevent me from glorying in my state of recently recovered health. Not so long ago, after all, I was practically written off as a chronic invalid, yet here I am, as fit as a fiddle – and proving my fitness, day after day, by the strength needed to wind up the most obstinate of the creaky ancient paddles. And it seems to me, when I'm sprinting along the top-planks, or leaping from boat to boat, or from fore-deck to towpath with a bicycle tucked under an arm, more like a sort of game I'm playing – a game I revel in – than hard work.

The bicycle we carry aboard is there in anticipation of

having another pair of boats travelling in the same direction just in front of us. We know that then the gates we are coming to are bound to be shut. So where the canal narrows to pass beneath a conveniently situated bridge, one of us (Eve or me; never chubby little Nina) will jump ashore, armed with the bicycle, and race on ahead to prepare the next lock, or maybe flight of locks, for our slowly following boats to enter.

Throughout the summer we've been wearing shirts filched from the wardrobes of brothers, and grey cotton dungarees, utility garments that take a minimum of precious coupons. In the hope of increased airiness I've shortened the trouser legs of mine, chopping them off to halfway up my shins: a compromise – Kitty has impressed on us the vital necessity of our remaining at all times decently clad, no matter how hot the weather or how dripping we are with sweat; and the importance of not, in particular, shocking the boaters' womenfolk, upon whose approval we Trainees rely. We must be especially careful, Kitty has said, to make sure we don't offend the susceptibilities of the older canal wives, many of whom still dress in full gathered black skirts descending to a few inches above their ankles.

I'm relieved to note that they have apparently accepted as eccentric rather than shameful the sight of me scampering about barefooted. During these weeks of summer I've dispensed with shoes altogether, partly because I find it safer to go unshod when scrambling on and off the huge beams of the lock gates, and partly for the agreeable touch of sun-warmed wood and cool flagstones on the soles of my naked feet.

It isn't with the deliberate intention of horrifying my mother that I'm not wearing shoes when I turn up one morning before breakfast at her cottage to begin six days' leave. Being barefooted is now natural to me; so much so I completely forgot, in a frantic rush for the last overnight blacked-out train to Dawlish, that it's normal practice, beyond the banks of the GUC, to have shoes on the feet.

Explanations are wasted. Since, according to my mother, no sane person would ever *choose* to run about on pavements, and in civilised railway carriages, barefooted, she presumes it's a combination of having finished my clothing coupons and the extreme rigours of a bargee's employment that has reduced me to this pitiable gypsy-like state.

'I've told you before, Mummy – I'm not a bargee – I'm a boater. Barges are much bigger than boats, wider, and they're pulled along by horses. Our boats have diesel engines –'

But to my mother, intent on searching out some of Harvey's rejected old tennis shoes for me, the distinction – bargee or boater – has little significance.

Her middle-aged village friends, all dedicated to performing their patriotic voluntary bit for the war effort, are surprised at Mrs Hallsmith's younger daughter, Elspeth, not being in any of the Forces (as is her sister Pam, and – belatedly – her brother Jim), or even in the Land Army. Nowadays, in this totally mobilised nation of ours, not to be wearing a uniform of some sort, and having a rank to go with it, is most unusual. They ask me, smiling interestedly, to describe my occupation – what exactly it is I do; but I can't. The world they inhabit and that from which I have just come are as different as the proverbial chalk and cheese, and the difference defies my powers of description.

If I speak of boats they can only envisage the sailing craft in Teignmouth harbour. And when I tell them I'm one of a number of girls who, working on the canal in teams of three, transport cargoes of steel, or aluminium, or occasionally sacks of cement, from London to Birmingham, and then, in Coventry, load up with coal for the return journey south, I

176

realise, as I watch them nod uncomprehendingly, I might as well save my breath.

How can mere dryly related facts convey the sights and sounds teeming inside my head? How is it possible to communicate with spoken words the magic, for instance, of early misty summer dawns, or clear starry skies far from town dwellings, in the silent heart of the English country-side? Or the curious thrill of being woken out of dreamless exhausted sleep by the chug-chug of a distant engine, draw-ing rapidly nearer, and knowing it's the beer-boat boys on their midnight run? (the only boats allowed, with shaded headlights and a cargo of barrels piled high, to travel through the dark). Phantoms, heard not seen, they swish past us at speed, and are gone, leaving our moored *Ascot* and *Crater* rocking gently in the wash of their bow-waves.

The haunting romance, for me, of these and similar exper-iences I'm unable to share with Holcombe residents, or anyone else except my fellow Trainees – and not always with them: reactions, as well as experiences, differ.

On joining the GUCCC I unconsciously crossed a frontier into a land I now perceive to be as alien to my upbringing as if it had indeed been foreign territory I was entering. I crossed a border for which I had, until then, held no passport, a border closed to me, forbidden, and by so doing acquired an unforeseen liberty: escape from the rigid inherited rules of conventional behaviour. This heady new-found freedom I will never, I promise myself, relinquish.

When factory workers in the London area lean out of open windows to yell down at me, '*Hi, Blondie!*', I raise a hand from the tiller of *Ascot* to wave back at them in acknowledgement of our camaraderie. When I'm bellowed at by a burly docker on the wharfside, '*Hey there, girl – get a move on, can't you? We ain't got all day to hang abaht,*' I hasten to obey him, unoffended: we are mates, he and I. Their world isn't remotely like the world I was born into, but its inhabitants – bargemen, boaters, dockers, lorry drivers, crane drivers, fitters, mechanics – have kindly accepted me into it on an equal footing as one of them, and I am aglow with gratitude for their tolerance, their undiscriminating welcome.

Back home in my mother's village for six days of respite from hard labour, there is time for me to ponder on how incredibly lucky I am to be licensed to come and go at will between these two fundamentally conflicting cultures and, by spanning the dividing line, to benefit from each in turn. Moreover, during my Holcombe visits (the reward earned by every four consecutive trips), as well as the luxury of frequent hot baths, and long hours of unbroken sleep on a soft mattress, and meals, properly cooked and eaten at leisure, I have the chance to gather much-needed information, to catch up at last with the current events of what has developed into a global war.

While on the Cut, absorbed as we then are, from sun-up to sunset, seven days a week, in the grinding business of getting our boats from place to place – loading, unloading, and immediately off again – we have only the haziest notion of what is occurring in all the far-flung battlegrounds. News, either good or bad, whether of success or failure, reaches us intermittently, like faint half-heard echoes, fragments, blown our way on the wind. But here in Holcombe everybody every evening listens religiously, avidly, to the six o'clock bulletin on the wireless, and discusses it afterwards in detail, argues about it, sticks rows of little coloured paper flags into maps pinned on walls; and thus am I, at intervals, brought up to date.

As secretaries in stuffy Blenheim Palace huts, it was hearing about the disastrous fall of Singapore with the Japanese capturing 150,000 of our troops and the desperate indecisive North African campaign, and the horrific sinking by U-boats in the Atlantic Ocean of convoys of merchant navy ships carrying life-saving food for the besieged British islanders, that had caused Eve Griffin and Damaris de Boulay and me to despair at being, we felt, uselessly occupied typing dreary pointless letters, and had determined us to engage, somehow or other, more actively in the great national struggle for survival against Fascism.

Now, in the late summer of 1943, thanks largely to millions of heroic Russians in the Soviet Union, and to battalions of American servicemen sent over from the United States under the command of General Eisenhower, the tide of war has finally turned. Our General Montgomery has defeated General Rommel in the sands of the Libyan desert; German U-boats have been chased from the Atlantic; the Allied armies have landed in Sicily and actually begun to push their way northwards up through Mussolini's crumbling Italy. If not yet in sight, victory, Mr Churchill has assured us, will undoubtedly – eventually – be ours; and we believe him. Hitler is going to be beaten.

Throughout the months of summer I can think of no wartime job I would sooner be doing than working a pair of monkey boats on the GUC. We have our setbacks, of course, the most usual being when our butty boat, *Crater*, goes aground on a mud bank and we are forced, willy-nilly, with straining muscles, to shaft it clear. Or, worse than mud, when *Ascot*'s propellor picks up floating debris and the engine coughs and splutters to a halt. Then one of us has the disagreeable task of plunging into the dirty water with a bread knife and sawing blindly through tight-wound pieces of cotton-line or strands of tow-rope before we can proceed.

Apart, though, from such minor misadventures, to be out

of doors in summery weather, transporting cargoes that we know are industrially essential, is an activity arduous but hugely enjoyable.

We have to struggle, it's true, in order to keep going as fast as the regular boating families, but the efforts we make are inspired rather by pride than by financial necessity. The boaters are in a perpetual tearing hurry, never dawdling, never pausing for an instant to gossip, but their unrelentingly rapid pace is maintained because they can't afford to slacken off: the money they earn is according to the content of their load and the speediness of its delivery, whereas we Trainee girls are paid a flat weekly wage irrespective of how quick or how slow is our progress.

And besides, the struggle for us has its periods of occasional relaxation when, traversing some of the longer *pounds* – those tranquil stretches of canal between locks – it's possible to navigate and read a book propped open on the cabin-top simultaneously. I've managed, bit by bit, while steering, to read the whole of Thomas Hardy's novel *Tess of the D'Urbervilles* and Christopher Isherwood's *Goodbye to Berlin*.

But summer doesn't last for ever. It evolves into a mild and beautiful autumn which is followed, all too soon, by the grip of icy winter; and with winter our entire existence undergoes a transformation.

No more bare feet for me. I wear clumsy boots now, and cross over the closed gates of a lock with extreme caution, clinging to the iron rail and edging my way step by step on the treacherous frozen surface: one slip could be fatal.

We keep a fire burning in the stove of each boat all day, every day, and hope, when we go to bed, it will stay alight until morning; but it seldom does and we wake, shivering, to a gloomy dawn. By day the steerer of either *Ascot* or *Crater*, standing with the doors of the hatches shut behind her, is exposed, from the waist up, to the full fury of the elements, rain or biting wind, or hail, sometimes even flurries of snow, while from the waist down her enclosed legs, planted unavoidably so near to the fiery stove as almost to touch it, are being roasted.

Nina Heseldine is the first of our crew to capitulate. Sniffing and snuffling and blowing her poor little red nose continually, she goes home for Christmas and doesn't come back. Her place is filled by Vera, an ex-hairdresser, and with her as our third crew member we plough doggedly on into the New Year.

But in January Eve's young man, David Henley, a Sub-Lieutenant in the Royal Navy, pays us a fleeting visit and is aghast at the hardships he finds his darling girl enduring. He begs Eve, *beseeches* her, for goodness' sake to chuck it in and apply instead to be taken on as a Boating Wren. Her canal experience will count, he argues, in her favour, and she would be keeping a connection with the water while wearing, like him, the spick and span uniform of the Senior Service. Eve dithers, protests, but eventually does allow herself – relieved, I think, secretly – to be persuaded.

And so I lose her too. When she and I met at Queen's Secretarial College learning the skills of shorthand and typing, we were both sixteen. It seems a very long time ago, and I shall miss her.

I've been told by our office manager, Mr Kempton, that a certain Mrs Curry will be joining me and Vera to fill the vacancy left by Eve's precipitous departure. At the time I couldn't think why he should sound so uneasy, telling me, but when we are introduced to our new crew member at the lay-by I realise the reason for his shiftiness.

Mrs Curry bears no resemblance to any of the Trainee girls currently working on the GUC. To begin with, she isn't

181

a girl: she's a woman in her thirties; the widow, Mr Kempton has informed me, grumpily, of a distinguished naval officer. Since Mrs Curry isn't, in my opinion, the sort of person Mr Kempton would be likely to select for the Scheme, I guess that his grumpiness is really annoyance because those in positions of authority higher up than his own have over-ruled him.

It's a rather tricky situation for us. Eve being gone, I've automatically taken her place as the skipper in charge of *Ascot* and *Crater* – Steerer Hallsmith – with Vera, slightly less experienced than me, as my second-in-command; and now this newcomer, Rita Curry, almost twice our age, is to play the part of what amounts to our cabin boy. But it isn't her age that makes her, we consider, such an inappropriate choice. Kitty Gayford, after all, is in her thirties, or possibly older. No – it's Rita Curry herself.

Her appearance, on arrival at the Depot's landing stage, is eyed by a number of boaters' wives leaning in their hatches, as well as by Vera and me, with silent disapproval. We judge everything about her to be wrong. Her lipstick is too bright and too scarlet: film-star lipstick. Her clothes are simply unsuitable for life on the Cut: expensive-looking tweeds and highly polished brogues with criss-cross laces. She is tall, Mrs Rita Curry, large of nose and imperious of manner, and even the dejected old cocker spaniel she holds aloft in her arms differs markedly from the canal dogs, a mongrel breed prowling the wharfside with the same air of suspicion as their owners afloat.

Mrs Curry's suitcase (containing, as it later transpires, two staunch travelling companions, a bottle of vodka and a bottle of pink gin) is carried by the dapper elderly gentleman escorting her, who turns out to be, we learn with some astonishment, His Grace the Duke of Grafton.

There's no point in our wondering *why* Rita Curry decided

to enlist in the GUC's Training Scheme – a move bizarrely, it would seem, out of character – or to wish, as we fervently do, that she hadn't been foisted on us. We just have to make the best of what Fate has decreed. The motor boat cabin, usually a prerogative enjoyed by the skipper, we allocate to her, and she presently emerges from it, still scarlet-lipsticked, it's true, but having otherwise effected a considerable improvement by changing into trousers and a polo-necked jersey.

And thus we set forth the following morning, an incongruous trio, accompanied by Rita's ancient semi-invalid spaniel, on our way down to the London docks.

As the wife, now widow, of a distinguished officer in the Royal Navy, Mrs Rita Curry is convinced, mistakenly, that she knows everything of any importance about boats, whether on an inland waterway or at sea; and this unshakeable belief, combined with my own failure to surmount the difficulty I find in giving her instructions, means our journey from London to Brum, and on from there, via the hellish Bottom Road, to the Coventry coalfields, has to be accomplished more or less two-handed by Vera and me. Working like a couple of demented demons at fever-pitch we manage to do it, Rita being much engaged meanwhile in caring for the ailing Hector, her spaniel, who suffers from a nervous condition and tends to have fits of hysteria and to need particular attention in the deeper locks.

But at Coventry a dramatic interruption to our established schedule provides myself and Vera, exhausted as we are, with a merciful, quite unexpected forty-eight hours of enforced idleness.

The boats have been loaded by nightfall, and we are prepared to start on the return trip south to Hemel Hempstead and Nash's Paper Mill, in spite of aching limbs, early next morning. Instead, though, I'm woken before daybreak in the

183

pitch darkness of the butty by the disembodied voice of Rita calling to me loudly from her berth in *Ascot*, moored alongside *Crater*: a summons to come at once – *at once* – and rescue her and Hector.

Rescue them? – from what?

'Rita,' I shout back, muzzy with sleep, 'what's happened? What's the matter?'

Sounding calmly controlled, but also desperate, she informs me that her cabin is flooded.

It can't be. '*Flooded*, Rita?'

'Yes – yes – flooded,' she cries, calmness deserting her. 'The water's pouring in – it's a foot or more deep. *We are SINKING!*'

And she's right. The motor boat *Ascot*, already inundated, is going down fast: is, in actual fact, sinking.

We have an emergency on our hands, a real and a rapidly compounding one, that requires immediate action. Rita buttons a coat hurriedly over her pyjamas and wobbles off on the bicycle to find and rouse helpers in this desolate landscape, leaving Vera and me, soon sopping wet ourselves, attempting to stem the flow by bailing out gallons of freezing cold water with the engine-hole bucket and the washing-up bowl. Only when day dawns and various Company officials arrive on the scene do we cease from our frenzy of bailing and feel able, relieved and thankful, to transfer the weight of responsibility on to the shoulders of these competent stalwart men.

The trouble is promptly diagnosed as being caused by a leaky stern-valve. *Ascot* has first to be unloaded, and then towed into dry dock to have the necessary repairs made.

Two blissful days ensue: days of doing absolutely nothing – days that are a gift bestowed by the gods, allowing us younger Trainees the chance to recover from an almost unbearable fatigue. After which interval of convalescence, with the motor boat mended, the cargo of coal re-loaded, and our strength fully restored, we complete the disrupted trip in record time, as if – a ridiculous notion – it's all down-hill from Coventry to Hemel Hempstead, and an easy run, even two-handed.

Once here, our loads discharged on to the wharfside of Nash's Paper Mill and me and my faithful uncomplaining shipmate, Vera, busily occupied in sweeping clean the empty holds, Mrs Rita Curry commandeers the Mill manager's office telephone and rings for a local taxi-cab to come and fetch her away. Shortly thereafter she appears on deck, dressed again in tweeds and brogues, and so presently, together with Hector *and* her suitcase, is whisked off by taxi up to London. And that is the last we see of them.

Another spring, another summer. Vera leaves the canal to get married. I'm teamed up with Elizabeth Glazier, a few years younger than me, and Mary Vanderpump, a few years older. And still the war goes on.

I wish it would end. It's all very well to be told that we, the Allies, are defeating the hated Nazis, but what a time it's taking, and the killing never stops. The Germans have started bombing raids again along the south coast, not only by night but also during the day.

Harvey writes from Holcombe to tell me he was sunbath-ing in the garden one afternoon when a solitary aeroplane came zooming low over the cottage, and as it banked he plainly saw, close above him, the black German cross painted on the wings. It was dropping bombs on Teignmouth, trying, supposedly, to hit either Shaldon Bridge or else the Morgan Giles miniature-submarine workshops, both of them prime enemy targets. Whichever it may have been aiming for, neither was hit, and having missed each and caused no damage, but only extreme surprise as much to the local anti-aircraft defences as to my schoolboy brother Harvey, the raider got clear away without itself being shot down, or even shot *at*. Harvey, of course, thinks his near encounter with a Luftwaffe Messerschmitt is terrifically exciting.

Then, at the beginning of June, what we've all been thinking about, and waiting for, and wondering if it was ever really going to happen, does happen. On 6th June the Allied Forces, which are a mixture of British and American and Commonwealth troops, invade France. The code name for this gargantuan operation is D-Day (although I don't know exactly what the *D* is meant to signify).

We are given very little detailed information in the newspapers or in the bulletins broadcast on the wireless of events taking place overseas: simply, we're told that the great long-expected invasion has at last been set in motion, and is forging ahead, successfully. It's a sort of Dunkirk in reverse: hundreds and hundreds of ships crossing the Channel, and thousands of men and tanks and artillery put ashore on the other side so as, first of all, to liberate occupied France, and then to carry on and conquer Hitler's Germany.

I remember how every morning when I was employed as a secretary at Blenheim Palace the coach driving me out from Oxford to Woodstock passed by the perimeter of that immense airfield where we could see huge gliders being towed off the ground. Once airborne they released the cable towing them to circle slowly, ponderously, in the sky above, returning almost immediately to land: rehearsing for what they are now having to support in deadly earnest – the D-Day invasion.

But it won't, we are warned, be a quick or an easy victory. Hitler doesn't intend to give up without a fight. Even though the gallant Russians have defeated him at Stalingrad and are advancing through Poland towards Berlin, he still seems to think his armies are capable of winning this war, aided by a truly devilish new weapon which his scientists have lately developed: an unmanned engine-powered rocket. By using the V-1, as the rocket is officially called, the Germans are spared having to risk the lives of too many more of their pilots, and saved the expense of manufacturing proper aeroplanes. These V-1 rockets have been nicknamed by the British: *doodlebugs*. Blasted off from launch pads concealed at intervals along the western coastlines of Europe, the V-1s are directed to fall chiefly on London, and particularly on the docks; but also pretty well indiscriminately anywhere, with the apparent intention of creating havoc and a general panic amongst our urban population.

Mary Vanderpump is being courted by Caspar John. She refers to him as her *beau*. He is the second son of Augustus John, the famous painter I can vividly remember having had pointed out to me years and years ago when I was a small child and he was a tall bearded figure striding through the streets of Newquay, distraught at the drowning in Vuggar Cove of Henry, youngest of his five sons. Now, more than a decade later, here I am meeting Caspar John, who from time to time, leave permitting, joins us on the Cut and, although a high-ranking officer in the Royal Navy, winds up those heavy stiff greasy lock-paddles with the alacrity and ease of a born boater, pumps the bilges dry, takes his turn at steering *Ascot*, and on one occasion probably saves my life.

He and I had gone ahead to make ready a downhill lock. We shut the lower gates, and after dropping their paddles, clankety-clank, raised the paddles of the closed upper gates which, as soon as the lock was brimful with water, we were able to push wide open. We then waited for our boats to arrive. But the gate of the beam I sat on, carelessly swinging my legs, wasn't completely open, and when the motor boat, gliding fast into place, struck and smacked it flat against the

187

lock wall, the violence of the collision bounced me off my perch and catapulted me directly in front of *Ascot*'s lethal bows. Caspar – trained for instant action – scooped me up, dripping wet, from what, a few seconds later, would almost certainly have been a watery grave.

His older brother, David, first of the five John sons, also sometimes visits us on the GUC and tries to help. But he, quite unlike Caspar, is vague and dreamy, a musician who plays an oboe in the RAF orchestra. It was David who, his mind on other things, no doubt (on Bach, perhaps: his passion), tied a rope from the foredeck of *Crater* to a bollard ashore when we were in a downhill emptying lock with nearly disastrous consequences: a mistake that Caspar, the sailor, would never have made.

Visitors are welcome. And luckily – a relief to us – the boaters don't seem to view the coming and going of our various guests as a source of scandal or in any way reprehensible. With such entertaining and agreeable company, and the fine warm weather, and the long light evenings, I should enjoy being on the Cut as much this summer as I did last summer, were it not for the plague of evil *doodlebugs*.

We see them, these *doodlebugs*, cruising across the sky, looking so innocent and pretty, like children's toys or some kind of Guy Fawkes fireworks. The rear end of each rocket is decorated with a bunch of flames, and the sound of its engine resembles that of a motor-mower cutting grass. Not, in reality, innocent at all, but sinister and frightening; we watch every V-1 as it bumbles playfully overhead, holding our breath in anticipation of the dreaded moment when, the game finished, its engine will suddenly stop and the *doodlebug* plunge instantaneously to earth, blowing to smithereens whatever and whoever has the misfortune to be beneath it.

Because of the V-1s we don't, nowadays, dally in Lime'us Basin. Once loaded we make haste to put as much distance as possible between us and the docks, delaying the necessary business of clothing-up the cargo until we've got as far, anyway, as the Angel, Islington, where we can moor for the night with a greater sense of security.

The boaters are even more reluctant than us Trainees to run the gauntlet – to venture, as we are all, however nervously, bound to do, in and out of Lime'us, or, it might be, the docks at Brentford. For them the undertaking is a more serious affair: they are having to jeopardise, as we single girls are not, their entire families and homes. At least, though, like us, they can load up and be away out of rocket range in between each trip. The twenty-four-hour threat to London dockers and bargemen who live in houses – buildings of brick that can't be moved – is unremitting and unavoidable.

Injuries on the Cut are an all too frequent occurrence, some worse than others. Towards the end of the summer season the crew of *Ascot* and *Crater*, regarded by me, thankfully, as being a dependable settled happy threesome, is abruptly deprived of its third member, little Elizabeth Glazier, who hurts herself sufficiently badly for her doctor, after he's patched his patient up, to forbid her returning to the boats: a veto that leaves me and Mary Vanderpump bereft.

We expect Mr Kempton to provide us with a replacement for our dear lost Elizabeth. But when summoned to his office I'm informed of a propaganda drive initiated by the HQ of the Ministry of Transport (which has assumed overall control of the Inland Waterways) to publicise an urgent need for volunteers to join the Women's Scheme, currently flagging: too many girls are departing, as in the case of Elizabeth Glazier, and not enough are signing on. To cope with the guaranteed influx of recruits, Mr K. tells me, additional trainers will be imperative, and I – Steerer Hallsmith – now counted as a veteran, am therefore to become one of these trainers, ably assisted, of course, by Mary Vanderpump, my second-in-command. Mary, when told of the proposed trans-formation, thinks it a tremendous joke.

But I don't think it's in the least bit funny, and protest vigorously. Apart from not wanting the burden of such a responsibility, I'm convinced I should be utterly hopeless at training anyone to do anything.

Mr Kempton refuses to listen to my protestations. He is inflexible, unyielding. Although the war undeniably is entering its final bloody stages, factories, he says, are going to have to have a continued supply of steel and coal, quite as much, if not more than ever, so as to manufacture peace-time goods instead of tanks and aeroplanes. When he mentions the word *duty* I automatically think of my mother, who holds it to be of paramount importance that everyone should perform his or her patriotic duty, no matter what the circumstances. So must I, then, agree, and accept my undesired promotion?

Kitty Gayford, from whom I seek advice and comfort, says it's true that the MOT is trying to increase, not lessen output; and there will certainly be a need for more trainers; and it isn't, she says, at all difficult to teach greenhorns the ropes (which I don't believe). In short, says Kitty, I should give it a go. Thus encouraged by her, and laughed at by Mary, I find myself soon in the ludicrous position of being a GUCCC trainer of Trainees.

The reasons why it doesn't last for very long are several. The first is my indignant discovery that Mrs Rita Curry – of *all* people – has been made head of the Women's Scheme, and the young ladies (debutantes, no less) enlisted by her and sent on to be dealt with by me are as unsuitable – to put it mildly – for turning into dirty dedicated hard-working canal boaters as she, Rita, once was.

Moreover – reason number two – I feel obliged, if I'm

honest, to admit to myself that the original overwhelming thrill of life on the GUC has latterly, for me, palled, and I've begun to be restless, to be dissatisfied; to want *something else*.

What is it, though, the something else I want, the something else I'm suddenly so afraid of missing?

Well, for a start, I've grown tired – yes, I have – of wearing dungarees in summer, and in winter my brother Harvey's old flannel cricket trousers; tired of the brass-buckled leather belt slung low round my hips with an iron windlass, for winding up the lock-gate paddles, tucked into it. I'm tired of battling against foul weather – sick and tired of being wet and cold and bruised and aching; tired of being always tired.

I want – I *yearn* – to wear pretty frocks, and shoes with high heels, and silk stockings, and lacy underclothes. I want to go to dances, as my sister Pam does. What I truly want, I realise – a blinding revelation – is not to be a boater any more, but a *real girl*.

And the most compelling reason, the one that has jolted me brusquely awake, is Mary Vanderpump announcing that she intends to be married in the spring to Caspar John, her beau.

Where is *my* beau? Where is the Prince that Eve and Paula and I sang about, pushing our bikes up the steep hill to Englefield Green, after watching the film of *Snow White and the Seven Dwarfs*? How long ago that seems: an age. Time, precious Time, is rushing past me, leaving me behind. I'm getting old: I shall be twenty-one on my next birthday.

My career as a canal boater I bring resolutely to an end in February 1945, two years almost to the day since I first laid eyes on the Cut at Bulls' Bridge Depot, Hayes, Middlesex. Despite some lingering regrets at all I'm leaving irrevocably behind me, I'm glad to go. I've had enough of poor food and clammy garments and insufficient sleep, of bedbugs and general discomfort: *enough*! The war in Europe, everybody predicts, is nearly over. Change is in the air, and I also need, I feel, a change. What sort of a change it may turn out to be I can't imagine. I'm able to visualise only a blank horizon.

The ambition I've cherished in secret from earliest memories of a storybook-infatuated childhood is eventually to become a writer. But my immediate aim has to be more practical. I have to find employment of some kind, such as will pay me a reasonable weekly wage while conforming to the Labour Exchange's still operative wartime regulations. The job I hope to succeed in presently getting must, however, be out of doors. After rejoicing in the untrammelled freedom of life on the GUC, I don't intend ever again to be stuck in a claustrophobic office, typing dreary letters.

Passing through London on my way home to my mother's Devonshire cottage, I stay the night with Caspar and Mary in a Chelsea flat they've borrowed as a temporary expedient from its absent owners. For a farewell treat they take me out to dinner in a fashionably bohemian club called the Gargoyle, to which they belong.

Everything related to this establishment is on a small scale, accounting perhaps for its discreetly intimate atmosphere. We eat our dinner at one of the tables encircling a small area of dance floor where a few couples are moving languidly in time to the soft music played by a small unobtrusive band. The lighting is low, subdued. I have never been in such a place before. It seems to me the essence of sophistication, and a million miles distant from Hammersmith's rowdy Palais-de-Danse, which I was taken to once by a fellow comrade of my brother Jim's during the days when he was a Conscientous Objector in the FAU and I was at Queen's Secretarial College.

The crowning moment of my Cinderella rags-into-riches

evening is when a tall dashingly handsome middle-aged man, a friend of Caspar John's, crosses the dimly lit room and invites me to dance with him. His name is Bunny Keene. Because I have to concentrate so hard on ensuring my feet behave as they should in a foxtrot, conversation is minimal. But the next morning, to Mary's great amusement, he rings me up and asks me if I would care to dine and dance – just me – tomorrow night as his guest at, again, the fabulous Gargoyle Club.

I wish – oh, how *much* I wish I could accept this glamorous stranger's dazzling invitation, but I can't. I'm not, I explain to him, stopping in London. I'm going home today – yes, today – to my mother's village in Devon, catching a 12.30 train at Paddington Station down to Dawlish on the South Coast.

And that, I think miserably, is that: a golden opportunity, gone for ever.

But no – wait! – it isn't gone! What, says the marvellous Bunny Keene, quite casually, is my mother's telephone number? When he's next in the West Country, as he shortly will be, on a business assignment, he'll make a point, he says, of looking me up.

Bunny Keene's business is documentary films: Caspar told me it was. And with a shock as startling as if being physically struck on the head, I'm roused from despair by the sudden revelation that *this* is exactly the creative activity I should like to be involved in myself: here is the perfect answer to those vaguely bothersome questions troubling my mind of what comes now. Of course! The problem has been solved! Why didn't I think of it sooner?

Except for having heard of (although not seen) Robert Flaherty's famous *Man of Aran*, I know nothing at all about documentary films; my ignorance of them is as total as it once was concerning canals, but I am fired by the same enthusiastic certainty as then, and convinced absolutely (as I was then) of the direction I have to take. Either a lucky accident or else Destiny (I prefer the latter explanation) has shown me my path. In 1943 it was canals; two years later it's documentary films. What could be clearer?

The movies I have seen, and I'm an insatiable cinema fan, were always highly dramatic, whereas documentary films, according to my imprecise understanding, deal with reality instead of fiction. *Documentary* implies – doesn't it? – being in the fresh air, travelling abroad, exploring exotic foreign countries far beyond the limits of Holcombe; it might even include a chance to write professionally: all, in fact, I've ever wanted or dreamed of. Awaiting me is a future no longer hazy, but glitteringly bright. I simply have to give Bunny Keene my mother's telephone number; which I do.

The weeks pass. The dream fades into oblivion. How foolish of me to have imagined so much could have resulted from so little.

The work I've managed to find is on Mr Whetman's market garden, a mile or so inland from Dawlish. Every morning, after an early breakfast, I bicycle out from Holcombe, with a packet of sandwiches for my lunch in an old school satchel, and every evening bicycle home to the hot nourishing suppers cooked by my good mother. When supper's done and the table cleared, I play Monopoly or card games with Harvey, a reminder of evenings in Oxford when I played rummy interminably with nice David Thompson.

My present employment consists of picking violets for sale in the shops of Newton Abbot. I've been taught the correct method of picking these little fragile flowers – keeping careful count of their stalks meanwhile, so that every bunch is the same size – and how to tie the completed bunch in its nest of green leaves, quickly and cleverly, with a strand from the hank of raffia hung about my neck. In due course there will be polyanthus to pick, and then anemones. Shall I still be here, I wonder, when it's the strawberry and raspberry season? Probably, yes.

Mr Whetman, by no means a slave-driver, is polite to me, incurious but friendly: rather shy! He employs two other workers, both young men from the nearby mental institution at Starcross. They also are polite and friendly, anxious to help me acquire the skills necessary for violet-picking. Bob has a slight impediment in his speech, and is big and lumbering, but the smaller neater Arnold has nothing perceptibly wrong with his intelligence, and I'm puzzled as to why he should be an inmate of Starcross asylum.

At midday we troop wearily down from the sloping field above to the cluster of ramshackle outbuildings below, in one of which, a large tool-shed, we assemble to eat our sandwiches, or whatever is the food we've brought with us, and to drink tea from Thermos flasks, using boxes to sit on and empty oil-drums for tables. Mostly we sit in silence, munching and gulping, but it's a companionable silence. Then I hand round my Woodbines, the brand of cheap cigarettes that we smoked on the Cut, offering them to Bob and Arnold as an alternative to their habitual shaggy roll-ups. Often Mr Whetman's three-year-old son, nicknamed Blue (in honour, I'm told, of a notable racehorse), will come running out of the house to stand in the doorway, staring at us inquisitively through the fug of smoke, until given a peppermint sweetie by Arnold.

This is the life I lead nowadays, an undemanding if monotonous existence, chiefly spent in hours of being bent double, stooping over and moving uphill, a step at a time: slow work indeed! I am out of doors, though, as planned, and I'm paid, not very much, but quite adequately; so I should be content. Why aren't I?

*   *   *

One day I discover a visitor waiting for me at St Bernard's Cottage. Sam Pyne, still an army officer, and returned intact from service overseas in India, has come to see me, with a gift of dress material by way of expressing gratitude for the dozens of dull short letters I dutifully, as promised, wrote to him. I unwrap the yards of gossamer fine silk, and kiss his cheek: thank you, Sam. Each of us kept faithfully to the bargain we made on Dartmoor's windy heights; but that was ages ago. We are older now, and Crapstone school holidays have receded into a past increasingly remote.

Laurence Brown – like Sam, a Crapstone survivor – also turns up unannounced in Holcombe, and from him I learn the precise fate of Robert Winnicott, the hero I disgraced – and myself as well – with my shamefully bad performance in Tavistock's Junior Tennis Tournament during the summer of 1939. He was killed, says Laurence, in France. I don't want Laurence Brown to tell me who else, besides beautiful Robert, has died; who else, of all the boys I played tennis or hockey with, light-heartedly picnicked with, swam with, have had their voices silenced for ever: those known to me, and the many many unknown others, as young and alive as Robert was, extinguished like the flames of candles that had only just been lit – I can't bear to think of them. Nobody is yet out of danger, nobody safe, or will be safe, until the last bullet has been discharged, and the last bomb dropped from the sky, and the bells in every church tower are allowed to ring and ring, ring and ring, proclaiming the advent of peace. But when will that happen? – *when*?

Jim, my older brother, having completed an unusually protracted RAF training in Canada, did succeed finally in achieving his wings as a sergeant-pilot (ex-COs forfeit their right to a commission, so I'm informed) and was posted to a bomber station somewhere in England. As crew member in a squadron of Lancaster bombers he has already been on raids over Germany, and will take part in more operational flights over enemy territory for as long as the war continues.

My sister Pam, the WAAF cipher-officer, comes home on a week's leave, but pleased as I am to see her, we lack any common wartime experience, and consequently lack a fund of topics to use for conversation. There is an unbridgeable gap between us. Then one day I happen to stumble upon her weeping in a corner of the cottage garden: Pam, the brave, the dauntless, a girl who never weeps! She's reading a letter from the mother of someone called, apparently, Geoff. I've not heard her speak of a Geoff before. And preoccupied as I've recently been with thoughts of Robert Winnicott, it now occurs to me, belatedly, how many young men on her various fighter stations Pam must have had as dear close friends, young men *she* laughed and joked with, drank with, danced with, who then flew off into the night and never returned.

Ricky, the Canadian boy I met in London, was one of those fighter-pilots who flew off and didn't come back. I remember him showing me, proudly, the ring he had put on my sister's engagement finger, and I remember being startled by the glimpse I caught of her unguarded expression: she *knew*!

This awful cruel war – when, oh when, will it be finished for good, and the killing ended?

'Somebody rang you up, Elspeth, from London – a man. I've left his name by the telephone. He wants you to ring him back.'

My mother has written on a piece of paper *Ralph Keene*, and a number, preceded by the letters FRO.

Ralph Keene – Bunny! – I can hardly believe it. He didn't forget. He meant what he said. I wasn't being so silly after all. How amazing!

'And who is this Ralph Keene of yours?' my mother enquires.

197

'He's not "of mine", Mummy – I've only met him once, when I was staying with Caspar and Mary – they introduced me to him. He's a documentary film director.' I try to make my voice sound uninterested, matter-of-fact, but I can feel my heart hammering and my eyes have blurred. 'He did mention that if he was ever down this way he might look me up.' And it's come true: he actually is going to look me up. Why, otherwise, would he have rung? Miracles do happen!

Ought I to call him Ralph, his official name, when I ring him back – or Bunny? Would *Bunny* be presumptious, taking a liberty? Better, perhaps, to avoid calling him anything. I steady myself with a deep breath and dial the magic number. He answers immediately, which flusters me even more; but if I'm in a state of dither, Bunny – or Ralph – is as cool as a cucumber, saying that since he's obliged to be in Salisbury over the weekend in order to meet a writer chap, he thought of combining business with pleasure by driving on to Dawlish for a whiff of sea air. Would I be at home on Friday? We could have dinner at his hotel.

'Salisbury?' says my mother, raising her eyebrows when I repeat these words of his, 'But that's nowhere near – it's miles away –'

'Well, I don't know, do I? Perhaps he has to see a writer chap in Dawlish too. I'm just telling you what he said.'

On Friday I bicycle home at breakneck speed, to be greeted by the incredible sight of a huge silver Rolls-Royce, a tourer, parked on the cracked concrete forecourt of St Bernard's Cottage, under the walnut tree. Ralph Keene – Bunny – has arrived before me. I open the front door to hear him laughing in the kitchen. He and my mother have dispensed with ceremony and are chatting vivaciously together on – it's obvious – the best of terms, with her at the Aga boiling the kettle again for another pot of tea. So that hurdle, thank goodness, has been safely cleared. Relax, relax!

I dash upstairs to bath and reappear ten minutes later wearing the one decent frock I possess. And then Bunny drives me into Teignmouth, a rather grander seaside resort than Dawlish, where he's booked a room for the night at the biggest hotel, the Royal, on the front.

'Charming woman, your mother,' Bunny Keene remarks, as we cruise majestically down Teignmouth Hill in his newly bought, second-hand fabulous car, of which he is endearingly childishly proud.

'That's what she thinks about you,' I dare to reply, risking a black mark for cheekiness. 'She thinks you're charming – she said so.'

'And she's right, of course – I am, I am,' says Bunny, patting my knee and roaring with laughter, hugely amused.

My mother could always charm people, a star quality she was endowed with at birth, to the bitter resentment of my father, who hadn't been similarly blessed. Plainly she, in her turn, has fallen under the irresistible spell of our visitor from London. As for me, by the end of the evening I've overcome my initial awe, and am as much at ease with Bunny Keene as is compatible with being totally infatuated. Here he is, at last, my long-awaited Prince from *Snow White and the Seven Dwarfs*: a walking talking living legend.

By the time we're sipping coffee and liqueurs (liqueurs!) I've plucked up courage enough to confide in him my ambition to be a writer, and furthermore a writer in – guess what? – documentary films.

I had fully expected – had feared – that my confession would get the derisive dismissal it deserved. But Bunny, nodding his head reflectively, sagely, declares that it isn't at all a bad idea, worth being given serious consideration. Greenpark Productions, he says, might well benefit from installing an assistant-scriptwriter on its permanent staff instead of having to depend, as it does now, on a string of unreliable freelance writers.

First, says wonderful Bunny, leaning towards me across the table and taking hold of my hand so as to add emphasis to his words, first I must think of a subject of some kind suitable for an educational film – what about canals, for instance? – and then write a Treatment, a summary of not more than a couple of pages, typed, and he will have its merits discussed and judged by a panel of the company's other directors.

Listening to him talk in the plush semi-deserted Royal Hotel dining room, I am dazed, incredulous. He makes it seem not in the least out of the ordinary, or ridiculous, but a perfectly reasonable, even attainable goal for me to aim at. Doesn't he realise that what he's offering me, quite casually, is my entire future?

By eleven o'clock on Saturday morning Bunny Keene has driven off at the wheel of his spectacular millionaire's car (which he insists he bought for a friendly price from a friend of his, Dick Wyndham) to keep the appointment in Salisbury with a certain Robert Henriques, who, Bunny is hoping, will be persuaded to write the script for a Greenpark Productions film commissioned by the National Farmers' Union. Just hearing of these negotiations makes me feel as if I've already entered the thrilling world of documentary films. But to push that door open I have to hurry up and obey instructions: there's no time to lose.

Bunny himself suggested canals as a subject, and the Regent's Canal Basin – Lime'us – down in the docks, would be an ideal setting – wouldn't it? – for a film. I visualise the towering cranes, the bustle of tugs and boats and barges, the various cargoes being loaded and unloaded. Action, shouting – *yes*!

But what on earth did Bunny mean by a *Treatment*? I should have asked him to explain; I didn't. He spoke, though, of a summary – two pages, typed: I can do *that*! I learnt how to summarise when I was studying English years ago for School Certificate. With a bit of bluff I ought to be able to concoct something that will pass for a film Treatment – whatever that is. I can do it – of course I can. Greenpark Productions Ltd here I come!

PART THREE

AFTER

I arrived in London on Thursday, and I've been invited round this afternoon, Saturday, to No. 1, Selwood Place, Bunny Keene's address, for tea. Events have moved so fast, lately: here I am, the tenant of a poky, but relatively cheap, attic room on the fourth floor of a house in Earl's Court and about to begin – as are countless others – a marvellous new peacetime life.

The war in Europe did ultimately, after more than five years, reach a conclusion, and the fighting ceased on 8th May when Germany capitulated to the Allies, and a document of unconditional surrender was signed by one of Admiral Dönitz's generals. Adolf Hitler couldn't sign it because, having been forced to admit irreversible final defeat, he had shot himself; although not until the Russian troops were practically at the door of his Berlin bunker where he was hiding.

The whole of Britain burst into a frenzy of joy, with a tumult of church bells ringing non-stop, and crowds of revellers dancing in the streets, and every sort of celebration erupting spontaneously. I stayed on in Holcombe for just long enough to participate in the village fun and games – a bumper tea party in the field at the top of the hill, and a hurriedly organised programme of competitive sports in which Harvey and I won the three-legged race – before packing my bag and boarding a train for London to start learning, as a Greenpark Productions employee, the job of writing scripts for documentary films.

Bunny Keene's house is very small and – like him – charming, the end one of a terrace, with a pub, the Selwood Arms, immediately round the corner. His cook-housekeeper, Mrs Crowe, is a chubby fiftyish peroxide blonde, a widow, wearing glitter-studded horn-rimmed spectacles, who sleeps on the ground floor in a tiny bedroom squeezed between an equally miniscule dining room and the kitchen. Upstairs an elegantly furnished, and rather more spacious, drawing-room – still small, but running the entire depth of the building – overlooks the street in front and a narrow garden at the back. Its French windows at either end are safeguarded by what can only be described as ornamental iron fenders, since they don't jut out far enough to be proper balconies.

Mrs Crowe brings us up a tray of tea and cakes, and shows an inclination to linger, acting as hostess, an error of judgement that earns her a snubbingly brusque dismissal from Bunny. His manner towards me remains affable. I, however, am tongue-tied, rendered speechless simply by finding myself here in the rarefied atmosphere of a fashionable London drawing-room, and being quite at a loss as to what to say or how to behave appropriately. He observes me gazing – gawping – at a big modernistic picture hung above the mantelpiece: it appears to represent a fat bulgy female figure, painted in a splurge of strong colours, red and green and blue, and bears not the slightest resemblance to the exact portraits my father used to paint, or to any of the illustrations I remember studying earnestly in his copies of the Royal Academy's annual summer catalogues.

'Do you like it?' Bunny asks me. I nod at him, dumbly; not

really truthfully. 'It's a Matthew Smith,' says Bunny, with careless pride. *Matthew Smith?* – who is he? I've never heard of him.

There's a scuffling sound in the street outside, and a man appears, climbing over the railing and tap-tapping at the French windows, which Bunny, laughing, hastens to open.

'Come in, Laurie – come in, come in. She's here, you see – my new girl, Elspeth, from the wilds of Devonshire. What do you think of her – eh?'

His new girl – is that what I am? And this is Laurie Lee, the famous poet, who lives, I learn, a few hundred yards away in Old Church Street, and whose slim book of selected poems, published by Messrs Faber & Faber, my brother Jim gave me before the war. I certainly know about *him* – Laurie Lee.

Then, five minutes later, we are joined by a person called Biddy Cook, with whom, it seems, I am to share an office on Monday when I start working for Greenpark Productions in Upper St Martin's Lane. She also lives close to Selwood Place, further westwards, somewhere off the Fulham Road, and arrives on her bicycle. Biddy Cook, aged, I would guess, about twenty-nine or thirty, is a very large woman; so large, indeed, that she makes Bunny's drawing-room, by no means extensive, feel even smaller and crammed uncomfortably full with too many people. But she has, I notice, the most beautiful sapphire blue eyes, fringed by long black lashes, and curly dark hair, and a warm embracing smile.

'Biddy's going to look after you, Elspeth, and teach you the ropes – aren't you, Biddy?' says Bunny Keene.

And when this nice large friendly smiling Biddy Cook promises to take me under her ample wing, I at once recover from my deplorable state of nervous paralysis, and instead of being stupid and gauche become calmly confident. If I fail to understand Laurie Lee's slyly clever jokes, or the reason for

Bunny's gales of merriment, it doesn't matter. I don't care. From now on, with Biddy as my teacher and my protector, all, I'm sure, will be well.

Thanks to Laurie Lee I've had the good luck to exchange my dismal attic in Earl's Court for a delightfully airy room on the first floor of a house in Markham Square, Chelsea, belonging to friends of his, Noel and Giana Blakiston, whose two grown-up daughters have left the family home. Noel is a writer, but gains a regular income by working five days a week as a civil servant in Somerset House where the records of births, deaths and marriages are stored. I see hardly anything of the Blakistons: they leave me alone, wishing, plainly, to establish a polite if slightly chilling distance between their lodger and themselves. I have my own front-door key and dodge in and out as hurriedly, guiltily, as if I were a criminal, always hoping to avoid meeting them, which I sometimes but not often do, on the stairs.

The minor awkwardness, however, of being (what I can't help feeling I am) an unwanted financial necessity, is far outweighed by the pleasure of living here in the heart of shabby bohemian Chelsea, a district inhabited by hordes of colourful impoverished artists and students for whom the King's Road is ideally suited to their – and my – economically straitened circumstances, dotted as it is with little inexpensive cafés and restaurants, and musty dusty second-hand antique shops full of old forgotten bric-à-brac going for a song. A stone's throw away from where I live is the Chelsea Cinema, in which can be viewed avant-garde French films for the price of tickets even I can afford.

At night I lie in my bed and watch, contentedly, the shadows from trees in the square flickering to and fro across my ceiling. Every morning I catch a No. 22 bus that carries me to Piccadilly, and on up Shaftesbury Avenue to Cambridge

Circus, from where I hurry, running in joyous anticipation of the day ahead, to Guild House in Upper St Martin's Lane.

I have not yet embarked, it's true, on learning how to be a scriptwriter – no; but that will follow, in due course. Meanwhile I'm perfectly happy to undertake whatever task I'm given – willing and eager to be treated as a glorified messenger girl and sent on errands to the British Film Institute in Soho Square, or told to convey tins of film to the Central Office of Information (a main commissioning agency of ours), where one memorable morning I happen to travel up in the same lift as Cecil Day-Lewis. He – naturally – doesn't even notice me; but I have no difficulty in recognizing *him*.

The fact is, I'm head over heels in love with everything remotely connected to the West End of London, an area so different from the East End and its docks, the only part of our capital city with which I have previously been familiar. Where I now work (if it can be termed *work*) is the centre for theatres and art galleries and big smart department stores, a crowded hub of bustle and excitement. Even the bomb sites – and there are plenty of those – seem to me beautiful and romantic, garnished like stage sets with sturdy colonising buddleia bushes and an invasion of wild-flowers from the countryside: acres of blossoming loosestrife and willowherb. The sun shines; the wind, blowing playfully in amongst this flourishing self-seeded camouflaging pink-and-green foliage, scatters a confetti of petals. Nobody speaks of the war. Nobody wants to remember it.

Nobody, none of us, wants to think about the war: it's over. Our eyes are fixed on what lies ahead: a wholly new beginning, where everything that was wrong before will be altered for the better. The very air pulsates with optimism, an exultant certainty that we, the British people, made wiser by tribulation, have learnt our lessons and outgrown past errors. Which is why, on 5th July, we vote in the General Election, not for Mr Winston Churchill to continue as our Prime Minister – he, the victorious heroic wartime leader – but for a somewhat younger insignificant-looking man, Mr Clement Atlee. The emergency coalition of political parties, being no longer relevant or needful, has disbanded, to resume its various different identities; and thus Mr Atlee is standing as head of a re-born boldly assertive Labour Party, determined, he declares, now that the war is won, to win the peace.

I am having my first experience of voting. So far as I can tell, at this decisive moment of British history we all in Greenpark Productions, including me, consider ourselves to be democratically left-wing enough to mark our crosses on the ballot papers as ardent supporters of weedy little Mr Atlee. And as thousands and thousands of our fellow citizens choose to do the same as us, the United Kingdom wakes up on the morning of 26th July to discover it has elected a Labour government to run our country. Poor Mr Churchill, grateful though we are for his years of inspiration in times of trial, has been pushed aside in order that we may welcome what we confidently believe awaits us: the rosy dawn of a new era.

Because we want so much to think the war has ended, we behave as if it has but of course it hasn't, not really. In the Far East, a very long way off, the agonising struggle is still being waged; until, on 6th August, a bomb, recently developed in Los Alamos, New Mexico – a nuclear bomb – is dropped by the American Air Force on the Japanese city of Hiroshima, obliterating it completely. Three days later a second bomb, also nuclear, dropped by another USA aeroplane on Nagasaki, has the identical result of annihilating its target – buildings, people: the lot. And with that second act of total destruction the war is finally, globally, ended.

210

But what are the implications of this extraordinary earth-shattering invention? What is the terrifying power discovered by scientists that can be contained in a single bomb, and harnessed or unleashed at will? What is meant by *nuclear*? I don't know, and nor can anyone I ask for information tell me. To be candid, we don't much want to discuss or worry ourselves about it, or about any aspect of the war, because we are so thankful it's behind us: what's done, is done! Our thoughts are focussed entirely on tomorrow, and on the future after tomorrow: on the prospect of a freedom that we, by desperate endeavours, have won at last, and the dazzling infinite possibilities we believe it holds out to us.

From the windows of the office I'm sharing with Biddy Cook on the first floor of Guild House we have a commanding view down Upper St Martin's Lane and beyond the Seven Dials to St Martin's Lane itself, which leads into Trafalgar Square. It's rather similar to being situated high up in the fo'c's'le of a ship at sea. Our office is in the middle of several occupied by, on the one hand, Bunny (here at Greenpark referred to always as *Ralph*: I *must* remember), sitting splendidly alone, as befits his eminence, and on the other hand by his team of film directors, John Eldridge, Charles de la Tour, and Ken Annakin, who come and go at random, depending on whether they are out and about somewhere actively engaged in shooting documentary footage, or using Guild House as a base between projects. Erica, who was a pre-war refugee from I'm not quite sure which Eastern European country, is assistant by turns to each of them, as and when required, and so she also comes and goes.

But Biddy, like an efficient policeman regulating traffic at a busy crossroads, remains immovably at her desk, her post, her telephone. She is the filter through which all communications pass, both inwards and outwards. Anybody who wants to see the boss, Ralph Keene, has to reach him via Biddy Cook. Everyone knows and is fond of Biddy, and never disputes her ruling: she can be formidable, largeness of size lending added weight to her authority.

Writers of reputation – Tambimuttu, the Indian poet, and John Sommerfield the novelist, for example – as well as lesser mortals, all of them hopefully in search of work, are frequent visitors, knocking at our door, putting their heads round it: 'Hullo, Biddy – is Ralph available, by any chance?' They stay on to chat to her, while I am sent scuttling off to the typists' pool to fetch hospitable cups of tea or coffee.

Oh happy times, with my London summer spinning on its axis like a golden ball! Of course the happiness, otherwise idyllic, does have its occasional darker moments, episodes, brief but searing, of excrutiating humiliation. Considering my abysmal ignorance, these disasters – luckily rare – are inevitable.

One day of dreadful memory I'm dispatched by Ken Annakin to Euston Station to meet and escort a couple of Yorkshire housewives and a shopkeeper to Merton Park Studios, a testing and responsible mission which I successfully accomplish, and arrive – regrettably, it's true – an hour later than scheduled, but nevertheless proudly shepherding my docile charges: I've managed to get them safely right across London! The bunch of amateur actors, my flock, are snatched away to have their make-up applied; and then, as soon as they are out of earshot, instead of the praise I expect from Ken Annakin, he wheels on me, and I am blasted into miserable atoms by the force of his fury.

'For God's sake, you little fool, don't you know better than to hang around waiting for Underground trains? Why on *earth* didn't you have the common sense to take a taxi?'

'I thought it would be too expensive, taking a taxi –'

'*Expensive*?' Haven't I any idea, he yells at me, how much

it costs our company to hire a floor for the morning at Merton Park Studios, or to have lights, technicians, a camera crew standing idle for a whole hour?

No – no; I haven't any idea, none at all. Shocked, ashamed, in floods of tears, hiccuping, sobbing, I can only repeat: 'I'm sorry, Ken – I'm so sorry, so sorry –'

It's a mistake I shall never make again.

But if I learn the hard way not to make that particular mistake again, there are plenty of other mistakes lying concealed like tiger traps dug in a jungle, ready for me to fall into.

Bunny takes me as a treat one evening after work to the Gargoyle Club, where we had our first meeting. We sit at the upstairs bar, waiting for a table to be vacant in the dining room below. The man sitting next to me by himself at the bar, hunched over a glass, is called Philip Toynbee. Bunny introduces us – rather, it seems to me, unwillingly. Almost at once Philip Toynbee and I become easily, deeply engaged in a conversation regarding the novels of Thomas Hardy, a recent discovery of mine. Following after *Tess of the D'Urbervilles* I've just finished reading *The Mayor of Casterbridge*. My new acquaintance – what a very nice man! – knows everything there is to be known about Thomas Hardy, and I am reluctant to have such a fund of literary information cut short by Bunny, who drags me off, grumpily, to a table and dinner downstairs; not, though, before Philip Toynbee has invited me to dine with him and continue our discussion here, at the Gargoyle tomorrow. All aglow from the flattering attention of this professorial erudite older man, I accept with alacrity; much to Bunny's annoyance.

'You silly girl – you should have refused,' he scolds me; scolding me as if I were a naughty child.

'Why? – why am I silly? We were having a very interesting

talk about books – ' I can't imagine ever discussing Thomas Hardy with Bunny. 'And besides, he's a friend of yours, isn't he?'

'Oh, I've known Philip for years – yes. But he drinks too much. And he's in a frightful mess with his marriage, poor fellow,' says Bunny, with lofty disdain, ignoring the fact that he himself is currently immersed in the complications of divorcing a second wife. 'And anyway, you're my girl – dam' cheek of him to go dating you under my nose –'

Being designated by Bunny *his girl* is beginning to lose its appeal. Bunny's feelings towards me are opaque. I'm growing daily more and more convinced that when we met he happened to be in need of someone, some girl pretty enough who would *do*, at any rate for the time being, to occupy the space created by the break-up of his marriage – his *second* marriage – and I was handy to fill the bill. But I certainly don't intend to be owned by Bunny Keene; I'm not his property.

Still as cross as two sticks, Bunny tells me again that I ought to steer clear of Philip Toynbee. 'He's not the sort of chap for a girl like you to get mixed up with.' And when I persist in my resolve, he repeats, grimly disapproving: 'Well, it's your funeral – don't say I didn't warn you'.

I choose not to heed his warning, but instead to assert my independence. The following evening, agog with happy anticipation, I hasten from Guild House to the Gargoyle, where I find Philip Toynbee hunched on the same stool as before, looking as if he hadn't stirred from it in twenty-four hours. He barely lifts his head to acknowledge my arrival, and he has obviously forgotten inviting me to have dinner with him. Sunk in an alchoholic fog, I doubt if he remembers who I am.

Not only is the disappointment acute, but I am also very hungry. Fifteen minutes of failure to rouse any spark of response in him having passed, I decide I might as well go home, and accordingly climb down off my stool.

'Goodbye, Philip –' He doesn't reply. Which is when a man who has been watching us from the end of the bar approaches, introduces himself as David Tennant, the owner of the Gargoyle, and gallantly offers to act as a substitute for Philip Toynbee. 'It's no use your expecting anything from Philip for the rest of today – he's a goner. Why don't you let me give you dinner?'

Oh, but how kind! The relief – starving as I am – is considerable, and I thank him effusively, my faith in the goodness of human nature quite restored.

Downstairs, sitting opposite each other at one of the little tables, the lights low, the band playing soft music, my host – my rescuer – orders dinner for two. And then, as I smile at him gratefully, he leans forward and addresses me, speaking clearly and slowly, with cruel emphasis, his eyes fastened on mine: 'Do you know, Elspeth – that is your name, isn't it? – you are the type of girl – I – simply – can't – *bear* –'

What does he mean? Why is he saying it? What have I done wrong? I jump to my feet, confused and frightened, knocking a wine glass off the table, stammering: 'I don't understand – I don't understand –'

How is it possible for David Tennant, my good Samaritan, to be transformed on the instant into a devil, a monster? And *why*? Weeping hysterically, I rush away upstairs to the bar, where Philip Toynbee is still crouched despondently on his stool. He produces an enormous handkerchief and proceeds to mop at my tears, meanwhile telling me not to worry about old David. 'He likes his bit of fun, ol' David. But tha' don' matter – I'll take you home. As a *marrofac'* I need somewhere to stay the night –'

Recoiling from the comforting arm around my shoulders, I thrust his handkerchief back at him. 'No, Philip – no;

215

I can perfectly well see myself home. You can't come with me – no!' The idea of turning up at Markam Square with him in this condition is horrific.

Will the nightmare never end? I'm safely in the lift when Philip pushes his way into it, alongside me. 'I jus' need a corner to lay my head – thas' all – jus' a corner – to lay my head –'

He lumbers down Shaftesbury Avenue after me, heaves himself aboard the same bus, staggers off it at Piccadilly Circus and pursues me down the steps of the Underground. 'All I want – is jus' – jus' a *corner* –'

The doors of the train I leap on to are too slow in closing, and he is there, forcing them apart. When I bolt up the stairs of South Kensington Station, he is following at my heels, his voice beseechingly loud: 'Jus' a corner – thas' all –' By now I am incapable of rational thought. Jamming myself into a telephone kiosk, I dial with shaking fingers, Bunny's number. Selwood Place isn't far off, and although Philip Toynbee, equally distraught and as mindless as I am, is hammering on the glass panels of the telephone box, when I see Bunny's tall figure striding along the pavement of the Old Brompton Road, suddenly I'm alone: my persecutor has gone, vanished into the night.

Holding me by the wrist, like a policeman making an arrest, Bunny marches me, angrily fast, back to his house. 'It's your own fault, you *silly* girl.' Then, more kindly: 'You really are as green as grass. Didn't I warn you?'

Sniffle, sniffle: 'Yes, Bunny – you did.'

These are the lessons that have to be learnt by silly green-as-grass girls.

In celebration of my new job and my wonderful new life, I've acquired a new name. *Elspeth Hallsmith* has always sounded ugly in my ears, clumsy and cumbersome, and I've decided that now is the perfect opportunity to get rid of it.

As a child I would have to listen, often and boringly, to my mother instructing shopkeepers in Newquay on the correct spelling of *Hallsmith*. It had to be written as one word, not as two: 'No hyphen!' I used to hear her say, again and again, and was irritated, even in those early days, by what I thought was tiresome unnecessary mumbo-jumbo. And *Elspeth* has been a name I've detested for as long as I can remember anything. *Ellie*, my sister Pam's version of it, I like, especially with the improvement of having an N added in front.

I therefore seize the chance to inform my Greenpark associates, when we are assembled in Ralph Keene's office for the purpose of dealing with the usual monthly agenda itemising works-in-progress and works-in-prospect, that I want to be known from now on as Nellie Smith.

To my dismay I'm told, flatly, that this is out of the question. *Smith* is acceptable – there are dozens of Smiths knocking about – but since my ultimate aim, I've confessed, is to be a writer, and since Nellie is a diminutive of Eleanor, and there already exists, it seems, a distinguished author called Lady Eleanor Smith, the present company agrees, unanimously, that I must adopt a first name entirely different.

Must I really? And what name, then, if not Nellie, my cherished own choice, am I to have? I wait humbly for the verdict of my superiors.

Laurie Lee provides the solution. With a flourish and the assurance of a poet, whose trade it is to render language euphonious: 'Emma,' he pronounces, plucking the syllables apparently out of thin air; and he repeats them, nodding in satisfaction. 'Yes,' he says, '*Emma*!'

I feel as ill-suited to being an Emma as for twenty-two years I have felt, and not enjoyed, being Elspeth, but I lack the confidence to resist a suggestion that has the enthusiastic approval of all the other Greenparkers. Ralph and Biddy and

Laurie, Charles and Erica, John Eldridge and Ken Annakin, are my respected, slightly feared elders and betters, and their time is much too valuable to waste it any further on the triviality of re-naming such a lowly junior member of the staff as me. So in five minutes the affair is disposed of, settled, and Elspeth Hallsmith has been consigned to oblivion. In her place is a young person with the name – undeniably less tongue-twisting and more convenient – of Emma Smith.

Pam has turned up in London, no longer wearing the uniform of a WAAF officer: she is a civilian now. Those who enlisted at the very beginning of the war, way back in September 1939 – how remote that seems! – are the first of the serving men and women to be discharged. Early in, early out, is the rule; and by the same token, late in, last out. Which is why Jim, her twin, will have to linger on for many months more in the RAF before he gains his release.

My sister has apprenticed herself to an Australian photographer of considerable renown, Douglas Glass. Her eye, her discerning discriminating accurate eye, inherited, although she would hotly deny it, from our father, is to form an intimate rewarding relationship for her, not with pencil or paint, or the other paraphernalia of an artist, but with the lens of a camera.

Douglas Glass lavishes praise on his pupil. Recognising a natural gift, a talent inborn, he has no hesitation in authorising her to cover some magazine stories without him, alone; and the resulting photographs, coming from his studio, but the actual product of her Leica camera, are infallibly of a professional fee-earning standard. Pam, in short, thanks to a combination of instinct and good luck, has found her career.

What I have found, to my unbounded joy, is the sister I lost when she was a brass-buttoned officer in H.M. Forces – a judgemental disciplinarian then – and I was running about the Grand Union's locks and docks in ragged dungarees, barefooted and dirty-faced. She, my missing sister, has now, as by a miracle, been restored to me.

Pam commemorated the declaration of peace with a symbolic gesture, immediately chopping off the plaits which were normally twined around her head like a sort of halo, and allowing her blonde hair to swing loose in a shoulder-length pageboy bob. This change of hair-style changed her appearance completely; and more than just her appearance. Overnight she reverted, effortlessly, to the character of an eighteen-year-old student, as though the war, that long dark passage of suffering and loss, had not after all been the destroyer of carefree youth, but merely, instead, an interruption to what could be resumed at the exact point where it had so arbitrarily been broken in upon.

I am proud to be seen in public with her, to share with her my friends, recreations, pursuits. When we were small it was Pam who taught me to read, Pam who was my protector, my leader, and I her willing slave. The alliance was a defensive one. We were inseparable because, in a threatening world, we needed each other. At Christmas we busied ourselves making bungled grubby presents for aunts and grannies (calendars, pen-wipers, cross-stitch embroidered tray-cloths). We invented games and competitions together, gave dramatic performances to entertain the Hallsmith family, whispered secrets from bed to bed in the dark. Our girls' club had a limited membership of two: Jim, a boy, was excluded from it. My brother Jim, though, maintained with me a comradely extraneous understanding that encompassed marbles and roller-skating and stamp-collecting, and didn't include Pam.

Growing up we grew, she and I, little by little, apart. The years passed, and here we are suddenly, in London, a pair of sisters again, but on an equal footing now, neither leading nor led, and as closely devotedly attached as it's possible for sisters to be. How wonderful!

In the spring of 1946 Greenpark's chief, Ralph Keene – Bunny – is in Cyprus with a camera crew shooting a promotional film for the Tourist Board. Laurie Lee has gone with them to write the script. As for me, my position has greatly improved, and from simply being available to run errands for all and sundry, I am now Ken Annakin's personal assistant. Ken is to direct a film commissioned by the Central Office of Information (COI) which will be distributed to our embassies, and to the overseas offices of the British Council, showing how admirably justice in Britain is upheld and administered. I am to help him research it, shape it, and get its budget accepted: this last being, in our post-war poverty-stricken economy, of paramount importance.

Money, whether domestic or Governmental, is tight. But there is also an optimism circulating, an energetic come-what-may determination to start afresh, to regenerate, and in this ebullient atmosphere documentary films are the benefici-aries of a honeymoon period. The need for propaganda that combines encouragement with useful instruction is almost insatiable, and when compared to the entertainment indus-try's feature films – amply supplied to our cinemas, in any case, by Hollywood – documentaries are relatively much cheaper and much quicker to produce.

My instant reaction on hearing that I was being assigned to work for Ken was one of near panic. His blistering rage, incurred by the imbecilic failure of mine to deliver a group of amateur actors to Merton Park Studios on time, was all too painfully clear in my memory. I needn't have worried, though. Nobody could be kinder to me than my new master. Ken Annakin is a bespectacled Yorkshireman, down-to-earth, straightforward, plain in face and manner, but giving credit where credit is due, and demonstrating his satisfaction, when pleased, with a huge smile.

He has forgiven, or perhaps forgotten, my original idiotic blunder and treats me nowadays as a trusted collaborator, not a brainless fool, inviting me home to his flat in Wimbledon to meet his nice Austrian wife, Blanka, and their little girl – a carbon copy of her father – who is nicknamed (I don't know why) Snicky. Having ceased to be in awe of Ken, working for him as his assistant proves to be a surprising pleasure.

My occupation during the next few weeks is to travel about London and various neighbouring towns, taking notes in magistrates' courtrooms of the cases – often quite minor offences – being tried there, and the rules and regulations involved in trying them. Later on, at Abingdon, I fill my notebook with descriptions of the colourful pomp and ceremony of its County Assizes. Finally, and most harrowingly, I have to attend, perched aloft in the visitors' gallery of the Old Bailey, two trials for murder.

The boy, aged nineteen, who accidentally shot and killed an American GI in Soho, while attempting to rob him, is found guilty of homicide by the jury, and sentenced to hang for his crime. But in the second instance I witness the prosecution and defence of a small wizened elderly man whose young wife mocked him unmercifully, until one day, taunted beyond endurance, he killed her; and I observe how his plight and his ultimate resolution of it rouses the sympathy of the twelve members of the jury, so that they acquit him of murder, bringing in a lesser verdict of culpable manslaughter, which doesn't carry the mandatory sentence of punishment by hanging.

I shall never forget seeing the judge, at the end of the first trial, place and carefully adjust the square of black material on top of his curled white wig to pronounce the dreadful sentence on the ashen-faced boy standing trembling in the dock before him. Nor shall I forget afterwards passing by the boy's mother huddled on a bench outside the courtroom, weeping, weeping for her son.

'It can't be right,' I say to Ken Annakin, '– surely it can't be? This law – our law – of capital punishment is wrong – is *wicked*. It makes murderers of us all.'

We are sitting as I speak side by side in deck-chairs at the edge of the Serpentine, basking in Hyde Park's unseasonably hot sunshine while endeavouring to draft, from the typewritten pages and pages of what had been my hastily scribbled notes, a rough preliminary shooting-script; Ken having pronounced, with his famous wide-stretching grin, that instead of us being cooped up inside his Guild House office, we could quite as easily sort out my copious jottings in the fresh air. How fortunate I am! What other working girl has a boss who declares that the unusually fine weather is a bonus too good to miss?

Is it any wonder I like working for Ken Annakin? And so, in due course, *British Justice*, the film, is scripted, and shot, and edited, and handed over to the COI for its dissemination throughout the civilized world.

I have had to relinquish my lovely big front room in Markham Square and be content with a much smaller darker room at the back of the house. This is on account of Laurie Lee deciding to swap his lodging in Old Church Street for accommodation, infinitely preferable, with the Blakistons; and, as their family friend, he naturally has prior claim to the best of the only two empty, and thus free-to-be-let, rooms on the first floor of No. 7.

Every day after school finishes Laurie is visited by Cathy. She arrives in her gym tunic, a schoolgirl of fifteen – or thereabouts – and having contrived a quick change of clothing, emerges from what used to be my and is now Laurie's room, looking every inch a woman (and a very beautiful woman) who could easily be ten years older than she actually is. Then off they go together, a couple not remarkable to the casual bystander for any obvious disparity in age.

The sophistication of Cathy's appearance when she's dressed up and wearing lipstick and mascara, belies the simplicity and frankness of her personality. Nothing to do with Cathy is in the slightest bit duplicitous or devious. She adores Laurie. And he, above all else, likes to be adored; especially by pretty girls.

Instead of poetry, Laurie has taken to writing prose, and is at present engaged upon an autobiographical account of his childhood in the Gloucestershire countryside. On some evenings there will be a tap at my door, and Laurie enters, bringing with him the last few completed pages of his manuscript to read aloud to me. I sit and listen, admiringly, enthralled a little envious too, and when he asks me what I think of his work-in-progress I tell him that it's brilliant; which, in my honest opinion, it is: witty, sparkling, and, of course – how could it not be – poetic. Would that I were able to write as well, as fluently, as brilliantly as Laurie does.

I joined Greenpark Productions in the capacity, I believed, of a junior scriptwriter. That expectation is yet to be realised, but its continued postponement has in no degree diminished my ambition to become, by hook or by crook, some sort of professional writer – not necessarily of film scripts. The novel I've spent weeks and weeks of my leisure hours working on relates to a rich old woman who, in spite of viewing all children with profound suspicion, adopts, as her moral duty, a boy from an orphanage. But while the creation of this fantasy absorbs and entertains me, I remain dubious as to the authenticity of the fictitious characters. Will they stand up to critical scrutiny? I'm not sure that they will.

Before delivering a full-length novel to the eyes of the

outside world, ought I to practise the art of writing, and gain greater experience, through the medium of short stories? And would it be better, I wonder, for me to select subjects with which I am genuinely familiar? Possibly, yes. The old lady and her orphan protégee are consequently shelved for the time being in favour of canals.

Owing to a stroke of good fortune, I happen to meet in Guild House the writer John Sommerfield on his way to or from a scripting session. Himself a well-known author, kind-hearted John Sommerfield takes an immediate encouraging interest in my incipient efforts, and after reading a few of the stories I am bold enough to show him, he says to me that in the current enterprising literary climate, with brave little magazines cropping up all over the place – as hopeful of future success as I am – he may very likely be able to place a story of mine with one of them.

And he does – indeed, he *does*! God bless John Sommerfield, my patron saint, my guardian angel!

Seven is the name of a newly launched modest little magazine containing articles and short stories, reviews and photographs. And there, in its third issue, printed on page twenty-three, is a brief, a very brief canal tale, entitled 'Albert and the Three Sailors', by – guess who? – Emma Smith!

I am in print. Hooray! I've been published. I am a *real writer*!

Greenpark Productions is prospering, and Ralph Keene, its proud owner, is in high spirits. The praise bestowed on the film he and his unit made in Cyprus has caught the attention and impressed the management of the Tea Board, an august body that has its headquarters in a street just off the Haymarket. One morning when Ralph – Bunny – is about to set forth on foot to meet by appointment various members of the illustrious Tea Board, he summons me at the last moment to accompany him, a summons I'm happy to obey, although I have to jogtrot briskly so as to keep up with the long strides of his long legs. Bunny never dawdles.

'You'd like to go to India, wouldn't you?' he remarks, as we're negotiating the traffic of Piccadilly Circus.

'India? – what, me?' He must be joking. 'Is that where you're going to film next – in India?'

'I certainly hope so,' says Bunny, with a careless air intended to conceal, I suspect, his true state of jubilation. India! Who wouldn't feel jubilant?

He introduces me as his assistant to the three men who rise from behind a big shiny desk and shake our hands cordially. We are given coffee to drink; not, as might have been expected, tea. I sit meekly silent, a little to the rear of my boss, pretending to jot down relevant facts and figures in my notebook, as a good assistant ought to do, but actually with my head whirling, so that the scribblings I try later on to decipher are a jumble of nonsense. *India*! *Me*? Did he really mean I am to go too?

Through a mental mist I hear them speak of Bombay, Calcutta, of tea gardens in Assam, and after an hour of jocular talk and laughter and more coffee, and a large-scale map being unrolled over the surface of the desk, the matter, or at least the preliminaries of it, have been settled. In the autumn of this year, 1946, a unit of Greenpark Productions will travel halfway round the globe to make an educational film by means of which the Tea Board will be able to demonstrate to their clients, and also to aspiring young tea-planters, the whole saga of how tea is cultivated, harvested, processed, shipped back in crates to the United Kingdom, sold in packets across the counters of innumerable grocery shops, and poured from the spouts of innumerable ladies' teapots. And I am to be with that unit: Bunny has said so.

For someone who has all her life dreamed of travelling

225

abroad, but who has never been out of this country, the prospect is deliriously exciting. *India*! I repeat the word to myself like a charm, again and again: *India*! There is a snag, though, and it is of such an awkward nature it could well be ruinous.

I, who a year ago was totally infatuated with Bunny Keene, am no longer, I've discovered, in love with him. To be his assistant is one thing; to be what, according to his description of me, I am – *his girl* – is quite another. And herein lies the problem I'm faced with: how can I agree to be the first, without being also the second?

Since living in Chelsea and rubbing shoulders with people of artistic eminence known to Ralph Keene, I've undergone what amounts to an awakening process of disillusionment. I used to imagine that famous painters and writers were as exalted and remote as gods, deserving, like gods, to be worshipped from afar by ordinary mortals. It was, I now consider, a naively erroneous belief. Fame – so coveted by my father – can induce, I've learnt, a false conviction of self-importance; can give rise to spitefulness, jealousy, back-stabbings, and any number of petty meannesses, not at all god-like. Besides which, people who aren't famous I have found to be, in general, much more fun.

It has taken just a few educational months for me to arrive at this conclusion. Bunny, with decades of experience to reflect upon, is as dazzled still by fame as a schoolboy. What seems to me a juvenile weakness is, nevertheless, to my mind, so endearing it may perhaps partly account for why, although I'm no longer in love, I am extremely fond of him. In my estimation Ralph Keene – Bunny – has infinitely greater worth, and finer qualities, than those friends of his he reveres and to whose faults he is blind: handsome, rich, aristocratic Dick Wyndham, for example – Bunny's hero, and as such beyond the faintest hint of criticism or censure.

On many occasions I have sat, silent, at Bunny's dining-room table, fulfilling my function of being his mandatory girlfriend, but ignored by the distinguished voluble guests who surround me, and consequently as free to listen and watch as if I was wearing a cloak of invisibility. And what I saw, and what I heard, I very often didn't like at all.

During the past year Bunny's attitude towards me has been gradually, imperceptibly changing. The change becomes apparent to both of us only when I pluck up courage enough in the summer to tell him I wish from now on to cease being *his girl*. He will have to find another girl, I inform him, to fill my shoes.

This ultimatum costs me a great deal of anguish to pronounce, for with it I am forfeiting the one chance in a million of going to fabulous India. But I have wrestled with my troublesome conscience, and my conscience has made ineluctably clear to me the agonising choice that lies between either Bunny and India, or no Bunny and no India; and has furthermore dictated sternly which of the two must be chosen.

Bunny's reaction to the speech I force myself to utter is bewildered incomprehension. He hasn't called me a silly girl for ages, but that's what he calls me now. 'You silly girl – you little goose – don't talk such rubbish! I know it's been hard for you – tricky, lately – but my divorce will be through soon, and then everything will be much easier. You can move into Selwood Place, if you want to – whatever you want –' He even mentions a possibility, at some indefinite future date, of marriage.

That he should be so upset and aggrieved astounds me. Is it the result of wounded pride, a refusal to accept that a mere chit of a girl has the cheek to turn down Ralph Keene? Or has he, over the preceding year, to my surprise and his surprise, grown genuinely fond of me – as I of him?

But when he presses me for a reason to explain my absurd decision ('I mean *why*, for God's sake – *why*? When we were getting on so splendidly together –') I am lost for an answer. I can't bring myself to declare the unequivocal truth, which is that having studied his circle of friends at close quarters, I don't want to join them. I'm uncomfortable in their company. I don't admire what they admire. To put it bluntly, I don't like them. As for becoming one day the third Mrs Ralph Keene, a union I would have bartered my soul for not so long ago, the suggestion appals me. But I'm unable to tell Bunny this; nor am I able to confess to him a crueller reason for wishing to cut the amorphous bonds that bind us: he simply is too old. Next time I fall in love I want it to be with someone of my own age: somebody young.

'Well, you can't start pulling out of going to India *now*,' says Bunny, huffily. 'All the arrangements have been made – you're a member of the unit. You've got to come. Look here,' he says, persuasively, '– if I promise not to lay a finger on you for the whole trip – will that do?'

I consult my mentor, my inconvenient conscience: will it do? Surely this promise of Bunny's offers an honourable way out of the dilemma – doesn't it? Yes, it does; it *will* do – and I can go to India!

On 5th October we drive down from London to Southampton to board the *Andes*. There are five of us in our unit: the cameraman, George Still, and his assistant Teddy Fader; Laurie Lee, who will write the script; Ralph Keene, the director, and myself, who on paper has the awesome sounding title of assistant-director, but who ought more aptly to be known as bottle-washer-in-chief.

At 6 p.m. we are waved goodbye from the quayside by a group of Greenpark well-wishers, Erica and Charles de la Tour and John Eldridge, and with music to celebrate our departure – a wistful tune, 'Indian Summer', relayed at full blast over the loudspeakers – we slip our moorings and slowly, majestically, leaving Southampton astern, cruise on into the English Channel. What, for the *Andes*, could be described as a second maiden voyage, has begun.

Throughout the war it served as a troop-carrier. Now the *Andes*, its re-conversion just completed, and resplendent with spanking white paint and polished brass, has become again the luxury liner it originally was, and we are amongst a multitude of passengers participating in the first trip of its brand-new peacetime career.

I stand on deck, watching the shore lights recede, and wondering what all the other lights winking and blinking across the water indicate. The coast of France, perhaps? I have no idea. Rather to my relief, I am found at the rail by George and Teddy and together we set off on a tour of exploration up and down ladders, from deck to deck, and realise the labyrinthine vastness of what is to be our floating home for the fortnight ahead of us.

Life at sea, we also discover, is regulated by inflexible rules. I am not allowed to have dinner with George and Teddy: their dining-saloon is for men only. Having missed the sitting I was supposed to attend earlier in a different saloon, obtaining a meal anywhere at the wrong time proves to be almost impossible: seats have been allocated, and rules are rules. The hubbub of voices and clatter of dishes is deafening. At last a kindly steward takes pity on my plight. After eating gratefully, guiltily, the food he smuggles out to me like so much contraband, I wander back up on deck. But the wind is too cold and too strong, the sea choppy, the night's huge vastness lonely. I've lost my companions. When I return inside I catch a glimpse of Ralph and Laurie at a table in one of the many lounges, cosily settled, drinks to hand, playing piquet. They don't notice me.

To reach my cabin, which I'm sharing with a little boy, Tom, and his mother, and three other women, it's necessary to ask for directions from the purser. I've managed to secure one of the top bunks. Climbing into it, exhausted by the exciting strangeness of everything, I lie and listen to the ceaseless rushing sound of the waves, and the ceaseless muffled beat of the engine that is carrying me on, I know, on and on, on and on, to India – to India . . . Lulled by the steadiness of these noises, I fall asleep.

Today we are in the Bay of Biscay. I spend hours by myself right up in the bows of the vessel, braving wind and rain and flying spray for the sake of being in the fresh air. I'm feeling not very well, curiously dizzy, giddy, and afraid that if I do go inside the queaziness may develop into something worse. Although the sea isn't really rough, the ship's continuous motion, rising and falling, rising and falling, has a destabilising effect on me. The *Andes*, apparently unaided by a crew, races ahead on an undeviatingly straight line, plunging through the dark water at a terrific speed towards an indiscernible destination, as if, hell-bent, racing to nowhere.

I skip lunch, but risk afternoon tea and a dry biscuit; and then, in an attempt to escape from the loud monotonous wailing of scores of unhappy children, retire, dinnerless, to the comfort of my bunk. Eyes closed, flat on my back is the way, I've decided, to survive. Tomorrow will be better.

And tomorrow *is* better. The weather has improved. It's warmer. I don't have to wear a coat on deck. Dolphins are leaping out of a greenish-blue sea, with a blue sky above, and like a mirage there is visible to one side of us a long honey-coloured streak or smudge, lying low on the horizon: land! We are off the coast of Portugal, and close enough presently to see small square white houses resembling lumps of sugar.

These recognisable signs of human habitation, the first we have had since leaving England on Saturday, are so far off and silent, voiceless, as to be unreal. We see them, and soon, still tearing south in the *Andes*, they are gone, lost to us for ever behind a band of intervening cloud.

I'm oblivious to our passage, sometime during the night, through the Straits of Gibraltar, but when I wake next morning we are in the Mediterranean.

It's very hot, and getting hotter. The strong wind, which never slackens, is gritty with sand, and presently we see the shores of Africa on our starboard side: vague brown contours of hills rising massively, layer upon layer. The swimming pool has been opened, a tiny patch of salty water, crowded with children.

We laze around in bathing costumes, reading, chatting, writing letters home. Laurie, despite the heat, is permanently active, pursuing in turn every pretty girl on board, and serenading them with the fiddle he made sure to include in his luggage. At night, under a full moon, there is dancing to the ship's band on F. Deck.

Travelling due east, always with the looming presence of Africa on our right hand, this routine of indulgent idleness continues, day after day, until interrupted one evening at eight o'clock when we come into view of Port Said's lighthouse. The *Andes*, reducing speed in obedience to its warning flashes, is met by a smart little launch bringing out the pilot who scrambles, as agile as a monkey, up the ladder lowered for him, and guides us to our anchorage.

We passengers have grown accustomed to the non-stop blowing of the wind, and to the ceaseless throbbing pulse of the engine, and to catching only fleeting glimpses of the lands we hurtle past. Now, moored and motionless, quite suddenly the wind has stopped blowing and the engine been stilled, and we are able to prop our elbows on the rail and gaze leisurely at the twinkling lights of a nearby foreign town – this exotic Arabian town, Port Said – and at the strange graceful shapes of dhows lining the jetties, their sails furled, their tall thin masts leaning haphazardly in all directions.

The unusual tranquillity is, however, short-lived. Soon after dropping anchor we are beseiged by a horde of ramshackle rowing-boats that gather like a swarm of predatory flies with the single frantic purpose of selling to gullible *Andes* passengers as many commodities – dubious in quality – at the highest possible price in the quickest possible time. And the resulting turmoil on the deep green water below us, illuminated in starkest detail by the steady glare of the *Andes'* watchful searchlight, is the opposite of tranquillity.

Forbidden to come aboard, each vendor balances himself upright in his dangerously bobbing dingy, holding his wares at arm's length so as to display and promote them in strident competition with fellow salesmen, who are all equally determined.

Leather bags, leather pouffes, boxes of Turkish Delight, sandals, cigarette cases, tasselled scarlet fez: 'You likey this, Madam? – Sir, Missie? – very cheap – very good value. For you, special small price –'

The favoured article is borne upwards – trustingly – in a basket attached to a piece of string for closer inspection, and either it, if rejected, or the money, if a bargain has been struck, then returned in the basket. The trading goes on for hours. Lying in my bunk, worn out by what, for us, is of no more importance than a game, I hear the shouts, the supplications, the laughter, the cries of joy or disappointment, resounding late into the night.

We leave Port Said at 7 a.m. and proceed at a stately pace to navigate the Canal. Moving so slowly, in order to create a minimum destructive wash of water, and so close to the bank, we are able to scrutinise everything with unhurried curiosity as we glide smoothly past. Studded with bollards at hundred-yard intervals, the sandy soil comes right down to the edge of the Canal. Tamarisk trees and clumps of date-palms and low scrubby bushes dot the surrounding arid landscape. The heat is stupendous. We see encampments of British Tommies, busy at some kind of work, all in khaki shorts and stripped to the waist. We see Arabs, men wearing what to us look like flapping white nightshirts; and naked brown beautiful children; and a group, at one point, of disconsolate camels waiting to board a cross-Canal ferry. And once we have to pull in to the side and stop altogether to let a ship of similar size to the *Andes* go by. Occasionally we pass a scattering of huts, too dispersed and impoverished in appearance to be described as villages, but skirted always by the black snake of a macadamised road running north and south from end to end of the Canal, with army vehicles, trucks and jeeps, racing along its barren surface.

Having left Port Said early this morning, our journey through the Canal has taken us exactly twelve hours. The *Andes*, after pausing only briefly at Port Suez, almost immediately gets up speed again and heads down the Gulf of Sinai and out into the Red Sea.

For the following two days we are off the coast of Arabia, as insubstantial and vague as a land in a dream. The nights are so hot I push the mattress of my bunk through the window and sleep on deck, under a now waning moon, to be woken at dawn by a member of the crew shaking my shoulder – 'Scrubbing decks in ten minutes' – and stumbling back to the stifling heat of the cabin. Our last sight of land before we reach Bombay is an indistinct view of Aden. Thereafter, with ocean stretching, unrelieved, to the furthest horizon, we

233

resume the daily routine of doing nothing – nothing but eat and drink, and bathe and doze, and be given, twice, the treat of a dance on F. Deck. And I assiduously, obsessively, write my diary, pages and pages of it. How else am I to keep alive, for me, for ever, my memory of this most extraordinary, wonderful adventure?

The lights of Bombay are first visible at 6 a.m. on Saturday, 19th October. A tug conducts us to our quayside mooring, and here, precisely two weeks from when we bade farewell to Southampton, our sea journey terminates, and India, that magical word, is transformed into physical seething raucous reality.

Throughout the morning confusion rages unabated aboard the *Andes*. Hundreds of passengers queue for the purser's office, queue for the lavatories. Distraught mothers lose and find and lose again their children. Families roam the corridors from deck to deck, searching for their luggage, searching for each other, all streaming with sweat in the overpowering heat, all desperate to get ashore. The noise, both aboard and on land, is deafening: a cacophony of shouting, crying, loudspeakers blaring directives, hooters honking.

We wait until afternoon before descending the gangplank, to be swallowed up in the jostling chaotic heterogeneous crowd below. Fending off a tangle of bare brown arms trying to snatch and carry our bags, we fight our way to the desks of immigration officials, answer their questions, sign their papers, recover our passports, and at last, escaping from this version of hell on earth, are driven in taxis, thankfully, to the cool immense haven – or heaven, indeed! – of the Taj Mahal Hotel, where we shall spend the next couple or so days before departing by train to Calcutta.

The Taj Mahal Hotel is vast, rising in five flights of wide

stone stairs round a central well, and topped by a glass dome. We luxuriate in its expensive comfort and acquire, for our even greater comfort, an Indian bearer (meaning a personal servant), who guides us to the local bazaars and assists us in buying Thermoses, necessary for the train journey ahead, and a supply of fruit and sweets and magazines. His name, he informs us, is Babu – a generic term, as we later learn, given to Indians literate in the English language, which our optimistic Babu can scarcely claim to be.

I can't get used to the superabundance of fruit piled high in the markets, oranges, pumpkins, melons, bananas – and not just to the quantity, but to the incredibly bright fresh colour of them. It dazzles me. My eyes, for years, were starved of colour, and it was a deprivation more disheartening by far than having to go without the taste of bananas or oranges. England in the war, and in the immediate aftermath of war, has been a country dressed, perforce, in the dull drabness of khaki and grey, navy and black.

And now, suddenly, I find myself startled by a veritable explosion of colour. Despite the obvious poverty and squalor of the crowded hectic streets, this prodigious wealth of colour is truly amazing. I feast my eyes on it. Colour is lavishly everywhere – in the bales of muslin and silk stacked on the shelves of shopkeepers' open-fronted stalls; in the hanging garlands of flowers pink and scarlet; in the saris women wear, as variegated and brilliant as the feathers of tropical birds; in the flamboyantly painted designs decorating every inch of space available on walls, buses, buildings. Clearly for Indians colour, whatever else they lack, is an absolutely essential vivid enhancement of life, no matter how humble that life may be.

Our preparations made, on Tuesday evening we go by taxi to Bombay's Victoria Station, and climb up into the fusty dirty compartment of a train bound for Calcutta. And so we are off again, this time crossing a continent, on the next stage of our long-drawn-out pilgrimage to Assam.

There is no connecting corridor on our train, and we judge it preferable, and possibly safer, to put up with the inconvenience of cramming ourselves, all five of us, into a single box-like compartment which has its own smelly lavatory and washbasin adjoining, rather than splitting into separate groups. As I am, according to an unspoken but generally held view, the least important member of the unit, my offer to be the person sleeping on the floor is accepted without argument. Ralph and George take possession of the two top bunks, Teddy and Laurie the two below.

At the first stop along the line our bearer, Babu, appears from wherever he has been concealed and taps on the window, beckoning to us urgently. We tumble out and chase after him the whole length of the train to the dining-car. Having eaten a meal of rice and chicken, we dash back, when it stops again, as fast as we can sprint, afraid of not regaining the security of our compartment before the engine chuffs off into the night, leaving us behind on the platform, stranded.

We needn't have been anxious: the train, as we very soon are made aware, is in no hurry to complete its journey. At every station the stops are interminable. Exhausted, we fall uneasily asleep, and remain for hours only vaguely conscious of the hullabaloo that bursts out at each successive halt – the squealing of brakes, the tumult of doors being slammed, and voices yelling, bells clanging, whistles blown – until we are woken at dawn by Babu bringing us a sloppy tray of tea and biscuits.

All day we rattle through a flat agricultural landscape of dry brown earth and small isolated villages. I sit gazing out at miles and miles, and miles and miles and *miles* of it: at oxen slowly pulling ploughshares, and figures dressed, not

236

colourfully as in Bombay, but wearing scanty cotton garments, invariably white. I see sparse clumps of trees, bony cows, kites or vultures wheeling above in a pale bleached sky, the infrequent glitter of water trickling thinly at the bottom of dried-up river beds, everything in sight reduced to insignificance by the impression of an enormous encompassing indifferent emptiness.

But no sooner do we arrive at the next station than, like a dream on waking, the impression vanishes and the empty void is replaced by its exact opposite: a platform teeming with people – people coming and going, old and young, a mass of bodies pushing and struggling either to get down from or else, more often, on to a train already suffocatingly overcrowded. Sellers of tea and sellers of water thread a practised pathway through the throng, and vendors of sweetmeats, knick-knacks and magazines raucously advertise their wares. Beggars, some of them blind, some hideously crippled, hobble about soliciting alms, the disabled being led or drawn on trolleys by those who are able. And always at our window, standing on tiptoe, are children, beautiful Indian children, holding their hands up, curved in the hope of receiving what they huskily, beseechingly plead for: 'Baksheesh, Sahib, Memsahib – baksheesh, baksheesh –'

Thus the day passes, followed by another steamy night, and then another day when the countryside grows greener and wetter, with paddy fields and water buffalo. And at last we reach Calcutta.

We have no wish to hang around in Calcutta for any longer than is absolutely needful. Our hotel, the Great Eastern, is a gloomy barracks of a building, as big as the Taj Mahal Hotel in Bombay but with none of its airy charm. Whether indoors or outside, an atmosphere of nervous tension prevails in Calcutta, the current widespread unrest seeming to warn of a lethal, hardly suppressed violence on the verge of erupting. The city's taxis are all on strike, and we have been advised to steer clear of the docks where bottles filled with acid are being flung about indiscriminately to demonstrate the extreme anti-Raj sentiments felt by certain sections of the population.

While knowing, of course – it's common knowledge – that the post-war British Government had agreed to allow India her Independence, we supposed the transference of power would be accomplished peacefully and calmly. Brought up on the description of India being the brightest jewel in the crown of the British Empire, we now discover, dismayingly, how the historic setting of that jewel doesn't inspire the same self-congratulatory pride in some of those who are ruled as it does in the breasts of us, their rulers: a discovery uncomfortable, to say the least.

Babu, our well-meaning but incompetent bearer, has been given a ticket back to Bombay, and in his stead we have hired a small brisk middle-aged Indian recommended by the manager of the Tea Board's Calcutta office. It turns out to be a stroke of remarkably good fortune for us. Thoroughly versed in the English language, efficient, capable, and reassuringly pro-British, Dil, our new bearer, is a blessing beyond price.

With Dil to protect me, I may venture safely on foot through the crowded streets of the turbulent city to buy various necessities at one of the markets; and in a frightening incident during our shopping expedition he proves his true worth as my guardian by steering us neatly and swiftly out of danger when a man, his eyes blazing with hatred, confronts me, spitting words of venom: 'What are you doing in our country, Miss? – *go away*! You British are not wanted here – go! *Jao, jao*! –'

Shocked by such naked unprovoked hostility, I shrink from him in terror. Almost equally shocking, though, is the explanation a boy on the hotel's kitchen staff gives me of why, when he brings my tray of tea before breakfast, it's minus a jug of milk: 'Sorry, Memsahib, no milk today. Milkman, he killed, Memsahib – milkman *dead*.'

Business has to be done, and vital appointments kept with agents of Kodak, with the British Overseas Airways Corporation (BOAC), and the London Tea Board's represent-atives on this side of the world; but once all arrangements have been satisfactorily concluded we are free to quit Calcutta, and are only too thankful to be gone. Ralph, our leader and mainstay, is becoming increasingly fractious, worn down by the multiplying difficulties of simply getting the unit he commands to the place where it can start work on the film we have been sent these hundreds and hundreds of miles to shoot.

He is accustomed, in his position of authority, to decide on something, and then for that something to be put into opera-tion *forthwith*. But in India this is not, he finds, the way it happens. In India nothing can be relied upon: the rules are different, or they don't exist. In India there are unforeseen hitches, inexplicable delays; orders are countermanded. Officials either misinform or are themselves misinformed; they say yes, when what they really mean is no, and any deci-sion that's made can, five minutes afterwards, be unmade.

Once more aboard a train but this time travelling north, en route for Assam, our puffing, whistling engine grinds to a halt again and again throughout the night; rails have been torn up ahead and must be re-laid; twice the communication cord is pulled for no valid reason by irresponsible passen-gers. Next day the ferry boat, on which we are to cross the mighty Brahmaputra river, is so retarded we miss our express mail-train connection on the other side and have to make do with a crawling rickety local train.

Under the prolonged frustration and stress of our repeat-edly interrupted rail-journey Ralph is rapidly going to pieces.

We draw in, finally, at the station nearest to Nazira, our ultimate destination, twenty-four hours after what had been the estimated time of arrival, to be met by a Mr Davies, the tea-planter selected to take charge of and act as chaperone to the Greenpark film unit. This big bluff Englishman's jokes and smiles and hearty handshakes have the effect of immediately restoring Ralph's confidence: *Thank God! – an Englishman! Now we shall be all right!*

Phew! Not a moment too soon! It was a close call.

We are being housed in a single-storey solid whitewashed building, once a hospital, appropriated by a committee of Nazira's tea-planters and prepared especially to receive us. Equipped with a minimum of furniture, it has tiled floors, lofty ceilings, and spacious interconnecting rooms with no doors between them but instead, hanging in their arched entrances, flimsy cotton curtains: privacy is thus as minimal as the furniture. At the top of the thick stone exterior walls are round holes, through which birds fly freely in and out. After the cramped conditions endured on those long stuffy rail-journeys we are delighted with the cool and unconfining openness of this palatial bungalow, our new quarters, and christen it the Ritz.

The Assamese staff installed to serve Greenpark's visiting film unit consists of Peter, speechless but willing, whose worried expression reflects a state of permanent anxiety, and his helper Ali, similarly speechless. There is also a cheerful bright-eyed young boy shuffling about on misshapen crumpled feet, and somewhere in the background a kitchen contingent of numerous cooks and their family supporters, eager to conjure up meals for us at any hour of the day or night. Dil, to his great satisfaction, is accepted gladly by the whole troop of them as their otherwise missing, much needed interpreter and general officer-in-charge.

240

We explore our surroundings. Opposite the Ritz is the British clubhouse, complete with a drinks bar, a ping-pong table, and a shelf of dog-eared detective novels. Beyond the clubhouse is the village, where we see shopkeepers and craftsmen, all busily employed: a silversmith, a baker, tailors, quilt-makers. As we pass by, they raise their heads calling out greetings, nodding and laughing, displaying none of the animosity we had experienced in the streets of Calcutta. Beyond the village is the river, and beyond the river acres and acres of green fertile plains, tea-gardens mostly, we are told, spreading away and away to the foot of the Naga hills.

A short stretch of road leads from the Ritz in the other direction to the residence of Mr Flux, the Company's elderly stout warm-hearted chief local manager, known as the burra-sahib, and his motherly wife, who have the luxuries of a tennis court and a swimming pool in their grounds. This evening we are introduced by Mr Davies – ('Call me Cappie') – to these nice hospitable Fluxes, and amble back later, sleepily, rather tipsy, through swarms of fireflies, under a sky brilliant with stars, to what we already think of as *home*. Glory be! – we have arrived. We are here; at last, at last, we are actually *here!*

Ralph and Laurie are conducted on a tour of the outlying tea-gardens, where the plucking season is in full swing, and to the factory complex with its drying-sheds and packing-sheds. Together they plan a shooting schedule, and make lists of the information that will have to accompany it. Then, a couple of days on we all, with our cameras, pile into the back of an open truck called an ammo-carrier, and having crossed the river – a branch of the Brahmaputra – by ferry, set off to start shooting our first film. The idea, hatched by Laurie and Ralph, is afterwards – if we have enough time left, and enough reels of spare material – to create a second film by way of supplementing the Board's commissioned and strictly educational documentary: a lyrical account of the courtship and marriage of two tea-garden workers.

Mr Brooks – Brookie – a bachelor (most of the planters are married), is the manager of Lakmijan Garden on which, after a quick survey of other neighbouring gardens, Ralph decides the unit will focus its attention. During shooting sessions my job is to be the continuity girl. Evenings at home in the Ritz are spent by me typing out readable copies in triplicate of the day's continuity notes; typing, as well, Ralph's business letters, and the progress report sheets that keep our London office in regular touch with the unit's activities. Any minutes remaining, if I can only manage to stay awake, are devoted to pages and pages of compulsive scribbling in my diary: the record I need in order to retain and remember everything, every fleeting detail of this Indian odyssey.

Ralph torments himself, and us, with agonies of doubt over the best method of ensuring the safe delivery of our daily 'rushes' to Calcutta, from where they will be flown back to Merton Park Studios for processing, viewing, and, we sincerely hope, approval. Despite his neurotic forebodings, the arrangements, made in advance, operate flawlessly, and the film that has so far been shot does arrive in London and is acknowledged with enthusiasm. Whereupon Ralph, our lord and master, relaxes, and, much to our relief, resumes his normal mood of breezy ebullience.

We have learnt the difference between Nazira's villagers, indigenous Assamese inhabitants maintaining their own independent self-sufficient lives, and the families employed on the tea-gardens, a workforce of imported labour dwelling apart in what are designated the coolie-lines. And then in Suntok Market we encounter the Nagas, the hill people, head-hunters of old: small, sturdy, bold, inquisitive, laughing men and boys, quite unlike in manner or appearance either the Assamese or the tea-garden workers. Almost naked, or swathed in colourful shawls, with scarlet leaves thrust jauntily through their ears, they have descended from their forested heights to barter the *paan* they harvest in exchange for ducks and piglets, mingling amongst the plainsfolk with swaggering, slightly contemptuous good humour. Brookie promises that before we go, if we are prepared to tackle the precipitously steep arduous climb, he will organise for us a visit to one of their high secretive *chungs*.

We have taken innumerable shots of the bushes being stripped of their glossy leaves by women standing in rows and filling, with nimble fingers, the deep cone-shaped bamboo baskets tied on to their backs. Both at long-range and in close-up we photograph the deft two-handed plucking motion that doesn't pause except when the char-pani wallah comes padding towards them on his flat bare feet to quench their thirst with a cupful of water or weak tea. We photograph him too, the indispensable char-pani wallah and his heavy burden, a gallon-sized re-used petrol tin slung, bouncing and swinging, at either end of the bendy bamboo pole he balances across his shoulder.

We film scenes at the factory, and we film scenes at the railway station. But by far the most enjoyable location is when we camp down by the river, shooting a fictional sequence to provide the preface for our documentary: Cappie Davies and Mr Flux, poled upstream in dugout canoes, pretend they are pioneers inspecting the lay of the land and supervising tree-felling, an essential preliminary to establishing the Company's original tea plantation.

So enjoyable is it, more pleasure than work, that the following day we return to the same beautiful tranquil length of river, not to film, but to reward ourselves for the previous week's hard labour with an afternoon of total idleness, picnicking and bathing in a green and golden paradise, where the only sounds in the clear air are those made by birds, and running water, and our own voices calling out to one another.

Signs of a waning season, the sun losing its heat and the evenings beginning to grow chilly, mean that this is the last opportunity we shall have for such an indulgence. When I stroll back from the solitary dip I routinely take at six o'clock in the burra-sahib's swimming-pool, I notice that the fireflies have disappeared.

On 1st December Laurie Lee says goodbye to the rest of us and departs alone for England. We wave him off at the station. By now, driving to work in the ammo-carrier through early morning mists, we are muffled up in jerseys, and at night feel grateful for the warmth of the kerosene stoves that our conscientious Dil has had installed, one stove in each room of the Ritz.

We still have a few final shots to take or retake – the tea workers queuing for payment of their wages, and some further scenes of domestic life in the coolie-lines – but once Christmas is behind us, and our main picture securely in the bag, we shall be free, if enough time remains, to film the touching love story of two tea workers, boy and girl, their wooing and wedding on Brookie's Lakmijan Garden. The idea – taken up with enthusiasm by Ralph – of giving the London Tea Board an unsolicited poetical bonus, was originally Laurie's inspiration. He plans to write the accompanying script, and attach it to the footage that we will have shot, at home.

The 25th of December is celebrated by an invitation from Mr and Mrs Flux to a lavish *al fresco* luncheon party. Quantities of festive food and drink have been spread out on tables alongside the tennis court, where an impromptu tournament, hilarious and progressively lacking in sobriety, takes place.

We are already well-acquainted with our fellow guests. Every Monday is club-night, a top-priority ritual the scattered planters and their wives all, unless forcibly prevented, attend. The sudden invasion, we realise, of Nazira's little conventionally regulated social circle by a raffish bunch of film-makers, and our non-conformist behaviour, could understandably have caused offence; but instead they have exhibited an easy-going mixture of amusement and curiosity, and a remarkable tolerance in forgiving us for breaking taboos of which we are plainly ignorant. I've earned the distinction, I'm told, of being dubbed 'jungly' for my habit of waving from our open truck at children in the road as we hurtle past them: waving at coolie children is absolutely beyond the pale, and the sort of thing only film people would do.

Today the whole British community is present, its widely dispersed members coming together as though to an unmissable family reunion; a show of solidarity, on the Fluxes' front lawn. 'It's a tradition,' Cappie Davies informs us, '– the burra-sahib's Christmas Day tennis party. A *tradition*,' he repeats again and again, with solemn emphasis, nodding.

Surely, I think, the tradition must have been suspended during the war – wasn't it? I think this, but I don't say what I'm thinking aloud because the war is a subject never mentioned here. Nobody ever *ever* speaks of the war: it might never have happened. The club-nights, the tennis and tea parties and sherry parties, are exactly the same, it would seem, as they were in the thirties; as if there hadn't been years of desperate bloody interruption.

At first this struck me as extremely odd, almost uncanny, considering that Nazira is practically on the borders of Burma, and the war so recent. But in London, too, nobody

245

talked of the war. And I remind myself of those days in the Meditteranean, aboard the *Andes*. Was I haunted, when cruising off the coast of Africa, by ghosts of the Libyan Campaign, of Mussolini, and Montgomery, and Rommel? No, I was not. I had my mind entirely fixed on the joys of sipping freshly squeezed orange juice and of dancing under a full moon on F. Deck. So who am I, Emma Smith, to throw stones at the glasshouses of tea-planters and their gossipy wives? The fact is, I suppose, human nature tends to forget what was unpleasant and is past: what it doesn't want to remember.

Returning from the Fluxes' jollifications we find that Dil and the staff at the Ritz have most touchingly prepared a further Christmas banquet for us, in appreciation of which Ralph dons a dinner jacket and bow tie, and I put on my long red crêpe evening dress. We raise our glasses and toast each other, and drink to our futures, and to the success of our films.

And that is how we four, myself and Ralph, and George and Teddy, have been spending the 25th of December, 1946, here in Nazira, Assam.

While staying with our friend, Brookie, in his Lakmijan bungalow we are taken by him to select from among the coolie-lines a young newly married couple who will be suitable to play the leading roles in our second film, and after some searching we have the good luck to discover Ramdas and his pretty wife, Mangri. Both of them, besides being charmingly photogenic, are highly intelligent, able and willing, with a natural poise and the confidence of professionals, to re-enact for us the days of their courtship and marriage.

We film Ramdas, once he has been accepted by Mangri's parents as her suitor, bringing her a necklace of beads, and other tokens of affection and esteem. We film Mangri, her silver bangles and earrings glinting in the sunshine, plucking leaves from the tea bushes, walking lightly, gracefully across a fragile bamboo bridge with a brass pot on her head, and hiding her face in the folds of her sari during the negotiations between Ramdas and her family regarding the marriage settlement. We photograph Ramdas beginning to construct a thatched hut on the plot of ground that Mangri's father agrees to give him; and as soon as the set, representing their new home, is established, I have the pleasureable task of furnishing it, finding such props as will lend a sufficient air of authenticity to the three-sided interior: tools and baskets, cooking utensils, a wooden-framed string-mesh bed.

And so eventually we reach the crowning scene of the ceremonial wedding. Resplendent in their bridal finery, the young couple, dignified and serious, go through the motions of becoming what they already actually are – man and wife. As always whenever the cameras are positioned, a fascinated crowd of spectators encircles us, the adults watching, spell-bound, in silence, the children chattering excitedly. It is Ramdas, by now an old hand at the game and with the authority of a seasoned performer, who hushes them sternly.

Darkness falls. Yet still the celebrations continue, on and on into the starlit, floodlit night, until finally, after bowing farewell to the assembled company, Ramdas and Mangri enter, hand-in-hand, their make-believe home, and shut the door. It's finished, over: the matrimonial drama concluded. Our floodlights are switched off, the flames of the fire inside the hut extinguished, the hut itself dismantled swiftly, and the props I had found and arranged with so much care either returned to their owners or else distributed as gifts to our cast of extras.

But then, standing alone in the dark on the deserted site, I am surprised – absurdly – by a sneaking wistful, quite irra-tional regret that the cosy little hut, which for several hours

247

had had the convincing appearance of a real home, welcoming, permanent, was just a pretence. How sad it suddenly seems: nothing lasts. The brilliant flickering moment passes, and is gone for ever: *Cut*!

With our mission for the Tea Board completed, here we are now, once more in Calcutta, en route for England, and staying at the Grand Hotel off Chowringee while organising our return journey, which will be by air and not, as we came, by sea.

Before we left Nazira Brookie had fulfilled his promise to take us on a day's climbing expedition to visit, somewhere high in the thickly forested hills, a Naga *chung*. George and Teddy, not wishing to make so strenuous an effort, declined his offer, but Ralph and I spent a desperate morning panting and puffing and scrambling for footholds up a path incredibly steep, half-hidden between impenetrable walls of vegetation, from which we emerged, exhausted but triumphant, into an open clearing on top of the world.

Greeted hospitably by the Nagas with the same faintly derisive amusement we remembered previously encountering in Suntok Market (they are brimful of teasing laughter), we were invited into one of their bamboo and palm-leaf houses. The *chung*, or village, was strung out along either side of a narrow ridge like a backbone, the entrance to each dwelling being consequently at ground-level, but leading through to a worryingly flimsy balcony propped on stilts over a precipitous drop, with a view of mountainous jungle stretching away and away to infinite distances.

We were also allowed to inspect an extensive dormitory-hut which constituted the sleeping quarters of their young unmarried sons and daughters. An immense tree-trunk, laid horizontally, marked the centre and provided the only division – strictly observed, we were told – that separated the young men from the girls. Everything we saw was very clean, very orderly, very disciplined, and the air at that height was exhilaratingly pure. I thought it well worth the uphill struggle of our ascent, and the subsequent almost equally difficult downhill slither, to have had this glimpse of where and how the Nagas live. They struck me as being a people robustly independent, and entirely different from their nearest neighbours, the Assamese inhabitants of the plains below.

On our last evening in an eerily empty Ritz, having our bags packed and piled, ready for early departure, we gave, as a gesture of gratitude, a goodbye drinks party, wanting thereby to express our thanks to the dear old burra-sahib and his wife, and Brookie and Cappie Davies, and the doctor, and all the tea-planters who, during the past few months of our invasion, have helped and entertained the Greenpark film unit. It was a huge success, punctuated by spontaneous bursts of song and sentimental speeches, and even some attempt at dancing, and everyone staying on until after midnight.

Now, in Calcutta, Teddy and George are consumed by impatience to get home. They have had enough of India, and are not inclined to linger for a minute beyond what is absolutely necessary. But Ralph has decided, prompted perhaps by the success of our Naga excursion, to occupy the time he has left at his disposal in travelling north to Darjeeling, from which vantage point there will be visible the magnificent snow-capped Himalayas, highest of all mountain ranges on the planet; and why don't I, he casually suggests, go with him?

With one further week to spare, the possibility had occurred to me of boarding a train for Delhi, and calling upon Sir Maurice Gwyer, my mother's acquaintance, to whose generosity and sponsorship I owe, indirectly, the circumstance of being where I am today. Delhi is the capital of India, and Sir Maurice is Lord Chief Justice of the whole British sub-continent, a position of unrivalled prestige, not to say grandeur, so it would undoubtedly be a memorable experience. But so too would seeing with my own eyes the fabulous Himalayas. Either is a once-in-a-lifetime chance, and I can't have both. Again, it's a matter of choice: Delhi or Darjeeling – which? I choose Darjeeling.

At least we don't have to scramble on foot up to the heights of Darjeeling, but instead can negotiate the sickeningly dizzy hairpin bends from the railway station in a taxi. Darjeeling is where for more than a century army officers and senior civil service officials have dispatched their womenfolk, and joined them when they could, so as to escape the stifling heat of the plains in summer.

Being out-of-season the windows of the many guest houses are tightly shuttered for winter, but we manage to secure lodgings with a Mrs McNab who opens her small claustrophobic rooms especially to accommodate us. These rooms contain, surprisingly, no hint of their situation on the map, no Oriental distractions of any kind: all the items of furniture, the carpets and curtains and antimacassars, could have been – and very possibly were – transported to Darjeeling directly from the damp Highlands of Scotland. Sepia Victorian prints of antlered stags and shaggy Scottish cattle adorn the walls. We wonder if the rest of the boarding houses are similarly dedicated as shrines of nostalgia to comfort the British in exile.

Outside our breath steams on the freezing air. The stillness is remarkable, almost uncanny. There is no wind. We gaze down from above on birds, eagles or kites, wheeling beneath us in leisurely circles; and individual sounds carrying clearly across great distances, like the rythmic thud, thud of an axe wielded by an unseen man at work on the other side of the valley, serve only to emphasise, not break, the vast empty silence.

Native-born residents, brown-skinned and rosy-cheeked, and encased from head to foot in quilted garments, toil through the steep tangle of lanes, leaning forward under heavy loads held in place on their backs by a leather strap around their foreheads. Or, occasionally, they clatter past us on sturdy little ponies; but when the hooves have gone, silence at once returns, just as water closes over the surface of a pool disturbed by a pebble dropped into it.

The impression I have is of our being suspended in a state of curious timeless unreality, halfway to heaven. And appearing as a sort of dream-image from beyond invisible borders of India, Sikkim, Nepal – seeming now near, sharply delineated, now remote and wreathed in cloud, but a presence forever *there* – are the peaks of the Snowy Range, the mighty Himalayas.

We stay three days in Darjeeling before setting off towards, at last, England. I have begun to feel ill, but tell myself the symptoms are those of a feverish cold, and try to ignore them. After stopping overnight in Karachi for our aeroplane to re-fuel, we land at Heathrow on 14th February in a snow-storm. More and more unwell, I part company with Ralph and hasten to reach the sanctuary of Holcombe, my mother's picture-postcard village in Devonshire, where Dr Courtenay diagnoses me as suffering from an acute attack of jaundice.

Convalescing from jaundice in my mother's cottage, with her doing duty as my devoted nurse, I decide – reluctantly, because my enthusiasm for documentary films is undiminished – that I have to find a different job.

Throughout the Indian campaign Ralph – or Bunny, which is what he has now reverted to being for me – did honour the terms of the bargain we had agreed upon in the summer, keeping his distance and treating me formally as, and only as, a member of our team (although the open-plan design of Nazira's ex-hospital where the unit was housed meant he had really no alternative).

In Darjeeling, however, he made it clear that the bargain we had struck was a mere convenience, a temporary expedient, and that when we returned to London I would automatically take up my former position of being *his girl* – of course I would! Look how satisfactorily we were getting along together nowadays, how suited we were as a couple! That ultimatum of mine was utter nonsense, the whim of a moment. India had proved it!

And to a certain extent he was right: India has indeed changed our attitudes to one another. During those months abroad we've developed the mutual respect that arises from a good working relationship. He no longer regards me as a fringe benefit of dubious worth, and I've grown to be genuinely more and more fond of Bunny, replacing what was my original dazzle of infatuation with an enduring depth of real affection. But I still don't care for his friends (hateful Dick Wyndham in particular), or his lifestyle, and the wide gap of our ages is an obstacle I have come to consider insurmountable.

Time rushes past at such a terrifying speed. Always I am aware, vividly, anxiously, of its rapid flight, and of how quickly – far too quickly – I'm getting older. But Bunny also is getting older; is already, actually, I can't help feeling, too old.

The inflexibility of my refusal to be *his girl* has got to be demonstrated, I resolve unhappily, by the sacrifice of bringing to an end my employment in Greenpark Productions. Yet again it's a choice: this or that; it can't be both.

I type an official letter, tendering my resignation, and enclose with it a personal brief handwritten note to Bunny saying '*sorry*'. Then I walk soberly, sadly up the hill and post it in the letterbox at the top. There! – it's done. I've burnt my boats. The question is – what now?

My sister Pam has taken over the room I once occupied in No. 7, Markham Square, the Blakistons' Chelsea house. Having no job I am unable to pay them the rent of thirty shillings a week, but I've been lucky enough to find lodgings with Biddy Cook a few miles off in Redcliffe Road, Fulham. Treated by Biddy, my generous former Greenpark colleague, more as a friend than a lodger, I give her, when I can, what money I can: which isn't often, and isn't ever very much.

Biddy, in my hour of need, is a loyal supporter, sustaining me, not only with free meals, and snippets of gossip brought back from the office we used to share, and suggestions and introductions helpful to my increasingly desperate search for work, but also with a contribution of even greater value: unequivocal encouragement. I have wanted, always wanted, to write, and Biddy buoys up my sinking confidence by her firm belief in my belief: the hope I cling to through thick and thin that I shall succeed, eventually, in making a career for myself as a professional writer.

Thanks to John Sommerfield, who staunchly, as well, supports my literary ambition, several short stories of mine have been published. But the payment by magazines for short stories is pitiful – miniscule – and while they may earn me a moment of glory, they will never earn me a living.

The closest I get to any sort of reliable wage is an occasional commission from Henry Cass, producer of feature films for ABC. My assignment consists of reading some novel or other and then synopsising the storyline, adding my personal evaluation of its filmic possibilities.

Anything being better than nothing, I try conscientiously to obey instructions; and fail dismally. When I submit a condensed version of Trollope's *The Eustace Diamonds*, and highly recommend it, Henry, scathing in his blunt rejection of the book, says it's out of date and a thorough bore. And when I dismiss the latest best-selling popular romance, *Forever Amber*, as a disgusting rubbishy bedroom romp, verging on pornography, he derides my poor judgement and ridicules my ignorance of the all-important tastes of cinema's ticket-buying customers.

'Darling,' says Henry, calling me what he calls everyone because it's a lot simpler than trying to remember names, 'darling, you are *so* wrong! *Forever Amber* is the ready-made script of a marvellous film – a winner – just asking to be screened –'

Plainly I am quite unfit to discover suitable stories for ABC. But I have to earn money, and what's more, to earn it soon; and who else will employ me? All I'm really good at is typing, and although I don't want to be merely a typist for the rest of my life, I lack other qualifications, and in the after-math of war, with such masses of people demobilised and jostling for work, any alternative seems tantalisingly out of reach; even typing posts aren't easy to come by.

Yesterday I met a friend of Biddy's, David Pearce, an engineer just back from Bremen, where he had been inspecting German tanks as a final job for the Ministry of Defence before the British Government dispenses with his services. Now he has to find, somehow, somewhere, a civilian engineering job, and the field, he tells me, is crowded.

Biddy has often spoken of David. He was her mother's lodger in Bristol during the war. Because of him having a first-class Cambridge degree, he was kept out of the Armed Forces and directed instead into what was called a reserved occupation; to do with, I think, aeroplane engines.

Extremely handsome, as well as unassuming and altogether likeable, I should be tempted to try my luck at capturing this beautiful smiling young man for myself if it weren't that the state of my entanglement with Bunny Keene (who lives dangerously close to Biddy Cook's Fulham address) remains worryingly inconclusive. The next best thing to pursuing lovely David on my own account is to introduce him to my sister Pam: an altruistic gesture rewarded by immediate success. But the bond they at once establish, while gratifying for its promoter, doesn't help me towards hitting on a much needed solution to my ever worsening problems.

I'm beginning to despair when, one Saturday afternoon, Claude Geoffroy-Dechaume, a jeweller by trade and another of Biddy's innumerable friends, happening to be up in London on a business trip, drops in at Redcliffe Road for a cup of tea and a convivial chat. As a Frenchman who has temporarily exiled himself to Surrey, he describes with nostalgia the Geoffroys' family home in Valmondois, a village to the north of Paris, where his mother and two of his brothers and a sister are still living. And he goes on to mention the nearby abandoned and semi-derelict old chateau they have recently acquired, in the hope of generating an income by filling it with affluent foreign students: a bold but, Claude fears, a decidedly risky venture. What they don't have, he says, and urgently need is somebody willing, in return for free board and lodging, to make the beds and clean the rooms and give these foreign students their breakfasts.

The message I'm receiving, loud and clear, is heaven-sent; a message, long awaited, bringing salvation. That *somebody*, spoken about so casually by Claude Geoffroy-Dechaume over Biddy's teacups, I instantly perceive to be myself.

Exactly a week later I'm ascending the gangplank of a cross-Channel ferry at Newhaven on my way to France, in the company of a certain Margaret Minns and the little French girl she's escorting. They too are en route for Valmondois. Antoinette, daughter of Antoine, eldest of the five Geoffroy-Dechaume brothers, is being restored to the care of her father having spent a holiday at the Hampstead home of Mr and Mrs Minns.

I was driven down to Newhaven from London by Bunny in the magnificent gleaming Rolls-Royce – a status-symbol to beat all status-symbols, and his most prized possession. On the quayside he asks me how much money I'm taking with me to France. I tell him: four pounds and ten shillings, which, after covering the cost of my sea passage, is all that remains of my meagre savings.

'It's not enough,' says Bunny, sounding irritated; '– not nearly enough. Good heavens! You ought to have more than that for a trip abroad.'

When I mumble, ashamedly, that this represents the sum total of my current finances, he first extracts from his wallet five one pound notes, and then digs about in various pockets and pours into my cupped hands a stream of loose change: half-crowns, florins, sixpenny pieces, threepenny bits – riches! I don't deserve such kindness.

Bunny, having failed to argue me out of what he describes as my latest idiotic fad, has come round to giving the scheme his grudging approval: a month or two of living in a strange country with a family of strangers, cut off from my own family and friends and obliged to fend for myself, might even, he's decided, be just the ticket – do the trick – bring me to my senses.

'Who was that handsome man,' inquires Margaret Minns, 'waving goodbye to you?'

'Oh – him. He's Ralph Keene, someone I used to work for,' I reply, confused and upset by a sudden surprising inclination to weep. Dear kind old Bunny! What am I doing, casting myself ungratefully adrift from the safety of his protection and trusting instead to the doubtful mercy of unknown foreigners? But it's too late for regrets. To deal with this enfeebling mood of tearfulness I explore the ship, and at the purser's office translate my English money into francs, a practical and thus an emotionally stabilising act. Then, standing on deck leaning over the rail and gazing ahead, with the wind in my hair and miles and miles of sea, nothing but sea in sight, I am overwhelmed by a surge, not of tears, but of excitement. It's an adventure I've embarked upon! I'm going to France – to *la belle France* – and everything, I tell myself, will be *all right*!

Thankfully, there is no need for me to worry about the intricacies of getting through the Customs at Dieppe, and then by train to Paris, and from Paris on by another train at the Gare du Nord to Pointoise. With Margaret Minns as my guiding light, I have only to follow and imitate her; although, by the time we reach Pointoise, darkness has fallen and I am exhausted.

Here, waiting for us on the station platform, is Antoine Geoffroy-Dechaume. Antoinette flies into her father's arms: '*Papa, papa –*' He embraces her, while simultaneously greeting Margaret, an old friend of his. When introduced to me, Antoine asks, in polite impeccable English, only very slightly accented, if I speak French.

'*Un très petit peu*,' I reply, modestly, but with the confidence of remembering my long ago School Certificate exam papers, and the credit I was awarded for proficiency in the French language.

Antoine corrects me: '*Un* tout *petit peu*,' he says. I am mortified. These are the first words I've spoken in French on French soil, and they are wrong – oh, how shaming!

We squeeze ourselves and our luggage into Antoine's dilapidated small car, and I, sitting on the back seat with

Margaret, doze off, lulled asleep by Antoinette's excited unintelligible chatter to her father in front.

Margaret is shaking my shoulder: 'Emma – wake up! We've arrived –'

Arrived? Arrived where? I stagger out of the car and into a house, into a room crowded with a blur of unfamiliar people, a blur of loud voices and laughter. Somebody hands me a plateful of food, and a drink of some sort, but all I yearn for is to lie down in a corner and be allowed to drop asleep again.

A tall young man, crowned by a crop of curly fair hair, rescues me from the desperate struggle I'm having to keep awake. He is, he informs me, Denis Geoffroy-Dechaume. Speaking English quite as well, or even better than his older brother, Antoine, he says, very cheerful and smiling: 'How do you do, Emma Smith – welcome to Valmondois.' I nod at him, dumbly, incapable of speech. Whereupon this nice understanding young Frenchman offers to conduct me, now if I want, immediately, to my apartment in the chateau.

Together we go out into the starry night, Denis carrying my bag, across a courtyard and up a flight of steep steps that lead us to what seems to be a steeply sloping vegetable garden. At the top of the garden a door set in the boundary wall opens on to a hill, similarly steep, and so rough underfoot I stumble. Denis takes hold of my arm to steady me. A few yards further, and all at once we are facing the chateau: a great grey square ghostly block of a building.

Obediently I climb the wide shallow staircase following my guide, turning right and stopping when he stops. 'This is your room, Emma,' he tells me. 'The W.C. is at the end of the passage –'

Despite my muzzy state I recognise the French pronunciation – *doobler-vay-say* – of those two letters in the alphabet, and their meaning. '*Merci*,' I venture, wanting to express my gratitude and appreciation for his helpfulness. I can't go wrong with *merci* – can I? '*Merci beaucoup.*'

'*Ah – mais non!*' Denis is laughing at me; not, though, unkindly. '*C'est à moi de vous remercier. Alors! Je vous souhaite une bonne nuit* – a good night's rest – yes? And we will meet again tomorrow. *À demain*, Emma.' And he leaves me.

The room I find myself alone in – my room – illuminated by a single dangling electric bulb, has a high ceiling and a window reaching almost the whole length from ceiling to floor. The window has shutters, half-closed, but no curtains. The floor is uncarpeted. A chair, a table and a bed are the only, but to my mind the quite sufficient, items of furniture: all I want, for the moment, is the bed.

How long have I been living in Valmondois? – I forget how long. I think this is a summer that will never end, a golden summer of unbroken heat and unclouded blue skies and sunshine: timeless. Day succeeds day, each as calm and blissful as the day that went before it.

My duties are not arduous. Every morning, early, I run down to the village, collect a supply of baguettes and croissants from the boulangerie, call in at the house for a can of milk placed ready for me on the kitchen table and hurry back uphill, laden, to prepare the coffee, and then rouse the students: English Charles and Swedish Jay and American Sally. We are joined for breakfast, a leisurely meal, by the two youngest Geoffroy sons, Jean-Pierre and Denis, who have also taken up residence in the recently acquired, airily empty chateau. When breakfast is over, and the students dispersed, I am free to occupy the tranquil hours lying ahead according to whatever I may be asked, or choose to do.

Sylvie, youngest of the ten Geoffroy children and approximately my age, lives with her widowed mother in the family home that borders, and opens directly on to the village street. Sometimes I help her in the kitchen, rinsing and chopping vegetables for the supper we will all of us later share, eating outside in the candlelit courtyard. On one occasion, our task having been completed and the last onion sliced, we reward ourselves by going for a swim, a cooling dip in the nearby river; and we've twice walked, she and I, the few dusty kilometres of country road from Valmondois to the local market in L'Isle Adam.

But whenever Sylvie doesn't require me, I offer my services instead to Denis and Jean-Pierre as fellow labourer on an ambitious project they've undertaken to transform the chateau's big stone adjacent barn into a theatre. Their aim, they tell me, is to create, as well as a much-needed source of income, a cultural centre where the performance of classical dramas and concerts will undoubtedly entice wealthy and discriminating audiences from miles around.

This, at any rate, is their hopeful proclaimed intention, although it must be admitted we don't apply ourselves very seriously to the business in hand. Midway through each hot sunshiny morning, a halt is called. We drop our tools and chase downhill to the village bistro for *un petit coup de vin blanc*: a treat I insist upon paying for out of the francs I stocked up with during the ferry trip over from England. Could there be any more enjoyable way to spend my nest-egg than on this delightfully idle daily indulgence?

We have such fun together, we three, lounging on the pavement, smoking pungent wispy Gauloises Bleu cigarettes (infinitely preferable, I consider, to English Woodbines), clinking our glasses, laughing. We laugh and laugh. The fun – the exuberant careless youthful comradeship – is exactly what I had missed and hankered after in London.

Increasingly, however, I am aware of a problem developing. The fact is, I have fallen head over heels in love, as I

260

begin to realise, with Jean-Pierre *and* with Denis: with both of them – an impossible situation. But how could it be otherwise? Both brothers are heroes of the French Resistance, bravest of the brave, young men who hid up in the hills and fought alongside the gallant Maquis, and by their indomitable courage saved the whole world from wicked German fascism. I am bound – am I not? – to adore them both.

My dilemma is, quite simply, solved one afternoon by Jean-Pierre: it is he who kisses me. There! – that settles it! I shall continue, of course, to love Denis, but from now on platonically, as a very dear brother.

What happiness! I am so happy – so happy! Jean-Pierre is the Prince I had always expected, always *knew* would one day appear over the horizon. Here he is!

Because the language most generally spoken in my hearing – except by Madame Geoffroy-Dechaume – is English, I've picked up scarcely more, unfortunately, than a smattering of French since I've been here. But having learnt a number of useful phrases by heart (*un petit coup de vin blanc*, for example), with a fair imitation of the correct accent, I can sometimes amuse myself by pretending to be a far better linguist than I really am. If I'm close to the house telephone when it rings, and a voice asks for, say, Denis, I'm able to rattle off, parrot-wise: *Il n'est pas ici à ce moment, Monsieur, mais ne quittez pas l'appareil – je vais le chercher.*'

And when, our supper finished, we remain sitting, a dozen or perhaps a score of us, round the long table in the courtyard, reluctant to move, and Madame Geoffroy, stout and elderly, modest and shy, is persuaded to sing, I can understand perfectly well, and shall remember always, the words of the beautiful hauntingly sad folk-ballads: '*Le Roi a Fait Battre Tambour*'; and another favourite: '*À La Claire Fontaine*'.

Of all my 1947 summer memories one of the most poignant will surely be the recollection of warm still evenings when the candle-flames hardly flicker, and the air is filled by the scent of roses clustering in profusion on the surrounding courtyard walls; and Madame Geoffroy lifts her chin, and closes her eyes, and her true sweet voice ascends without a quaver, floating up, up into the starry skies above: '*Il y a longtemps que je t'aime/ Jamais je ne t'oublerais . . .*'

Throughout the sweltering months of June, July, August there is a continual coming and going, often unexpected, always welcome, of visitors to Valmondois. Some of them are old friends from abroad, eager to renew the ties disrupted by years of intervening war. Some are members of the extensive Geoffroy-Dechaume clan, birds of passage pausing briefly on their way elsewhere. Amongst these last is Marie-France and her husband, Dermod MacCarthy, a British paediatrician whose father is the eminent writer, Desmond MacCarthy. Newly married, they are travelling back to England after their honeymoon. Marie-France, fourth of the five sisters, was decorated by General de Gaulle with the Croix de Guerre, equivalent of our V.C., and the Medaille de la Résistance for her heroism in the French Resistance. I watch from a discreet distance – not as an outsider, but as a sympathetic interested observer – the meetings and greetings, the joyous reunions. How could I feel an outsider when I have the private happiness of knowing I am Jean-Pierre's beloved, and therefore practically a Geoffroy myself?

Antoine, eldest of the brothers, also fought with the Resistance, though, unlike Denis and Jean-Pierre, he was captured by the Gestapo, imprisoned and tortured. A musician, dedicated to playing the harpsichord, Antoine lives in Paris and we seldom see him at Valmondois. Consequently François, second in the fraternal hierarchy, has assumed

Antoine's role as head of the family and the responsibilities that go with it.

While hospitality is never refused to the guests who turn up – frequently unannounced and always hungry – the vegetables that Sylvie and I so industriously chop and slice are wholly inadequate to satisfy their appetites; but any possibly resulting embarassment is avoided by François' ingenious method of concealing the deficiency.

François too lives in Paris, and being a career diplomat receives, presumably, a considerable salary, enabling him to drive down late every afternoon bringing with him tray-loads of sophisticated dishes, cooked in advance, with which to augment the basic and not very plentiful food obtainable locally, besides relieving the strain on household finances. As an emergency measure his extra provisions are invaluable, but they cease to be absolutely vital when, week by week, fewer and fewer visitors, and finally none, arrive in Valmondois.

For the summer I had believed would never end, is ending; is imperceptibly merging into autumn. Gradually the days are losing their heat, evenings grow chillier; fallen rose-petals litter the courtyard's flagstones. The students have packed their bags and departed to register at the start of their various university terms. Even Denis has gone. Intent on learning an agreeable and remunerative trade, he has apprenticed himself to a Parisian printer. Now Jean-Pierre and I are the only inhabitants of the hilltop chateau. After such constant society it might be thought we should find our isolation dull by contrast, but we have each other and having each other is company enough.

Then one Friday evening François, immediately on arrival from Paris, brusquely bids me report to him in what he calls his bureau – his office. He doesn't say why, but because we are all, including Madame Geoffroy, his mother, somewhat intimidated by François, I have to steel myself for the interview. He has always, I know, viewed me with displeasure, tinged by suspicion. He thinks I'm a raffish interloper, a little Miss Nobody who, without any supporting credentials, represents a threat to the prestige of his distinguished family. Too bad! – François is going to have to get used to the fact that, like it or not, I'm here to stay.

Detecting an attempt of Jean-Pierre's to sneak off unobtrusively, I grab hold of his belt and lug him with me, despite his manifest unwillingness. There's no point in our postponing it further: this is the crucial moment to announce that we are a pair, and that nothing and nobody in future can divide us.

But before I've managed to utter a single word, François speaks, informing me, coldly and clearly, that it's time I left: high time, indeed. The purpose of my being here – to look after the students in the chateau – no longer exists, and the Geoffroy-Dechaumes can't afford, he says, the continued expense of having to feed another mouth for no good reason.

Another mouth? Is that all I am? *For no good reason*? Why doesn't Jean-Pierre say something? *Tell* him? I turn round, and Jean-Pierre isn't where he was, behind me. I'm on my own, alone. Alone! And it's then the dreadful truth hits me with the shattering force of an explosion.

I've made a mistake, a horrible humiliating mistake. I am not Jean-Pierre's beloved, as I had believed I was, and as he is mine. I was never more than just his summer girl, and the summer is over. How could I have been so stupid, so blind – so *deaf*? Was I not warned by the song Madame Geoffroy sang? *Adieu, ma mie, adieu, mon coeur/ Adieu mon espérance* . . . Didn't I hear the warning, understand it was meant for me? No, in my silly happiness, I didn't.

Séparons-nous d'ensemble . . .

* * *

264

I am in Paris, having been rescued by Elisabeth, née Geoffroy-Dechaume, and given shelter in the attic room of the apartment-block flat where she lives with Paul, her husband, and their three little girls.

For Elisabeth, seen at Valmondois as rarely as Antoine, to have been there on that awful occasion was not, I'm convinced, coincidental. She must have had prior knowledge of the axe that was about to fall on me, and had come especially so as to soften the blow and be able to carry me off directly afterwards by train without a moment's unnecessary delay. Her intuitive kindness and prompt action spared me the ordeal of having to sit through supper with everyone at the table aware of my shame. Everyone, I'm certain, on reflection, did know before it happened that I was going to have to be got rid of by François – knew of my impending ignominious dismissal. The only person who didn't know of it was me.

Good kind Elisabeth is upset and indignant on my behalf, strongly criticising her brother François to Paul for what she describes as the undeserved brutality of his ultimatum. But I argue in defence of François, maintaining that he had right on his side and was fully justified; that I, not he, was in the wrong. Having plainly outstayed my welcome and my usefulness, I should have had the common sense to go sooner, and François was bound, in the interests of his family, to tell me so. I don't blame him, I say to Elisabeth – not *at all*. And indeed, I don't.

Regarding Jean-Pierre, though, I am silent; my heart is too sore to mention his name. But in the solitude of my small bedroom under the tiles I force myself to admit the culpable naivity of my error. How could I have failed to perceive that what for me had been the classic romantic happy ending portrayed in countless novels and films, for Jean-Pierre was neither more nor less than a frivolous delightful summer flirtation? It was my fault entirely; not his. He had made me no promises, never said he loved me, never deceived me. The fault was mine alone, and mine alone the penalty of heartbreak.

Grateful as I am to Paul and Elisabeth for their hospitable kindness and consideration – and I am deeply grateful – it's their three charmingly pretty little daughters, Isabelle, Marie-Christine and Lucile, who by their affectionate companionship provide, unwittingly, balm for my wounds. Every morning I help them to wash and dress; I brush and braid their long fair hair, escort them to school, and fetch them away when lessons are over. We spend our afternoons in the lovely neighbouring Jardins du Luxembourg amongst the many statues and sparkling fountains, the close-clipped lawns and gravel paths where nursemaids push babies in prams, and dogs gambol, barking, and children bowl their hoops and sail toy boats on the ponds. In the mild autumn sunshine we four play games of hide-and-seek and skipping with a rope, of hopscotch, and throwing and catching a ball, until the light begins to fade, when we walk hand-in-hand homewards, to our evening meal.

For me it allows a blessed breathing-space wherein to repair my battered self-esteem. But it can't, I realise, last; it's only a stop-gap. Winter is approaching and I have to decide what move to make and what I must do next.

Then, astonishingly, I receive a letter forwarded on to me from London, written by someone called Phoebe Prince of Messrs Curtis Brown, the literary agents. Her attention has been caught, she informs me, by a story of mine printed in a magazine, *Modern Reading*, using material gained by my Grand Union Canal wartime experiences. If, says Phoebe Prince, I can complete a full-length book on the same subject, she thinks it probable a publisher could be found for it.

The letter is nothing short of miraculous: an answer once

again, to prayer. Can I complete a full-length book dealing with life on a canal? Why, of course I can! In a trice I've embraced dear Paul and Elisabeth, hugged and kissed the three little girls, and got myself aboard a cross-Channel ferry from Dieppe to Newhaven, en route for the ever-open door and sanctuary of my mother's cottage in Devon and salvation in the shape of my portable typewriter.

I'm going to have to learn a new technique. So far I've written and had published only short stories, but the discipline of brevity won't at all do for a full-length book. Or will it, I wonder? Luckily, the three weeks of a round trip on the GUC presents a shape already structured and moving forwards: a beginning, a middle, and an end; and if I describe a typical journey it could, perhaps, be treated almost as a sequence of separate short stories, with a chapter for each day, strung together to form a continuous account. Such a plan strikes me as being both feasible and within my capabilities. Worth, at any rate, a try.

During the two years I was working on the canal I kept no diary, but I remember vividly the countryside, the docks, the wharves and cranes, the boating families and the London bargemen, the seasons, the weather, what we wore and ate and did and endured. It was the 'we' that varied. In those two years the girls who were with me on the boats kept changing. Different girls bicycled along the towpath, windlasses tucked into their belts, to make ready the next flight of locks; different girls ran acrobatically from stern to bows on the top-planks, clothed-up the cargoes, let go the boats at first light, shafted us off the mud, tied us up to bollards or iron rings or trees at nightfall. That's where the difference was from trip to trip: in different girls.

Besides, therefore, cramming into the time-frame of one journey the scenes and events that, although real enough, had involved an assortment of girls over a period of many months, I must also invent for the book a couple of young women to be my unvarying companions, my regular crew. Actually, the idea of incorporating an element of fiction, and the freedom of imagination it will allow, into the hard grist of fact, rather appeals to me. And with the aim of avoiding a wearisomely intrusive repetition of the first person, I've decided to refer to myself throughout the narrative as 'Emma'. Will the device of combining 'Emma' with 'us' be annoying for a reader – too unusual, too odd? Perhaps, but I'll chance it.

My small St Bernard's Cottage bedroom upstairs is where, every morning after breakfast, I shut the door and settle down to write. The table I work at is by the window. Whenever I raise my head I see a field full of Mr Rowe's placid cows on the opposite side of Holcombe's narrow valley; whenever I lower it I see instead the lock-gates opening, hear the chug-chug of approaching boats.

Careful not to interrupt, at eleven o' clock my dear devoted mother tiptoes in behind me, and having silently put a mug of tea and a slice of cake on a plate by my typewriter, tiptoes out again. She knows that later, when we've had our supper, I shall read aloud to her the typed pages, needing, and sure of getting, her unstinted approval.

The weeks fly past. The pages accumulate. It's Christmas, and Harvey arrives home on holiday from Sherborne College, his boarding school. Unlike my mother, who only ever praises, he is a critical listener. But Harvey's passion for the stage, and the plays of our leading English dramatists, has given him, my schoolboy brother, a discernment beyond his years, so that I appreciate his comments, and take due note of his opinions.

When the first few chapters of my canal saga have been corrected and rendered into neat orderly typescript, I post them off to Phoebe Prince of Messrs Curtis Brown, the literary agents: a sample, as agreed, of what's in the pipeline. And Phoebe Prince responds almost at once with a letter saying that the publisher she had predicted might be interested, a Mr Herbert van Thal, *is* interested; and that he is prepared, furthermore, on the strength of what I've already written, to offer me a contract.

A contract! We gaze at each other, my mother, Harvey and I, in disbelief – no, in belief! I'm a real writer – an author. I've written – or very nearly written – a real full-length book. I'm being offered a contract! A *contract*! It's true! Quick, quick – I must finish it! And by mid-February, finished it is.

The day before I've arranged to meet Phoebe Prince in London, bringing with me the draft manuscript, now completed, I get a letter in the morning post from somebody, a Mr James MacGibbon, of the publishers Putnam & Co. Ltd. His letter, to my astonishment, is practically a carbon copy of the historic missive I received last October in Paris from Phoebe Prince. He too read and was impressed by, he tells me, a short story of mine in a magazine. Have I considered, Mr MacGibbon enquires (exactly as Phoebe Prince did), writing a whole book? And he goes on to say that he would very much like an opportunity to discuss the possibilities of this proposal. When might I be next in London?

When? – why, tomorrow; I shall be in London tomorrow! And I've done more than simply *consider* writing a book – I've written one!

My mother, as excited as I am, persuades me to ring up Mr MacGibbon there and then – never mind the cost – and explain, which I do, the circumstances accounting for my imminent London visit; the result of our expensive telephone conversation being that next day Mr James MacGibbon is at

Paddington Station to greet me as the train pulls in, and to whirl me off in a taxi to a smart little restaurant for lunch.

It takes less than five minutes for me to feel as if we've been friends for ages. He asked for permission, straight away, to call me, not *Miss Smith*, but *Emma*, and I'm obeying instructions to call him – although he's almost old enough to be my father – James.

Big and bluff, with a big laugh and a big friendly smile, he knows – I've told him – that Phoebe Prince has fixed an appointment for me tomorrow afternoon with Mr van Thal, at which meeting I'm to hand over the manuscript and sign a contract. However, James, my new friend, says that before I give away the manuscript to Mr van Thal, he would like very much to read it himself. May he, please, borrow it – just borrow it; just for the night?

Since there can be no harm, surely, in my lending it to him for twenty-four hours, and since, as well, I'm tremendously flattered that he should be so keen to read what I've spent the winter writing, I say yes, of course he may borrow it. And so, on the warmest of terms, we part, Mr James MacGibbon having scribbled down the telephone number of Biddy Cook, with whom I shall be staying, and carrying off with him my precious manuscript, which he has sworn to guard with his life.

At nine o'clock the following morning he rings me up in a great burst of enthusiasm. I am to cancel – he is insistent that I *must* cancel the undertaking made on my behalf by Phoebe Prince of Curtis Brown, and agree instead to have my canal book published by Putnam's.

'But I can't,' I say, aghast and thrilled at the same time. 'It's too late – I'm seeing Mr van Thal today – this afternoon. He has a contract ready waiting for me. I've *promised* him –'

'Oh, don't let that worry you,' says James MacGibbon, breezily. 'Leave it to me, Emma. I'll get in touch with Bertie van Thal. He's a very nice man – I've known him for years. I'll soon square Bertie –'

So I do leave it to James MacGibbon, and he does square Mr van Thal, who certainly is a nice man; for when I type him a note, apologising guiltily, abjectly, the generosity of his reply quite overwhelms me. The house of Putnam's, he says, will be able to launch and promote the work of an aspiring young writer at the beginning of her career, as I am, far better than he could with the resources of his relatively modest firm; and he sends me – kind Mr Herbert van Thal – his best wishes for my future success.

Wonderful news! David Pearce and my sister Pam are going to be married; and soon, too. There's no point in their prolonging the engagement. David is now employed on the staff of a reputable engineering firm, Messrs Paxman's of Colchester, and his father, Maresco Pearce, a painter of some considerable renown, has rendered practical assistance by advancing them the money with which they have bought a small cosy nest of a home, Mill Cottage in the Suffolk village of Polstead, ten miles outside Colchester.

Because furnishing material is exempt from coupons, Pam makes her wedding dress of the white-spotted muslin sold in drapery shops for curtains; and I also buy coupon-free curtain material – flowered chintz – for my bridesmaid's dress, as does Jenny, the second bridesmaid and the youngest of David's three sisters. Pam and I decided together on the stuff and the designs of what we mean to wear, but in every other particular our mother – born organiser that she is – has commandeered the wedding and taken over management of everything to do with it: food and drinks, the floral arrangements, the hiring and placing of a marquee on her lawn, the list of guests to be invited and catered for (Guthrie, her husband, our absent father, is, not unnaturally, missing from

271

the list) – *everything*. She has even resurrected a previously unheard-of clergyman from her distant past to perform the nuptial ceremony.

As Pam has very strong opinions of her own (besides being accustomed, when she was a WAAF officer, to issuing orders and having them obeyed), inevitably a good many heated pre-marriage exchanges flare up in St Bernard's Cottage between parent and elder daughter, causing me to exclaim eventually, out of sheer exasperation, that should I ever happen to get married it will be a completely private affair, and I shall tell no one about it – least of all my mother – until afterwards.

'If you were to marry, Elspeth, without telling me – in secret –' declares my poor wounded reproachful but, as always, dramatic mother, and showing, by use of my discarded baptismal name, her displeasure, 'it would break my heart.'

Oh, pouf! It takes more than that to break a heart. I ought to know: I have a broken heart myself.

On their wedding day the sun shines brilliantly. David's parents are here, and his brother John is best man. Pam, beautiful in her floating white muslin, walks the few yards uphill to the tiny village church on the arm of *her* brother, Jim, who is again a civilian, demobilised at last from the RAF and with the job of piloting a light aircraft for an agricultural crop-spraying enterprise. Old Mr Crewe, a benevolent neighbouring friend, plays the part of father-figure and gives the bride away. The road on either side is lined with cheering spectators. And when, in our mother's garden, the cake has been cut and distributed, glasses raised and speeches uttered, off go Pam and David Pearce, now man and wife, to the fishing port of Brixham for a fortnight's honeymoon.

And I, once the celebrationary dust has settled, retreat to my upstairs bedroom and resume work on re-reading, word by word, and making final corrections to the pages of a book which Pam has entitled for me, *Maidens' Trip*.

I'm back again in France and living on the Left Bank of Paris at a corner of the Rue Saint-Sulpice, in the minute and very cheap Hôtel de Tournon, where I plan to write my second book, a novel. It's going to be a fictionalised version of the Indian diary I kept so assiduously when on location with the Greenpark film unit.

Before leaving England I learnt a piece of extremely encouraging news: I've had bestowed on me, by something called an Atlantic Award in Literature, a sort of scholarship which renders financial aid to impecunious would-be authors. Grateful as I am for the money – a most welcome £250 – my biggest thrill was to discover that Louis MacNeice, the poet I revere above all of our modern poets, had been a member of the Award's panel of judges and must therefore have read, and more than read, have particularly commended the half-dozen short stories I submitted for consideration. To receive such an accolade from Louis MacNeice, my hero – whew! – what an honour!

And so, the moment of extra confidence engendered by my Award being seized and the plunge taken, here I am in Paris, artistic centre of the world. Who can resist the legendary lure of Paris – Paris! – with the romantic appeal of its boulevards and buildings, its cafés and squares and bridges over the Seine, made famous by Impressionist paintings and a host of literary giants, past and present? But I was driven on throughout the Holcombe winter by an even more powerful incentive – the urge to show myself to Jean-Pierre in the new light of what I've become since he saw me almost a year ago in Valmondois. The insignificant little Nobody I was then is now a Somebody, winner of a short-stories prize and author of a book – a real book – soon to be published. This impulse had fluctuated, however, between on the one hand strengthening my resolve, and on the other causing me deep uneasiness; for I couldn't help knowing, uncomfortably, that if my altered status, with which I'm seeking to impress Jean-Pierre, does impress him, does enhance my value in his eyes, I shall find his being thus influenced despicable. Why should my success in writing change his feelings for me? Am I not exactly the same girl now as I was last summer?

Torn by these contradictory hopes and fears, I might, as it turns out, have spared myself the anguish. Jean-Pierre, love of my life and object of my pilgrimage, isn't in Paris when I get here, or in Valmondois. He isn't in France. He's visiting friends in – of all places – Wales.

Nobody had informed me that Parisians, during the summer months, habitually flee *en masse* from their beautiful capital city, leaving it to be filled with tourists and students, mostly Americans, and me.

Denis hasn't left Paris, and occasionally he drops in to see me; not often though. His life is as socially crowded as mine is solitary, and he, besides, is currently in pursuit of a very pretty Australian student. One evening, she being temporarily unavailable, he takes me instead of his Australian to the theatre, and from high above we gaze down, down at a tiny little woman standing in the centre of a bare stage, a chanteuse who stuns her packed audience with the extraordinary disproportionately loud harsh volume of her voice. 'Non,' she sings, defiantly, triumphantly, '– non, je ne regrette rien . . .'

But this outing, alone with Denis, is a rare treat. I fight shy of accepting invitations to join his easy-going intimate circle of companions, who seem to be mostly a bunch of students from abroad and full of an uninhibited joie de vivre in which I am not able to participate. I tell Denis, by way of excuse, that I must work, that I have a book to write – which is true; and so I immerse myself in it, to the exclusion of everything else.

This state of self-imposed isolation means that whatever I hear spoken around me is in largely unintelligible French, and as a result I'm developing a curious hunger for not just the sound but the sight also of my native language. Instead of pinning postcards and magazine reproductions of paintings to a wall of my Hôtel de Tournon bedroom as decoration, I've fastened up sheets of paper with 'Ode to a Nightingale' and 'Ozymandias' typed on them. And in my pocket I carry always a small scarlet cloth-bound edition of Shakespeare's Sonnets: portable comfort, the reassuring familiarity in a foreign land of inspirational English literature.

It is to my poor unhappy father I owe, and am grateful for, my obsessive ineradicable love of words, the result of his passion for poetry. But words are dangerously seductive, and unless disciplined can all too easily degenerate into the aberrant luxury of indulgence. I remind myself that as a writer – a *professional* writer – I must never forget the primary purpose of words isn't to please me, but to build a bridge of communication between myself and the invisible reader I'm trying to reach.

The people I associate with on a perpetual hourly basis are the people I'm inventing for my story, in particular the four main characters: middle-aged neurotic Mr Digby, escaping headlong from the clutches of his estranged and predatory wife (who remains unseen, off-stage) by travelling half across the globe, he and their schoolgirl daughter, Theresa, mistakenly hoping to find protection with Ruth, his older daughter, and her tea-planter husband in Assam, India.

These are my chief protaganists, and I worry in case the storyline that has to account for their journeying is too thin, too fragile to bear the weight of that still daunting prospect, a full-length book. The fictional connecting thread, while necessary, is really a blatant pretext for me to have the pleasure of retracing my own colourful experience, as recorded at the time. My notebooks contain copious material for authentic background – yes – but to transform the scribblings of a personal diary into a readable novel requires me, as well as editing the hotch-potch into lucid grammatical prose, somehow to combine and make believable what I really had heard and seen, with the lives of imaginary individuals. Can I manage to do this?

The day-to-day routine I follow is undeviatingly simple. Early each morning, while the air retains a degree of its night-time freshness, I buy croissants and milk for breakfast in the neighbouring market, and for my picnic lunch later on, a baguette, plus a twist of butter, a slice of cheese, and an apple or pear. I've already obtained from a stall at the same local market a glazed yellow faience jug, and a plate, and a cup and saucer. Madame la Concierge allows me to have an electric kettle, in which I can boil up water for coffee or tea. These things are enough to satisfy my culinary requirements.

Immediately after breakfast I leave the dim interior of my claustrophobic little room and hasten out into the blazing sunshine of the summer streets. Armed with typewriter, briefcase and food for lunch, I walk to work, as if to my office, down the Rue de Tournon and the Rue Saint-Jacques, towards the river and the Pont Royale. Halfway across the bridge is a double flight of steps leading to the extreme tip of the Île de la Cité, and it's here, with trees behind me and the Seine in front, and few if any pedestrians to disturb my peace, that I settle myself on the flagstones for a whole day of concentrated mental labour.

My mind is focussed so intently elsewhere, visualising

scenes in far distant Calcutta, I ignore and try to remain oblivious to a wandering photographer taking snapshots one day in the vicinity of where I'm sitting. But next evening, returning from supper eaten as usual at a nearby noisy students' café (head bent low over a book I'm pretending to read amidst a vociferous boisterous mob of strangers), I'm surprised by Denis turning up unexpectedly to show me the centrefoil of a newspaper, the day's *Paris Match*, filled with hot-weather pictures illustrating the different ways that Paris keeps cool out-of-doors during a heatwave. And amongst them is the photograph of an anonymous girl, bare-footed, bare-legged, with her typewriter balanced on her knees, hard at work beside the River Seine!

Except for Pam and David calling in to see me en route to an international engineering conference in Italy (when my sister tells me she's pregnant), and infrequent glimpses of Denis, I have otherwise no visitors. The days and the weeks go by, dedicated uninterruptedly to the process of writing, writing, writing; until, just as summer is drawing to an end, I too reach an end, and type the final sentence on the final page of *Theresa*. There! It's done, for better or worse; and I consign the manuscript to a friend of Biddy Cook's who, happening to be passing through Paris exactly when I need a dependable courier, offers to take and deliver the draft version of my new novel to James MacGibbon in London.

As soon as she, and *Theresa*, have gone I'm aware of a disconcerting sense of emptiness, a yawning void of having nothing to do. Not wanting to hang about idly while awaiting a verdict from James, and feeling quite suddenly miserable and lonely in Paris by myself, I jump aboard an overnight train at the Gare Saint-Lazare, and wake up to the sight of palm trees and corrugated pink roofs in the South of France on the coast of the brilliantly blue Mediterranean Sea.

* * *

277

I am the only guest in the only hotel in Ramatuelle, and the only foreigner, I think, in this very little, very ancient fortress of a town perched high up in the hills, a bumpy bus ride of some ten or so kilometres to the west of Saint-Tropez, which is centred around a harbour criss-crossed by countless bobbing masts and spars arising from the many sailing boats and fishing vessels anchored there.

It was James MacGibbon who mentioned Ramatuelle to me, saying that he and Jean, his wife, had discovered it when they were holidaying in the South of France during the thirties. I ought, he said, before returning to England, to see something of the Midi – so entirely different from northern France – and in particular he recommended Ramatuelle, as being typical of any number of miniature medieval towns, walled, as they were, against Arab invaders infiltrating the not far distant Spanish border.

I remembered the name – Ramatuelle – for its poetic lilt, and thought that now was the perfect opportunity, having time on my hands, to take James MacGibbon's advice and travel south to the *département* of Var for a first glimpse of France's semi-tropical Midi.

In Ramatuelle the houses are all joined together – crammed together – some of them actually incorporated into the encircling outer wall, so that their windows on the further side serve as look-outs keeping watch over the plain below for approaching marauders. The maze of tightly interlocking alleyways all tend upwards, leading to an open roughly triangular space, shaded by the branches of a single central elm tree, the reason why Ramatuelle's only bistro is called the Café de l'Orme.

The Hôtel Bellevue, my present address, was built, if counted in centuries, at a date comparatively recent. It stands just outside the perimeter of the little town, on the extreme edge of what is the upper of two roads connecting Ramatuelle with Saint-Tropez, and the view from a glass-fronted dining-room running the whole length of the hotel where I sit alone eating my meals, more than justifies the promise of it being *belle*: the view is breathtaking, stupendous.

I gaze from this high unimpeded vantage point, as from a bird's nest, clear across miles of absolutely flat farmland, thinly populated, to the Plage de Pampelonne, a straight elongated line of sandy coast bordering the Mediterranean. At night I see the moon appear magically above the far horizon casting a silvery glittering pathway over the water. And except when a dog barks, and other dogs answer it, there is silence for miles; and for miles a complete stillness: nothing stirs.

By day, armed with a stout stick, I explore the surrounding landscape, roaming widely, down to the sea, along to Cap Ferrat, and up into the wild hilly hinterland; always with a faintly pleasureable sense of riskiness, engendered partly by the environment's brooding air of untamed primitive savagery and partly by the utterances of Madame Batiste, the hotel's *patronne*, who interests herself in my welfare and *tutoyers* me as if I were a child. '*Fait attention!*' she advises solicitously. '*Les types paysannes qui travaillent d'alentours ne restent pas toujours gentille, tu sais* –' Madame herself isn't a native of the region. She has a more refined accent than prevails hereabouts, not pronouncing, for instance, the *z* in Saint-Tropez with the harshly Spanish inflection habitual to the local patois.

I do pay attention, but although I'm eyed with a wary curiosity by such inhabitants of the little impoverished, thinly scattered farmsteads as I happen to encounter, their greetings are invariably civil, if brusque. It's the dogs that threaten me.

I've been afraid of dogs ever since early childhood, and my worst misadventure here is when I'm confronted on the outskirts of one hamlet by a snarling, barking, bristling monstrous animal, from which I flee in terror. Attempting to bypass the village and its ferocious guardian, I become entangled most painfully in a thicket of brambles and prickly cacti, and am able to extricate myself only at the cost of torn clothes and torn skin. Madame Batiste, administering balm to my bloody scratches, clucks her tongue over them with motherly concern. Did she not warn *Mad'moiselle Smit* how unwise it was for a *jeune fille* to ramble about the countryside *toute seule*?

In the hurry of leaving Paris I omitted to bring a book with me, a serious deprivation, remedied by the good fortune of lighting upon an English Bible that some previous Bellevue guest had left behind. Having nothing else to read, I read the Bible, and beginning with the first sentence of Genesis work my way steadily through the collection of fables and stories, poetry, prophesies, lamentations, exhortations, historical records, the four Gospels, the Acts of the Apostles, St Paul's Epistles – a veritable treasure trove, unsuspected and unsurpassed – until I reach the last sentence of Revelations, at which point, coincidentally, the news I've been waiting for arrives by post from James MacGibbon in London: news, generally speaking, favourable. James, on the whole, approves of *Theresa*, but suggests the benefit of making certain drastic alterations to the text, such as cutting out the whole preliminary section and beginning the book in India. I'm appalled. Clearly he hasn't understood the fundamental *shape* of my narrative. Discussion, explanation, defence of my writing position is vital.

It's time to go home; time to say farewell to Madame Batiste and the Hôtel Bellevue, and to lovely fairytale Ramatuelle. The past fortnight has been for me a dreamlike interlude, wholly detached from the reality of a familiar world, to which I now must return. Life, real life, has to be resumed.

In Paris I retrieve my typewriter and the luggage I had stored with the concierge at the Hôtel de Tournon, and arrive back, twenty-four hours later, in London's Fulham Road.

Whether or not the exceptionally good reviews of *Maidens' Trip*, just published, have influenced James MacGibbon's judgement, I don't know, but after a second reading he has changed his opinion, agreeing to leave *Theresa* – which I have re-christened *The Far Cry* – as it is. He no longer thinks that to chop off the beginning would be an improvement, but assures me it will be published without any further alteration. Warmly encouraging, he is urging me to make a start on the next book, and his urgency is partly because, as I learn, he is in the process of departing from Putnam's and setting up, with his friend Robert Kee, an entirely new publishing house. *The Far Cry* won't be published by Putnam's after all, and in a generous gesture they have relinquished their rights to reprinting *Maidens' Trip*, so MacGibbon and Kee's first two books will be my first two books, and James wants to make sure there is already a third on the way.

One evening he takes me to a party at the private residence of a Mrs Llewellyn Rhys and her sister. My hostess is the widow of an RAF pilot killed in the war. Before the war he had been a writer with a promising future, and in his memory she has inaugurated a prize to be given each year for whatever first novel is judged the best. Standing in front of her fireplace in her crowded drawing-room she announces that this year the prize has been won by Emma Smith for *Maidens' Trip*. Emlyn Williams, the famous playwright, hands me a cheque with his congratulations, and everybody claps.

I'm astonished, dumbfounded, and can think of nothing to say except 'Thank you – thank you –' again and again. It has come as a complete surprise: I had thought the party was the sort often held in literary circles for no particular reason. James had known what it was for, but he hadn't told me.

These last twelve months or so have been full of surprises. First there was the Atlantic Award for my bunch of short stories. Then I was given the John Llewellyn Rhys Prize for *Maidens' Trip*. And now, most wonderful of all – although hardly a surprise – on April the 7th Daniel Maresco Pearce is born in Colchester Hospital and will duly be christened in the church of Pam and David's village, Polstead. I am staying with them for the time being in Mill Cottage, their snug little home by a stream, and I envy – *how* I envy – Pam for her beautiful baby. What happiness! I would so much like to be more than only a godmother – to have a real live baby of my own. But this, of course, in the present circumstances, is impossible. I have to write another book: it's expected of me. And if I wrote, as I did, those first two at top speed in twelve months, it is naturally to be supposed that, with the wind in my sails, I can achieve a third novel inside a year.

But the awful fact of the matter is, I can't.

Why can't I write a third best-selling novel for James MacGibbon? I *try*. I've spent the past last few weeks of spring and summer once again in the Hôtel de Tournon, *trying*; but to no avail. Why should I have come to a full stop, as though finding myself at the foot of an unscaleable cliff? In my head I have a distinct picture of three main characters and a rough outline of their interlocking stories. I've written pages and pages, scene after scene, some of them set in the English countryside, some in London, some in France. But it's no good. The various episodes ought, by combining, to form a single continuous chain of events, instead of which they remain obstinately separate and unrelated. Something, I know, is basically wrong with my embryonic novel; only I don't know *what*.

Then a letter from John Moore, who is a writer living in Gloucestershire and who reviewed *Maidens' Trip* enthusiastically when it was first published, offers me a respite from my ever-increasing frustration and sense of failure. He tells me that Cheltenham, as part of the post-war resurgence of artistic life, is putting on a Festival of Literature, and I am invited to be one of the speakers at it. Perhaps, he suggests – ironically, in the circumstances – I might give a talk entitled *Why I Write*.

I accept his invitation with gratitude, thankful to have an excuse for abandoning, even temporarily, my futile struggles. October seems to be unworryingly distant, a dot on the horizon. But of course it doesn't stay safely far off – it draws closer with alarming speed. I have never before had to stand on a platform confronting row upon row of strangers' faces, all tilted attentively towards me, and the prospect of doing so becomes daily more and more terrifying. However, the die being cast, I apply myself to composing a talk which has to last for an hour and has to sound, when spoken aloud, as though I'm delivering it spontaneously, impromptu.

This is because, in my ignorance of public speechifying, I think it's against the rules to *read* a speech. You are – so I believe – expected to be able to invent your observations as you go along; or in any case to appear to be inventing. Consequently, having completed to the best of my ability what reminds me of producing a school essay on a given subject, I then learn it painstakingly by heart, every pause, every emphasis, every falsely off-the-cuff joke, every word.

Yes, but suppose in the middle of it I forget the lines I've learnt, and my mind is quite suddenly a blank? Without a script at hand for reference I shall be lost! Oh, what a nightmare! Why on earth did I agree to let myself in for this torment?

Inevitably the fatal day arrives, as the day of execution always does, and having crossed the Channel, I board a train from London to Cheltenham, escorted by my dear kind publisher, James, whose intention it is to protect me from panic attacks and to bolster my flagging courage. We have been booked for the night into a first-class hotel, and the next morning here I am, standing before a horrifyingly real audience: rows of actual flesh-and-blood people, who have all paid good money to listen to whatever it is I have to say, all waiting in silence for me to entertain them.

I must pretend I'm not frightened. I must pretend to myself it's easy. I must – I *have* to open my mouth and begin speaking. And once I've started, miraculously the sentences committed to memory reveal themselves as being securely stored in my brain. I'm saved! My confidence revives. I am in full flow when two middle-aged women sitting in the very front seats get up and stump crossly down the centre aisle and out of the hall. Their departure, unmistakeably indicating that in their opinion I'm talking rubbish, practically destroys me, but somehow, although severely shaken, by a supreme effort of will I carry on until the hour is up and the final word has been uttered, and it's over. Rubbish or not, I've survived to the end: it's done, and I'm free!

Paris is on strike: no electricity, no buses or Métro. There are queues to buy candles and oil for lamps. The weather is cold and dark, more wintry than autumnal. Customers of the Café de Flore and Les Deux Magots are all sitting inside, instead of being served at tables on the pavement, as they were in the summer. There is no longer, as then, an air of gaiety in a crowded Boulevard Saint-Germain dotted by girls wearing, with bold insouciance, the long full swinging skirts and flat ballet-type shoes of Christian Dior's New Look.

Depressed by the current gloominess and reluctant to

resume my fruitless labours on the typewriter, I'm glad to get a card from two American acquaintances of James MacGibbon's, two men I haven't met before, inviting me with polite formality to dinner and an evening out at the Folies Bergère.

Although they are only, I know, performing a duty to please James, anything is better than nothing. On the date of the invitation, there being no public transport, I hail a taxi, give the driver, who has a friend alongside him, the address of my hosts, living some distance away on the affluent Right Bank, and off we go. The two *copains* are in high spirits, laughing and joking. Over their shoulders they engage me in lively conversation. I am English – yes? From London, perhaps? They have once, they inform me, visited London, for a weekend, and they mention Piccadilly. Do I know Piccadilly? I say I do and likewise Buckingham Palace and Trafalgar Square. Marcel, the driver (we have exchanged first names), announces that these happy connections must be celebrated, and to seal the bond *un petit coup de vin rouge* is imperative. With a squeal of brakes, he pulls in at a café.

Why should I hesitate? Do I not believe ardently in the brotherhood of man? And are not Gustave and Marcel a heart-warming example of *fraternité*, *egalité*, and hands-across-the-sea?

So we have our drink, which they insist on paying for. We clink glasses and toast Great Britain's King George, and Churchill, and their own gallant Charles de Gaulle. But when they call for the *garçon* to refill our glasses, I refuse further hospitality, having realised by now that their extravagant hilarity is the result of a good many – too many – earlier little *coups de vin rouge*. I shall be late, I say, for my party. We must go. Yes – *now*!

We pile back into the taxi and again set off, driving danger-ously fast in exactly the opposite direction to the one we ought to be taking. When I point this out they roar with laughter. They are taking me, they say, to a different party, to *their* party.

'Ne t'inquiétes pas, Mad'moiselle Emma – restes tranquille. Tout va bien –'

When I beg them, in my bad French and my panicky English, to stop – please, please to stop – they only laugh all the more uproariously, and instead of stopping, begin to sing.

Oh, what a fool I am! How could I have been so stupid, so gullible? I seem to hear Bunny's voice: *You silly girl*. Silly indeed. Whatever am I to do?

When Marcel has to slow down momentarily at a red light without a second thought I wrench open the door and leap out in high heels on to cobbles, and run, run, as fast as I can, pausing once briefly to snatch off my shoes so as to be able to run faster. But when I've climbed into another taxi, driven by a very old man – discernably sober – it's then I discover that I've left my pretty black velvet bag behind on the seat of my wicked kidnappers' taxi. What a disaster!

The Americans are kind enough to pay my fare as well as lending me the money that gets me back to the Hôtel de Tournon at the end of a miserable evening. I hate the Folies Bergère, and my hosts are entirely taken up by their other much more interesting and important guest, the famous film-actor, Charles Laughton.

As well as my bag I've lost everything that was in it: money and a powder compact, a handkerchief, a comb, a lipstick and a packet of cigarettes. The one point of contact I have with the villianous Marcel and Gustave is the café where we had our ill-fated drink. In the morning – since, however hopeless, there is nothing else I *can* do – I re-trace on foot that initial taxi journey, to be greeted by a smiling patron of the café, and the instant production from under the counter of my black velvet bag.

'*Voilà, Mad'moiselle – vous avez de la bonne chance, n'est-ce pas?*'

'*Ah, mais oui, M'sieu – merci mille fois M'sieu –*'

My faith in the goodness of human nature is immediately restored. They weren't villains really, my kidnappers. They were just high-spirited French boys, out for fun, and the only item missing from my bag is the packet of Gauloises Bleu.

The euphoria generated by the recovery of my cherished possession and its contents doesn't last. Paris has failed to inspire me as it did a year ago when, day after day, I wrote *The Far Cry* in an uninterrupted burst of productivity.

Tired of sitting at my typewriter for hours on end with nothing worthwhile to show for it, I wander the back streets and alleyways of the Left Bank and the Île de la Cité, and notice what I hadn't paid much attention to before. Again and again, in obscure nooks and crannies, I come upon what can only be described as modest shrines marking the spot where a Resistance fighter had been chased and cornered and shot dead by Nazis during the Occupation. What strikes me forcibly is that the flowers in the jam-jars, four years after the war ended, are always fresh, constantly renewed, even as the sorrow and pride of each loss never fades. And the sight of those faithful simple memorials makes me feel ashamed for being so upset when I thought I had lost a mere black velvet evening bag.

On the several occasions this year when Jean-Pierre came up from Valmondois to Paris, we met, and the meetings were amiable and easy: comradely, no more than that. But whereas I have grown to accept the reality of not being, nor ever likely to be, the love of Jean-Pierre's life, what has surprised me is to find that neither is he mine. How can such an all-consuming passion have slipped away quietly when I wasn't looking?

The vacuum it leaves is part of a dreary echoing emptiness by which I am now surrounded. Here I am in Paris, unable to write, alone and lonely: *homesick*. What is the cure – the only possible cure for homesickness? Surely it is to go home? So I do.

Bunny has finally given up on me ('*Silly girl . . .*') and while retaining a warmly affectionate friendship with my sister Pam and my brother-in-law David, has married somebody else. Good! She – the third Mrs Keene – is as tall as Bunny himself, half his age, and, moreover, beautiful.

With a view to settling me down and giving me a place to call my own, Pam and David have bought, on the spur of the moment, a terraced row of cottages – Beech Cottages – in Stoke-by-Nayland, the larger village situated a mile or so up a steep hill from Polstead, where they live. No. 3, at the end of row, is empty, and would be ideal, they think, for me to rent from them at the nominal sum of fifteen shillings a week. When their proposal is put to me, tentatively, I am ecstatic and agree without hesitation. Yes, yes, *yes*!

The immediate task is for my cottage, No. 3, to be swept and scrubbed throughout. Then it has to be furnished. This entails my sister driving me here and there, with Dan strapped in the back seat, to wherever a big house in the neighbourhood, having been sold, is advertising the subsequent sale by auction, on site, of its contents. Auction sales constitute a new and exciting game for me, but Pam is an old hand at them, and under her expert tuition I learn how to bid for various items more and more boldly; and so in time become the owner of three upholstered Victorian chairs, all in tip-top condition (but going cheap because they came from the nursery and servants' quarters on the attic floor), a very small sofa, a brass fireguard, a sturdy kitchen table to work or eat at, and all sorts of other jumbled-up odds and ends which are disposed of higgledy-piggledy in job lots.

Together, guided by Pam's discerning eye, we forage like treasure-seekers through many dim little junk shops. In Colchester I buy rush matting for the floor, and yards of stripy cotton for curtains. Furnishing a home – *my* home – from scratch is so much fun for me, and so absorbing, that the last thing I allow myself to worry about is the awful difficulty of writing a third book.

I'm reminded guiltily of this obligation when James MacGibbon rings up to say a well-known journalist, Montagu Slater, has been asking if he and his photographer, Kurt Hutton, can pay me a visit in Suffolk for an illustrated article to appear in the popular weekly magazine, *Picture Post*. James is, naturally, delighted: publicity sells books.

On Saturday he comes down from London with them, and Pam and I, leaving Dan, now seven months old, to be cared for by David, are driven over to Woodbridge, where James keeps his boat moored – the boat in which, during several past weekends, he has taken me sailing on the Norfolk Broads. It's thought that to photograph us all out at sea (except for Monty, who is thankful to be spared such an ordeal), battling with choppy waves in blowy weather will provide exactly the right sort of lively magazine material. I keep wishing my hair hadn't been cut, by mistake, so unbecomingly short the day before. Kurt Hutton is far more interested in focussing his camera on Pam than on me, and no wonder!

Back on shore again, and having tea and cakes in Mill Cottage, I can't help being secretly amused by the deference with which my interviewer, Montagu Slater, treats me today, in contrast to those memories I have of him at the COI when I was a humble messenger-girl, carrying tins of film to and fro for Greenpark Productions Ltd. Although I remember Monty well, he doesn't remember me – of course not: the unimportant are, generally speaking, invisible.

James, when Montagu Slater and Kurt Hutton leave, stays behind, and I tell him, as I think I now must, that the book he is eagerly awaiting, the next best-seller to increase and boost MacGibbon & Kee's budding list, will never be written. I am so sorry, I say, so ashamed, but it has defeated me: I just can't manage, somehow, to do it. Even the James Tait Black Memorial Prize, awarded to me in March for *The Far Cry*, hasn't acted as a regenerative spark to reignite the burnt-out fires of fictional invention.

On hearing my woeful confession, James MacGibbon – good, kind, considerate friend that he is – doesn't blame or reproach me. I've been trying, he declares, to write the wrong book, that's all. *Maidens' Trip* and *The Far Cry* were drawn from my real experiences, and what I need, says James, is another real experience to inspire me.

He may, in his publisher's wisdom, have divined the cause of my failure, and the solution to it, but how in the world, I wonder, are we to manufacture deliberately a real book-inspiring experience for me?

James MacGibbon posts me a copy he has made of a notice pinned up on the Yacht Club's board: *Crew required to sail yacht for holiday cruise among the Greek islands. All applications should be addressed to me here at the Yacht Club. Signed – Aylmer Simey*. Underneath James had scrawled in his large untidy handwriting: How about this?

How about it? In my imagination I picture the yacht, an elegant three-masted schooner, painted a dazzling white, with gleaming brass portholes, and the legendary Greek islands for our destination – what a dream! I fear there must already have been dozens of applications to join Aylmer Simey's crew, from people much better qualified than me. Well, I'm not actually qualified at all, as I have truthfully to admit in my letter: two years on a canal and the ability to splice a rope don't really count as qualifications for sailing a yacht – a schooner – in the romantic Aegean Sea, but I might as well have a go: nothing venture, nothing win!

To my immense surprise I receive a telegram next morning from the yacht owner. It says: *Come to Cowes tomorrow for trial trip to Cherbourg stop will meet 12:30 ferry from Southampton stop Simey.*

I share the thrilling news with Pam and David, and I ring James. I don't ring my mother: she would only be worried and make a fuss. Twenty-four hours after getting the telegram I step off the 12.30 ferry-boat on to Cowes landing stage, where I am accosted by a smallish dejected-looking middle-aged person who introduces himself as Aylmer Simey.

It's raining steadily, as it has been all morning. At his suggestion we have a fish-and-chip lunch in a nearby café, a meal eaten almost without either of us uttering a word. He is somebody not, I decide, by nature talkative, but his silence infects me, so that I can't think of anything to say and become tongue-tied. After lunch he does some shopping, and then we climb into a dinghy and Mr Aylmer Simey rows me out to his yacht.

It isn't a three-masted schooner. It's a very pretty little ketch with its name, *Winkle*, on the bows, and it's tiny – a toy sailing-boat. We have to wait overnight, I'm told, for a certain Mr Potter to join us. Mr Potter is to be the third member of our crew and as soon as he arrives we will set off across the English Channel, heading for Cherbourg.

Down below in the cabin this evening, with rain drumming on the deck above our heads, I do learn a few facts regarding my skipper. He had a farm in Kenya – what sort of a farm he doesn't specify – and he was married. When his wife died he sold the farm and used the proceeds, on his return to England, to buy *Winkle*. A friend had advised him that the Greek islands were well worth a visit.

After our supper of eggs, bacon and sausages, cooked on the gas stove by Mr Simey, I lie down on one of the two narrow side-beds fully clothed, with a blanket to cover me, and in spite of some serious doubts that have arisen about what I've let myself in for, instantly fall asleep.

The following morning rain is still pouring down from a darkening sky, and there is a strong wind blowing, whipping the sea around us into white crests.

We crouch in the cabin, listening to weather forecasts on the radio, all of which give warning of worstening conditions. The third crew member, Mr Potter, when we meet him off the ferry, turns out to be elderly, cheerful, and as garrulous as Mr Simey is taciturn. He has spent his working life, we are told, in the accounts department of a ship-building firm, and his practical knowledge of sailing is as limited as mine, consisting mainly – like mine – of occasional greatly enjoyed outings on the Norfolk Broads, crewing for a neighbour who owns a converted fishing-smack. Unfortunately his wife, says Mr Potter, disapproves of what she describes as her husband's hobby, and has given him permission most unwillingly for the Cherbourg jaunt. (Presumably he would never be allowed by Mrs Potter to sign on for a sailing holiday amongst the Greek islands, and so it seems as if his trial cross-Channel trip will be a trial for going nowhere!)

All afternoon small craft are running for shelter, making their way back from the Channel's rough outer waters to seek the security of an inshore berth. But because Mrs Potter has permitted her husband three days' leave of absence, and only three days, we will have to make the crossing, Mr Simey decides, tonight, stormy weather or no stormy weather.

Consequently at five o'clock, fortified by mugs of tea and thick slices of bread and strawberry jam, Mr Simey (as I still politely address him) and I set about hauling up the stern

292

anchor, while Mr Potter on the foredeck unties the line mooring *Winkle* to a buoy. In our busy preoccupation we fail to
observe the Southampton ferry's untimely arrival at just this
critical juncture. With no weigh on, and under loosely flapping sails, we are caught in its wash and swept unresistingly
to one side, as helpless as a drifting leaf. Whereupon Mr
Aylmer Simey, his hand on the ineffectual tiller, says to me –
to *me*! – 'What shall I do?'

It's then that I truly realise, with a sinking heart, the
dangerous folly of this enterprise: I, who know nothing
about sailing, am on the verge of embarking on a Channel
crossing at night, in a storm, with old Mr Potter, who also
knows nothing about sailing, skippered by a man who turns
to *me* asking 'What shall I do?' when his boat is tossed to one
side in the wash of the car ferry. But it's too late now to
change my mind and save myself. The sails have filled, and
Winkle, powered by the irresistible force of a tempestuous
wind, is scudding, hell for leather, out to sea.

At eleven o'clock I'm roused from the cowardly sleep in
which I'm endeavouring to hide my fears by Aylmer Simey
shouting: 'Miss Smith –' I can dimly see him standing above
me in the hatches, and I know that the dreaded moment has
come when I have to take charge of what he termed the
middle watch. It has to be me: old Mr Potter is too old to do
battle with the savage elements.

I scramble blurrily up the steps to be engulfed instantaneously by the wet wild howling battering darkness outside.
Aylmer Simey is bawling in my ear that we are lucky to
have a favourable following wind, blowing south-east and
holding steady. I have simply, he yells, to fix my eyes on the
compass and keep *Winkle*'s bows pointing the way they
are now. Whatever happens I mustn't let the wind and
waves push *Winkle* off course. If we seem in danger of

being run down by one of the big steamers whose paths we are cutting across I am to shine the torch, which he gives me, on to the mainsail.

Then Mr Aylmer Simey hands me the tiller, and saying – or shouting – that he will relieve me of my watch at four in the morning, disappears below decks, where old Mr Potter, oblivious to the storm above his head, is peacefully snoring. And I am left by myself to struggle alone in the night's vast blackness against the violence of wind and the huge waves that rise up ahead of the boat, one after another, each a mountainous enemy intent on swamping us, drowning us. But the little *Winkle*, amazingly, bravely, rides up each precipitous wall of water, and slides down the far side unharmed, again and again, again and again. Sitting in the hatches I jam my legs as wide apart as possible to prevent myself toppling overboard, and I grasp the tiller with all my strength, wrestling to keep control of it, my eyes riveted on the illuminated circle of the compass in front of me, so as to make sure the flickering needle goes on pointing in the right direction, the direction of Cherbourg and survival.

Now and then I see the lights of steamers, always, mercifully, in the distance, and I hear in the rigging a mysterious unintelligible murmur of voices and once or twice the tempest tears a ragged hole in the clouds to reveal a pale yellow crescent of moon. And the hours pass. My arms and legs, and my eyes, ache; every bit of me aches. Curiously, the monotonous rise and fall, rise and fall of gigantic waves and the bright hypnotic dial of the compass have a lulling effect on me, so that in spite of the discomfort of my position, legs braced, and the unremitting effort required to maintain mastery of the tiller, I'm fighting to stay awake and alert; for a few terrifying seconds my eyes do close and I almost allow *Winkle* to gybe. But the noisy commotion of disregarded sails and rigging brings me to my senses just in time to avert a disaster. And there, low on the horizon, is the first long streak of dawn.

When Aylmer Simey emerges to take his turn at steering, I tumble down the steps and roll, exhausted, on to the side-bed opposite Mr Potter's recumbent form; and the next thing I'm aware of is our entrance into Cherbourg harbour. We *have* survived the night and, by a miracle, reached the coast of France.

Because the foresail has ripped, presumably when I nearly gybed, we are obliged to loiter around in Cherbourg for two days while it's being mended. Oh, blessed two days! The weather improves. The sun shines. We drink coffee and wine at quayside cafés, laze on the beach, explore the town, have picnics aboard *Winkle*, perched on the cabin-top. I would be happy staying idly on in delightful Cherbourg, practising my feeble French in the bistros, for a whole week – for weeks, for ever. But old Mr Potter, anticipating a scolding from his wife, is fretting at the delay. And so, as soon as the mended sail has been collected, our skipper decides we will immediately make the return journey cross-Channel to Cowes, again at night, even though clouds are gathering ominously, the wind rising, and the radio bulletins forecasting stormy conditions.

And again, in the fading daylight, we are the only craft heading out to sea. A group of men standing silently together in the well of a fishing-boat as it passes close by us, homeward bound, all at once pull their caps from their heads and flourish them in the air, shouting, whether kindly or mockingly, '*Bonne voyage!*'

For me the voyage is far from *bonne*. On the previous crossing I had felt, but wasn't, sick. Tonight, though, during my middle watch at the tiller, I *am* sick; and not just sick, but sick, sick, *sick*. 'Aylmer,' I call, dispensing in a crisis with

polite formality, 'you'll have to take over, Aylmer. I can't –'
And then, before I'm able to say another word, convulsed by
an extreme spasm of sickness, I lose control completely of
the tiller: *Winkle* gybes, and pandemonium ensues. At least
the masts, instead of snapping in half, are still intact, although
the foresail, and perhaps the mainsail too, may have ripped;
but I am past caring. Aylmer manages, with Mr Potter helping, to get us back on course again, and I spend the rest of the
night huddled at his feet in the hatches, retching and dozing
alternately.

He must be a better sailor, Mr Simey – Aylmer – than I had
given him credit for, because in the early morning he steers us
in past the treacherous Needles, navigates the Isle of Wight's
notoriously tricky currents, and drops anchor finally by the
very same buoy we started from three days – a lifetime – ago.

I've lived through a *real* Channel-crossing experience and
am back on dry land – which for quite a while seems to be
oddly unsteady under my feet – but it was not, as I have to
tell James, the experience to inspire a book. Nor shall I, one
fine day, be cruising aboard *Winkle*, skippered by Mr Aylmer
Simey, amongst the Greek archipelago.

I've enjoyed spending Christmas with my mother and Harvey
in Holcombe, but as soon as it's over I hasten back to No. 3
Beech Cottages. I have to prepare myself for the next *real
experience* that James MacGibbon, undeterred by the disappointment of the cruising project, is in the process of fixing
up on my behalf. If he succeeds in his attempt I will shortly
become assistant to a priest in Naples who has taken on the
praiseworthy but daunting task of rescuing abandoned
orphan children from the streets and providing them with
food and clothing, shelter and education. Never having been
to Italy, and fond as I am of children, it appears to me to be
a very interesting and rewarding proposition.

But meanwhile there are New Year festivities pending. Pam and David have friends, Leslie and Robert Goodden, living nearby in the village of Nayland and Robert's brother, Wyndham, has invited them, and the three of us, to join with a group of other people he knows who are buying tickets for the famous fancy-dress dance held annually on New Year's Eve in the Royal Albert Hall.

I'm reluctant to accept this invitation. Wyndham Goodden is divorced, with teenage daughters, and I suspect he may have his eye on me to fill the marital gap, which I have no wish to do. My eye, in any case, is fastened on the approaching date of the Neapolitan street-children-rescue undertaking.

'I don't a bit want to go to a New Year's Eve fancy-dress ball,' I say to my sister. 'You and David can go. I'd much rather be left here, looking after darling Dan.'

'Oh, but that's ridiculous – of *course* you must come,' she replies briskly, refusing to listen to any of my excuses. She thinks I'm depressed and in need of cheering. 'It'll be fun – and easy. We can pretend to be pirates, and then all we shall need for fancy-dress are spotted red handkerchiefs and scarlet sashes. You've *got* to come, Ellie – Emma – I won't go without you.'

My sister Pam can be very forceful. So finally I'm persuaded, and on the 31st of December we motor up to London, taking Dan with us to be cared for by David's mother, Anna Pearce, who lives in Chelsea's Old Church Street, while we, with the spotted cotton handkerchiefs knotted round our heads, and brass curtain-rings dangling from our ears, and daggers made of cardboard thrust into our sashes, proceed to the house of Sir Robin Darwin, Principal of the Royal College of Art (where Robert has a teaching post), for the pre-ball dinner that he most hospitably is giving as a send-off to us band of merrymakers.

We meet the other guests. Amongst them is a very beautiful girl, Elizabeth Jane Howard, a writer, married to the painter, Peter Scott, and who, instead of bothering with the nuisance of fancy dress, has decked herself out in a necklace of fabulous emeralds borrowed for the occasion from the owner of Cameo Corner, a famous jewellery shop. There is also in the party somebody called Richard Stewart-Jones, wearing a hired snuff-coloured Victorian gentleman's outfit. When the main course of steaming hot vol-au-vents, piled high on an immense and probably priceless china platter, is dropped – horror of horrors! – just as it's being carried into the dining-room, and the platter broken in half, Richard Stewart-Jones, without losing a second, goes down on his snuff-coloured knees and saves the sumptuous dinner of a distraught Robin Darwin from seemingly total ruin by scooping the creamy vol-au-vents on to several smaller dishes, while exhorting the appalled company of would-be diners not to despair.

'None of it's gone on the floor – look! It's all right, still – perfectly all right for us to eat –'

I admire his presence of mind, his speediness of action, his adroitness in transforming a catastrophe into what can be related as an amusing anecdote. Later on, finding myself sitting beside him, aloft in our Royal Albert Hall box, I offer my congratulations for his brilliant extempore performance. We talk; we laugh. What a lovely jokey man he is! Presently, by mutual consent, we forsake our grandly exclusive box and our fellow party-goers, to descend from above, and mingle with the hundreds of revellers, dressed in every sort of colourful carnival costume, who are thronging the arena below. Dancing, in that great crush of gyrating bodies, to music being relayed over deafeningly loud loud-speakers, is difficult (and anyway he's a hopeless dancer), so we soon give up the feeble jogging pretence of foxtrotting and make our way to the bar.

We are so deep in conversation that we hardly notice time passing until suddenly, with midnight upon us, the music stops, the dancing stops; everything stops. We stand in a crowd of friendly strangers, waiting, motionless, for the long pause of absolute silence to be ended by the slow solemn strokes of Big Ben, introducing the first minutes of that unknown year lying ahead of us all, the year of 1951.

I stay for the night – or for what remains of the night – at Biddy Cook's Fulham address. Pam and David and Dan drive home to Polstead after lunch, but I decide to prolong my London visit for a while. And sure enough, as I had hoped, and more than half expected, Richard Stewart-Jones rings me up. How lucky it was I did stay on! At seven p.m. I make my way from Redcliffe Road down to the Embankment to have supper with him in the house he has recently acquired and in which he is now living.

One hundred Cheyne Walk is imposing, both outside and inside. Everything is on a big scale: a big entrance hall, paved with big black and white flagstones, a big staircase leading up to a very big oak-panelled drawing-room with an ornate marble fireplace at either end, and big windows looking out on to the River Thames. He conducts me round this latest acquisition of his which would have suffered, he says, had he not bought it with money raised from selling the house next door, the ignominious fate of becoming a showcase for the sale of expensive cars. What unspeakable vandalism! To ensure the future safety of 100 Cheyne Walk he has handed it over to the guardianship of the National Trust, and the NT has leased it back to him for a hundred years at a peppercorn rent.

The Ellis family, mother, father, and two children, occupy, also as NT tenants, a self-contained flat at the top of the house, with a separate front door and separate stairs. But except for them, and Elsa, his giggly young Italian cook, he is the sole inhabitant of this palatial, sparsely furnished mansion. Such furniture as there is perfectly matches its surroundings, being large, handsome, antique, and – I would imagine – of considerable value.

I'm impressed and rather overawed by the grandeur and the size of everything, and relieved that on the ground floor Richard has a comfortable little snuggery facing out on to an ancient mulberry tree in the back garden, and serving as his sitting-room, his dining-room, his office: in short, as his cosy untidy little nest. It's here, beside a roaring fire, that Elsa brings us our supper.

Richard Stewart-Jones is unlike anyone I've ever met before. How can I describe him? He is very amusing, a joker; a person it's fun to be with. But also – I'm guessing – warm-hearted: a loveable person. I want to find out more about him.

He is the owner, apparently, of several more houses in Cheyne Walk, and he has lodgers in two of them. He works on and off for the National Trust and for the SPAB (an acronym meaning *Society for the Preservation of Ancient Buildings*), but exactly what is the work he does I'm still not certain. I learn, however, during our evening in the snuggery, that Richard's abiding passion is for ancient buildings and their preservation.

It's practically midnight when he escorts me back on foot to Redcliffe Road, and because we have still a great deal to say, so many interesting topics merely touched on, we agree to meet again tomorrow. And we meet the next day as well, *and* the day after, when it occurs to us that our continual traipsing to and fro between Chelsea and Fulham is quite unnecessary and a waste of time. It would be far more sensible – practical – if I were to move into 100 Cheyne Walk – there's enough space available, goodness knows! And so I do. And in the following three weeks, except for occasional sightings of the upstairs Ellis family, and of Elsa who cooks our meals, and Mrs Anderson who crosses over Battersea Bridge daily to clean the place, Richard and I see each other, and only each other, almost exclusively. It's as though we are the last two people in the world, castaways, washed up, alone, on an idyllic desert island.

What have we done during the past three weeks? I can't really remember. It's a blur. But there comes a time when Richard, pacing up and down, the inevitable cigarette in a corner of his mouth – he is a chain-smoker – says to me, 'Mitzi,' he says (this is a private and inexplicable nickname he uses), 'don't you think, Mitzi, that we're getting rather fond of one another?'

'Yes,' I answer, cautiously, nodding. 'You may be right. Perhaps we are.'

'Well then,' says Richard, 'what do you think we ought to do about it?'

'I don't know,' I say. 'What do *you* think?'

After a few more turns about the room, he says: 'How about us getting married, Mitzi?'

'Oh – married?' I consider the proposal for a minute; a minute is long enough. 'Well, yes – why not?' I nod at him again. 'It's a good idea. Let's – let's get married.' James MacGibbon and the unwritten third book vanish into thin air; as also does the priest in Naples and the poor starving street children – all of them, in a matter of seconds, disappear clean out of my mind.

'Stephan's the chap to marry us,' Richard is saying. 'I'll give him a call.' And straight away he dials the number of Stephan Hopkinson, vicar of Battersea Church on the other side of the river, a friend of his and husband of Anne, a Stewart-Jones relation.

Stephan Hopkinson, an extremely busy vicar, tells Richard

he happens to have an hour free next Friday, when he would be delighted to perform the wedding ceremony in our Chelsea parish, providing the incumbent vicar agrees. Richard goes off to somewhere in the City to obtain the vital Special Licence. I go off to Peter Jones in Sloane Square to buy a hat. And together we go to the Aladdin's cave of Cameo Corner, and from its treasure trove select a Victorian ring, the circle of gold completed by two symbolically intertwined hands. And when this is done, we are ready.

On the appointed morning, as soon as breakfast is finished, and just before leaving the house, I telephone my mother in faraway Devon to announce, very quickly (so as to give her no opportunity for saying anything), that in ten minutes I shall be getting married, forgetting to mention, in my hurry, to whom. (My agitated mother, as she later dramatically describes to me, having rushed up the hill to the village church and dropped on her knees, found herself praying for a blessing to be bestowed on her daughter Elspeth – no, Emma – and a Somebody nameless.)

Outside it's cold, a wintry day, but with the sun shining and the sky blue. Richard and I walk, hand in hand – as though imitating the clasped hands of our wedding ring – silently, seriously down the road to the ruins of Chelsea Old Church, which a direct hit from a land-mine in the war utterly demolished. By an extraordinary chance, or else by a miracle, the chapel of Sir Thomas More, running along one side of the church, was left intact; and here, assembled in a group, are Stephan and Anne Hopkinson with the parish priest who *has* very kindly given permission, and a Warden and the Chapel cleaner.

So it is we two, standing side by side in front of the magnificent surviving Stanley monument, are joined by dear Stephan in holy matrimony: married. Richard had some difficulty forcing the ring, a tight fit, on to my finger, but it was an emotional moment and we both, much moved, let fall a few tears. Our favourite hymn, 'All People that on Earth do Dwell', is sung beautifully, unaccompanied, by Anne, who had trained as an opera singer. Then we sign our names in the Register, with the Warden and the obliging cleaner for our witnesses. And Amen: it's over.

But only when Mrs Anderson, the daily housekeeper, who has always punctilliously referred to me as *Miss Smith*, addresses me in the hall of 100 Cheyne Walk on my return from church, as *Madam*, only then am I hit by the astonishing realisation that I have become a married woman.

I telephone my mother again to tell her I am now married, and – this time – to whom I am married. She mustn't, I declare, feel in the slightest bit excluded by not being present at the actual brief ceremony. We told no one before of our plan to marry, and I am bringing Richard this very day to meet her.

At Paddington Station he and I board a train bound for the West Country. We travel in a first-class carriage, which is something I have never done before, and at Dawlish, instead of the usual transport by bus, we take a taxi to St Bernard's Cottage, where my darling mother greets her new son-in-law – thank heavens! – with open arms. As I watch them forming an immediate alliance, talking and laughing, it's plain to see I have nothing to fear. My mother's heart is *not* broken. I knew it wouldn't be.

So that's all right!

Afterword

In the autumn of 1957 Richard died, aged forty-three, having suffered three heart attacks in a year, the last of which killed him.

He left me two children, our son Barnaby, and our daughter, Lucy Rose.

In due course Barney, with Elizabeth, had Luke and Hugo; and Rosie, with Ben, had Joe.

My children and my grandsons have been the greatest joy of my long life.

Thank you, Richard.

Acknowledgements

I would like my brother Jim to be remembered for a remark he made to me when he was an old man, the year before he died: *The only thing that really counts is kindness.*

A NOTE ON THE AUTHOR

Emma Smith was born Elspeth Hallsmith in 1923 in Newquay, Cornwall, where until the age of twelve, she lived with her mother and father, an elder brother and sister, and a younger brother. Her first book, *Maidens' Trip*, was published in 1948 and won the John Llewellyn Rhys Memorial Prize. Her second, *The Far Cry*, was published the following year and was awarded the James Tait Black Memorial Prize.

In 1951 Emma Smith married Richard Stewart-Jones. After her husband's death in 1957 she went to live with her two young children in Wales, where she proceeded to write and have published four successful children's books, one of which, *No Way of Telling*, was runner-up for the Carnegie Gold Medal. She also published a number of short stories and, in 1978, her novel *The Opportunity of a Lifetime*. In 2008 *The Great Western Beach*, her memoir of her Cornish childhood, was published to widespread critical acclaim.

Since 1980 Emma Smith has lived in the London district of Putney.